AUTOBIOGRAPHY

BOOKS BY A. A. MILNE

A. A. MILNE

AUTOBIOGRAPHY

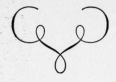

by

A. A. MILNE

With a frontispiece

E. P. DUTTON & CO., INC.

Publishers   *New York*

PUBLISHED SERIALLY IN THE ATLANTIC MONTHLY
UNDER THE TITLE "WHAT LUCK."

1880–1929

TO THE MEMORY OF
KENNETH JOHN MILNE
WHO
BORE THE WORST OF ME
AND
MADE THE BEST OF ME

CONTENTS

INTRODUCTION

WHEN I read the biography of a well-known man, I find that it is the first half of it which holds my attention. I watch with fascinated surprise the baby, finger in mouth, grow into the politician, tongue in cheek; but I find nothing either fascinating or surprising in the discovery that the cynicism of the politician has matured into the pomposity of the Cabinet Minister. It was inevitable. So, too, is it inevitable that the composer of one opera should compose other operas, and, if not inevitable, at least not surprising that a reputation founded on the first should grow with its successors. Nor is it surprising (nor particularly interesting) that any man moderately well known should meet other well-known people; for as soon as he has made himself known he will dine with Lady X; it is for Lady X to write her own autobiography and tell us who else were there. What we want to learn from the composer is how he came to compose an opera at all. Tell us why the boy became an apothecary, and how the apothecary found himself writing *Endymion,* and let us guess for ourselves that the author of *Endymion* will meet Wordsworth and Shelley, and surprise neither of them with an *Ode to a Nightingale.*

There is no vanity in supposing that even one's own early life may have this interest for others. Most of us must have wondered about the making of those we meet. This man who has come to mend the telephone: that man who has come to mend the chair: why not the other way round, this one mending the chair, and that one the tele-

9

phone? Our lawyer, our doctor: what accident, what environment, what determination placed them where they are? The painter with whom we had supposed ourselves intimate says casually: 'I remember when I was a schoolmaster at Eastbourne,' and it is as startling to us as if he had said: 'I remember when I was prospecting for gold in the Carpathians.' So *that* was how he began! How interesting!

Feeling like this about other people I feel like it also about myself. In this book, as in everything which I have written, I have humoured the author. Whatever happens to the public, the author is not going to be bored. I have enjoyed looking back on the past, and if others now find enjoyment in looking over my shoulder, I am as glad as my publishers will be. But let us be quite clear that this is my party, not theirs. There is no index for their entertainment. Even if there were an index, there would be very few names to put in it. I had the honour of meeting a world-famous golfer once. We were introduced, but naturally my name meant nothing to him. Our introducer, wishing to do his best for me, added kindly, 'The writer, you know.' The golfer looked uncomfortable and said, 'Oh, yes.' I should have been content to leave it there, but my friend was more persistent. '*You* know,' he said doggedly; 'the dramatist, *Mr Pim Passes By*.' Amazingly the golfer's face lit up. He beamed at me. 'Oh,' he said eagerly, 'then you know a lot of actresses!' I do; but this is the autobiography of a writer, not a book about a lot of actresses. It will be a disappointment to the golfing world.

A good title for the autobiography of any writer would be 'It's Too Late Now.' This does not mean that if I had my life again I should be an engineer or a clergyman or a stockbroker or a better man, and that unfortunately it is too late now to be any of these things. It means that heredity and environment make the child, and the child makes the man, and the man makes the writer; so that it is too late now—it was probably too late forty years ago—for me to be a different writer. I say this neither regretfully nor complacently, I state it as a fact. It is a habit of modern criticism to condemn the author of the book criticized for not being the author of somebody else's book: for not writing, that is, in a style alien to him. He who is at home among the leisured classes is urged to take a 'bus down the Whitechapel Road and see how the poor live; and he whose heart is in the Whitechapel Road is rebuked for his 'inability to draw a gentleman.' The optimist is reproached for not despairing of the world, the pessimist is urged to take a lesson from the optimist. One begins by reading such criticism hoping to profit by it, and one ends by realizing that it is too late to profit by it; the criticism should have been made to the child, even to the child's parents before they married. One writes in a certain sort of way because one is a certain sort of person; one is a certain sort of person because one has led a certain sort of life.

This is the life.

When I had my first story published in an American magazine, the editor asked my agent for a short account of this unknown author for his monthly article 'Something about Our New Contributors.' My agent passed the letter on to me, and I did what I could for him. A few weeks later my first published book in America was due, and again some information about the unknown author was required. Again I wrote happily about myself. Back came an indignant letter from the agent: 'Hi! This life is the same as the other one!'

You see, it was too late even then.

A. A. M.

CHILD

1882–1893

Chapter One

1

'ONCE upon a time there was a man who had three sons' —this was how we began, this was how the fairy stories began. And as our governess read them aloud to their inevitable end, Barry looked at Ken, and the two of them looked at Alan, and I looked as little complacent as I could, knowing that the third son was the good one, yet in a way sorry that his character was so blameless, his destiny so assured. Perhaps, after all, the others would get more fun out of life. In another moment Barry would be turned into a toadstool, and Ken into a two-headed bear; interesting, interesting; but the third son would only kill the same old dragon and come into the same old Kingdom, just as he had done a hundred times before. Oh, to be Barry or Ken for once, to miss this easy good-fortune by the simple and attractive method of being rude to a godmother, how exciting that would be!

Rudeness, alas, was for the others only. We could stand in a row and put our tongues out at an unpopular governess, but my tongue would not be noticed. Miserably I would withdraw it, and wait to be held up to the others as a model of propriety. It was true that I had blue eyes and long flaxen hair; true that these were the Little Lord Fauntleroy days, and that on occasion I wore a velvet suit and lace collar; true that my hair curled naturally on my shoulders, after it had spent the night in papers. But this was equally true of all of us. Why, then, was I treated so unfairly?

AUTOBIOGRAPHY

In the circumstances Barry and Ken behaved well. Barry, secure in his position as the bad boy of the family, regarded me with kindly condescension. He had nothing to regret, being one of those boys who are sent to governesses solely (it seems) for comparison. On the one hand, let us contemplate George Washington, the young Nelson and James Watt; on the other hand, Barry. Which of these exemplars were Ken and I following? Later on it was my privilege also to contemplate Ken. Was I going the way Ken was rapidly going? Honestly I tried to, but the fairy stories were against me. I remained the third son of the family, for whom good-fortune waited . . . 'Once upon a time there was a man who had three sons,' read our governess.

Governesses came and went. By the third day we had made up our minds about them, as they, no doubt, about us. Only one stayed, and her we loved dearly. There was argument as to which of us should marry her, but though historically she would have fallen to me, Barry claimed her by right of conquest. When Barry was in this mood, it was a case of History against One on the Nose, and History said no more. Fortunately she had two sisters, Trot and Molly. Trot had been an occasional visitor to our house, so that when Ken proposed to her and accepted himself, there was no surprise in the family. This brought Molly and me together. I had seen her photograph; she was the Beloved One's sister; she was the only one left; it was enough. I would marry Molly.

We all chose houses for ourselves in Priory Road, for it was up this road that we walked every morning on our way to Miss Budd's kindergarten. I thought at the time, and still think, that Molly's and mine was the prettiest house. Ken's was dark and gloomy, but he had found a buff-tip caterpillar just outside the front door, and it had seemed to him that the house, for some reason, might be

attractive to buff-tip caterpillars. Barry's artistic nature
was satisfied when he had assured himself that he was settling down as far as possible from Miss Budd's. But my
house had a virginia creeper all over it, and was bright
and sunny. Being in the neighbourhood the other day I
walked up the Priory Road, and looked for it again. It
was still the prettiest house in the road. I never really got
to know Molly's tastes (one can do so little with a photograph), but I think that she would have liked it as it looked
that autumn afternoon. Where is she now? Married, I
suppose, to somebody else.

2

Molly would be about seventy now, which makes me
feel that Miss Budd must be well over a hundred. If so,
she will not mind my saying that she looked like the
Duchess in *Alice in Wonderland*. At Miss Budd's we began morning-school with a hymn. In reward for I know
not what good or bad behaviour one or other of us might
be called upon to choose this hymn, and my choice on
these occasions would fall upon *'All things bright and
beautiful'*; possibly because it was the only one I could
remember in my sudden embarrassment. But indeed I
liked it, in as far as one can like a hymn, for it had a scent
of the country which distinguished it from its fellows.
'The rushes that we gather by the stream-side every day'
opened up a vista of enchantment and adventure to a
London child along which he could wander happily
through the Arithmetic lesson. 'A very pleasing choice,'
Miss Budd would say, 'but we will omit the third verse,
for unfortunately it is not quite true of those of us here
to-day. We do *not* make a habit of gathering rushes. Now,
Miss Florence, please, omitting the third verse.' And Miss
Florence Budd at the piano would strike the appropriate

chord. Unimaginative Miss Budds. I had gathered rushes and fallen into that stream a hundred times.

We lived, as perhaps I should have said before, in Mortimer Road. In those days it was Mortimer Road, Kilburn, and none the worse for that; now it is become more respectable (or Kilburn less) and is known as Mortimer Crescent, St John's Wood. Priory Road was just across the railway bridge; and day and night, beneath that bridge, trains roared their romantic way to Scotland. I always thought of them as going to the right to Scotland, but I see now that they must have gone to the left, and that every train which I watched so enviously into the heather was in fact burrowing its way ingloriously back to something worse than Kilburn. Possibly I should have been a different man if I had got the truth of this as a child; possibly not. But the Milnes came from Scotland, and I ought to have known where to look for it.

Every morning then, in charge of Miss Beatrice Edwards, we leave Scotland on the left and make for Miss Budd's. It is probable that Barry is no longer with us, being already too big, or too bad, for kindergarten. Before he was in double figures his life diverged from Ken's and mine never to come back to it. 'We' through all my memories of childhood is Ken and myself, and was to remain so until he was eighteen. Now I am six, Ken seven. We cross the bridge, the beloved 'Bee' in the middle. She holds a hand of each, and repeats to us the twenty-third Psalm. We have half-an-hour yet before school begins; we shall walk all up West End Lane and then slowly back down Priory Road; and by the time we get to Miss Budd's we shall (it is hoped by Miss Budd) know Psalm 23 by heart.

'The Lord is my shepherd, I shall not want,' says Ken. 'That's easy.'

'He maketh me to lie down in green pathturth; he

18

leadeth me bethide the thtill waterth,' say I, leaving it
uncertain whether it is the Psalmist or I who is lisping.
'Oh, look, thereth a caterpillar.'

'I saw it first. I saw it *years* ago. Yea, though I walk
through the valley——'

'No, darling. He restoreth my soul——'

Time goes on inexorably. We are getting nearer and
nearer to Miss Budd's. Nothing now can keep us from
getting there. Surely goodness and mercy shall follow me
all the days of my life, but what's the good of saying it
after Bee, when I don't really remember it, and *why*
didn't we start learning it sooner?

The sun is shining, goodness and mercy are to follow
me (it seems) for ever, but fifty years from now I shall
still dream at times that I am walking up Priory Road, an
unhappy middle-aged man wrestling with a psalm which
no father of fifty-six should be asked to learn. The hymn
and the psalm: this is all that is left to me of Miss Budd's
educational system.

3

Ken was sixteen months older than I and fifteen months
younger than Barry, so he could be as young as the one
or as old as the other, whichever he preferred. Fortunately he chose me for contemporary. We were inseparable; sometimes, when fighting, so mixed up as to be
indistinguishable. We never ceased to quarrel with each
other, nor to feel the need of each other. Save for the fact
that he hated cheese, we shared equally all belief, all
knowledge, all ambition, all hope and all fear. Sometimes
at inns or in strange houses we shared a bed. I remember
once asking an elderly visitor if she didn't agree with me
that sharing a bed with somebody else was the most horrible thing which anybody could be asked to do. Before

she could tell me, my mother interrupted. 'Talking of bed,' said my mother calmly . . . and I knew as I 'ran along' that I had been a fool to mention the subject. I only mention it now, because I wish to put it on record that my love for Ken, as his for me, survived six holiday weeks in the same bed; with a fight every morning, when one of us found that the tide of clothes had receded in the night, leaving him bare and beached.

It was, of course, I who gained most from this friend-ship. When Ken did a thing I did it too, and this meant that I was always sixteen months ahead of him. In any contemporary estimate of Shakespeare and Marlowe the few months between them would not be held to matter; but as between two boys, every day is a day in which the younger may overtake the older. 'When I am Ken's age, how much more I shall know than he knows now.' So I could think then. But I can make myself no promises to-day as to what I shall know when I am Shaw's age. Strange, for surely I can learn more quickly now than I could when I was a boy.

All through Ken's schooldays, then, it was a reproach to him that his younger brother was intellectually his superior. If, by reason of his greater age, he could enter for, and did in fact pass, some examination before I did, nobody had any doubt that I should pass it before the sixteen months were up, and with more distinction. Every triumph had over it the shadow of my impending tri-umph. When he was only twelve, he surprised the family by getting a Westminster scholarship; congratulations were sincere, but kept within reason. There was (surely?) something better to come. There was. Within six months I had got a similar scholarship . . . and I was still only eleven.

Do you wonder that he was jealous of me?

But he wasn't. A boy can do a great deal in sixteen

months, but he cannot change his nature, and Ken had
one advantage of me which he was to keep throughout
his life. He was definitely—nicer. On going into the matter with Dr Murray I find that the word 'nice' has fourteen meanings, none of which gives the clue to Ken's
superior quality. Yet I still say that he was nicer than I;
kinder, larger-hearted, more lovable, more tolerant,
sweeter tempered—all of that or none of that, it doesn't
matter, he was just 'nicer.' If you knew us both, you preferred Ken. I might be better at work and games; even
better-looking, for he had been dropped on his nose as a
baby (or picked up by it, we never could decide which);
but 'poor old Ken' or 'dear old Ken' had his private right
of entry into everybody's heart. Anybody less nice than
he would have found me, and left me, insufferable. If, in
later years, I have not seemed insufferable to my friends
over any success which has looked in on me, I owe it to
him, in whose company complacence found nothing on
which to batten. And if I have taken failure less well than
I should have done, it is because I am still sixteen months
behind him in humility, and shall never catch up.

But in these days humility and complacence were unknown words to us, and examinations had not come seriously into our lives. The only competition between us
was for the larger half of the holiday bed. In bed or out
of it, we looked (except for Ken's nose, and there may be
precedent for that) like two angels not yet fledged—or, as
one might say, entire cherubim. Any old lady could be
trusted to adore us, any normal boy to have the urge to
kick us. Both would have been wrong. To some extent
we were unkickable anyway, being now at our father's
school; but without its protecting walls we had to take
our chance. There was an occasion during a summer holiday at Sevenoaks, Ken being eight and I seven, and both
of us too winsome for words, when we were rounded up

by a gang of savages in the ruins of a deserted house. What dreadful fate would have befallen us I do not know, but Ken created a diversion while I escaped, and becoming himself a prisoner was inspired to say that he lived in a village three miles off, and if given two hundred yards' start would never be seen again. The lust of the chase was too much for the hunters; they could beat the quarry up at leisure afterwards. Gleefully they gave him to just short of the cottage down the road, and set off after him with loud halloos. So Ken trotted into our cottage and joined me in the kitchen, to the relief of the cook, who was being hurriedly organized for rescue.

On another occasion, in what was then St Mary's Fields, but is now, I suppose, a network of appendices to Priory Road, we found a big boy knocking about a smaller friend. Ken thought that we could appeal to the big boy's better nature; I thought that we should be late for tea as it was. However, we intervened. There was never any doubt of our success. As soon as we came into the battle area, our superior claims were recognized. The small friend was forgotten; Ken was punched on the nose; the big boy, with all the blood on his hands which he wanted, slouched off defiantly; and I, who relate the story, gallantly picked up the wounded. It always was, it always would be, poor old Ken.

4

We lived at Henley House. Ken and I re-visited it after the war; not with any idea of putting up a plaque, though he was now a C.B.E., but to discover whether caterpillars really had frequented Mortimer and Priory Roads with the persistence which memory alleged. It was less of a shock to find no caterpillars than to find that Henley House was now two houses, the gravelled playground at the back two gardens, and the road on which we had learned to bicycle (how many years ago) wearing the less homely name of crescent. The house had been two houses before it had been turned into a school; the playground two gardens; and certainly the road had always had the shape of a crescent; so perhaps Time had been more gentle with our birthplace than we had a right to expect. It might have been a Cinema de Luxe, with Shirley Temple (whom at one time we had resembled so greatly) enchanting and infuriating, as we did, all Kilburn.

Our father had come there—let me get one authentic date into this book—in 1878. His was one of those private schools, then so common, now so unusual, for boys of all ages. At eight I was the youngest of them, and the oldest may have been eighteen. Of the fifty boys, perhaps fifteen were boarders. One of my early contributions to English literature describes a typical football match, or fight, in the playground between Boarders and Day-boys. I spend a good deal of time to-day telling young writers that it is the actual writing and not the personal introduction to the editor which counts, but of course it does depend upon how young they are; under the age of ten one wants to know the editor. An early introduction to my father gave me the password into the *Henley House School Magazine,* my first fully-signed article carrying beneath the signature the disarming apology 'Aged 8¾ years.' One wishes that one could still apologize. In this account of the Fifteen-Years-War between Boarders and Day-boys a more mature writer was at work, aged nine years. In the first flush of inspiration I wrote 'The Day-boys have thousands of chaps all crowding round and the Boarders never have more than eleven, but of course the Boarders always win. Hoorah for the Boarders.' Of all my memories of those years the one most clear to me is this of myself at my desk in the big schoolroom biting the end of my pen into splinters, and acknowledging sadly to myself that 'thousands' is an exaggeration, and that in the pursuit of truth I ought to get it down to 'hundreds.' Reluctantly I got it down to hundreds. Hundreds? There were only thirty-five Day-boys in the school, and some would not be playing. Perhaps 'twenty' would be the truth. Yet must one keep to the strict truth? Never! So, in my last clean copy for the printer, the Day-boys had 'about fifty chaps' . . . and in all that I have written since I have held to my creed that Art is exaggeration—but in fifties not in thousands.

Really, I suppose, we were qualified for both sides, and could have played for either, as does Royalty in the annual golf-match between Generals and Admirals. We outboarded the boarders in that we were there even for the holidays, but even the Day-boy who went home for dinner (as most of them did) could not (as we did) slip through the dividing door during the morning break, and take a glass of milk with his Mama. Boarders, however, we called ourselves, and as boarders hacked the opposition, and shrilled 'Shoot!' and cut our knees on the gravel, and screamed, 'Shut up, you cad,' and 'No, I didn't' and 'Come on, boarders!'

Most of the games in that playground were rough or mildly dangerous or both. Our favourite was a form of leap-frog called 'Foot-it.' A taking-off line was drawn in the gravel, a boy bent down and the others jumped over him. At the end of every round he moved one foot's length away from the line, so that at the end of six rounds the others would be taking off for the jump from about five feet away. Anybody who knocked him over took his place. At a suitable distance 'one foot in' would be allowed, one foot, that is, in the sacred ground between line and boy; then 'two feet in' and so on. In the end the boy would be at the far end of the playground, and the

rest of us would be allowed eight flying strides before putting our hands on his back and vaulting him.

It was a game, as you see, which provided for an in-
spiriting number of crashes; a game in which the nine-
year-old, however active, however certainly the Headmaster's Benjamin, was due for more than his share of
them. Shortness of stride left him with a succession of
almost unreachable, surely impassable, obstacles to nego-
tiate, and on picking himself out of the ruins, he had to
bend and wait with beating heart for the thunderous approach of the heavy brigade, beneath whose weight he
would become one again with the gravel. Yet we loved it,
and were deeply disappointed to find that for the public
schools it had no message. Our other favourite game was
'Sunday-Monday.' Each boy was given a day of the week
or of succeeding weeks (as it might be 'Monday fortnight') by which to remember himself, a ball was thrown
up against the high school wall, and a day called out. The
owner of the day had to catch the ball, and, catching it,
himself throw and call out a day. If he missed it, he could
only save his 'life' by throwing the ball at any boy in
range and hitting him. One sees, I hope, the dilemma
which was the game's attraction. Being Tuesday, and seeing a high ball coming to Monday, what should one do?
Remain close at hand in case he catches it, and lobs an
easy one for Tuesday. But if he fumbles and misses? Then
one must be as far away as possible. The climax of the
game was the Victor's Reward, he being allowed three
shots across the playground at the stationary behind of
each player; or, if he preferred it as offering a wider target, six shots at the concerted behinds.

In one corner of the playground was an erection known
as The Gymnasium. Whether one can still buy a 'gymnasium' I do not know; nor how one would ask for it, nor
at what shop begin. Without the utmost freedom of ges-

ticulation one might return with anything from a mouse-trap to a small nonconformist chapel. It is one of the curses of descriptive writing that one has to translate every instinctive and reinforcing movement of the hands into fixed words; words, to the writer, so uncommunicative. Well then, the gymnasium was a piece of scaffolding fifteen feet high, which consisted of two inverted 'V's' and an ornamental crosspiece. Of the four 'V' sides, one was a ladder, one a slider, and the other two were sliders with projecting rungs. The ornamentation had been by Time's fell hand defaced, down-razed and finally destroyed, so that it was now possible to proceed over the narrow cross-piece either cautiously on the stomach, or more daringly in a sitting position; and one boy, otherwise unremembered in history, but at this time famous, had walked across it. Even the most lethargic old gentleman must feel that a game of Follow-my-leader or Keep-the-pot-a-boiling over this gymnasium, up the ladder of one V, across the top, down the slider of the other V, with each boy treading on the hands of the boy behind as they go up the ladder, being kicked by the boy in front as they cross the abyss, and receiving the full weight of several boys behind as they shoot down the slider—even the most lethargic old gentleman under *The Times* must see that this was fun. But there was even more fun to be got out of the gymnasium. From the crosspiece depended a swing; so catalogued, no doubt, but to us a flying trapeze. The swing was set in motion, we ran at it from the far end of the playground, took off from a spring-board, jumped, caught it, swung off at the other end, and left it swinging back for the next boy. Every game has its ecstatic moments; indeed, life offers quite tolerable diversions apart from games; but for a prolongation of ecstasy one must return to the flying trapeze: the year at the spring, morning at nine, and oneself a few months younger. Child-

hood is not the happiest time of one's life, but only to a
child is pure happiness possible. Afterwards it is tainted
with the knowledge that it will not last, and the fear that
one will have to pay for it.

The private sitting-room of the family had its windows
over the playground, and it is to be supposed that our
mother, looking out from time to time, and seeing her
little ones balanced precariously fifteen feet over the
gravel, or crushed into it by some bigger boy, said 'Oh,
dear' to herself, and 'Must they?' But she showed none
of this, knowing that a mother's job is not to prevent
wounds, but to bind up the wounded. In any case she had
the Victorian woman's complete faith in the rights of a
father. It was he who was bringing us up. He conceded
her the Little Lord Fauntleroy make-up (for I suppose it
was she who liked it) and did his best to nullify its effect.
We were to be 'manly little fellows' . . . and manly little
fellows we were. If I were a psycho-analytical critic, and
if I thought that this Edwardian writer Milne were worth
one of my portentous volumes, I should ascribe everything which he had done and failed to do, his personality
as revealed in his books and hidden in himself, to the con-
sciousness implanted in him as a child that he was battling
against the wrong make-up. There was a music-hall song
of those days whose refrain was the simple exhortation:
'Get your hair cut.' It is possible that an accidental sight
of me inspired it. It is also possible that my mother's need
of the reminder inspired, for better or worse, much of
my life.

5

From time to time people have said to me 'You *are*
lucky,' meaning by this that I was leading, as far as they
could see, a happy, successful and not impoverished existence. But there has been a suggestion in the tone of

their voice (as there has been in mine, when in imagination I have so addressed my opponent at golf) that if the luck had been evenly distributed, the success might have rested elsewhere. Fortune has been over-kind to the lucky ones. Now I suppose one's instinct is to deny hotly that Fortune has had any sort of hand in one's career. On the contrary, madam, I have carved out my career for myself; every penny I have spent I have earned; I owe nothing to the advice or the patronage of others. But as soon as one has said this, one sees how absurd it is. It is true that I have never walked up Shaftesbury Avenue with a play in my pocket, and bumped into a man who was walking down Shaftesbury Avenue looking for that sort of play. It is true that no languishing work of mine has received the accidental stimulus of a royal or episcopal reference. Fortune has reserved her more spectacular appearance for others. But she must have been there in an unobtrusive way from the beginning, for how else could one begin at all? We may 'carve out' careers for ourselves, but our parentage gave us the implements with which to do it, and we certainly didn't carve out our parents. Everybody's luck, good or ill, begins on the day on which he was born. I was lucky. It is time that I tried to explain how lucky I was.

My father, John Vine Milne, was the eldest son of a Presbyterian minister. My great-grandfather was, I believe, a stone-mason in Aberdeenshire. If he shares responsibility for the average cemetery display of Aberdeen granite, I hope that I have inherited nothing from him. But I am not even sure that he was a mason. A second cousin of Father's died intestate in 1892 and left thirty thousand pounds, this being the only money that any relation of ours has ever left. Unfortunately she also left thirty second-cousins. A first-cousin had died a few months earlier, leaving, more characteristically, three silver teaspoons, two of which went to my father and one to my uncle; and it is reasonable to suppose that the £30,000, if she had survived to come into it, would have been divided in the same proportions. As it was, a genealogical tree had to be prepared, proving the equal claims of all these second-cousins, and in this way I learnt all about my grandmother's family; which included (to the gratification of a boy of ten) an uncle of hers who had been one of Nelson's captains at Trafalgar, and still had a monument to himself in Bath Abbey. All this may have crowded out any knowledge I had gleaned of my grandfather's ancestry; or it may be that we were snobs about it. But I seem to remember thinking of my great-grandfather, not even as a carver of tombstones, but as the man who sat by the roadside, chipping stolidly at little heaps of granite, and trying not to get too much of it into his eyes.

Grandfather Milne was the world's most unworldly muddler. He was born in 1815; came from Aberdeen to England as a minister; went out to Jamaica as a missionary; converted another missionary to the belief that she could love, honour and obey him; returned to England as a married man; retired from the ministry and started a school; started with equal optimism twelve other schools in other parts of England; fathered hopefully ten children; returned to the ministry; and died in 1874—leaving behind him a widow and four sons to tell themselves that, after all, he was a good man. He was a very good man. His income was never more than eighty pounds a year; his children when they were not dying lived exclusively on porridge, and were educated for twopence a week at the village school; but he could come home triumphantly from a chapel meeting to tell his underfed family that he had promised twenty pounds for the new pews. And somehow the twenty pounds would be paid. It was for The Lord. Yet he was neither sanctimonious nor fanatical. He just believed quite simply that nothing which happened in this world mattered to a good man; to a man, that is, who believed in God and would return to Him. It mattered not if his sons were dukes or dustmen, so long as they were good. Nor did it matter if his wife did all the housework. And if the housekeeping could only allow one egg a day for the whole family, no doubt he ate it himself in an unworldly and absentminded way before giving the tramp at the door the last shilling in his pocket. It is difficult to explain to a tramp that being good is more important than beer.

I never knew my grandfather and grandmother. I suppose I must have seen their photographs in the family album, but photographs of grandparents, taken in the days when one leant self-consciously against an aspidistra or the rigging of a yacht, give no impression of character. It may be that they loved each other wildly through all their troubles; my father wouldn't know, and it was from him that I drew all my knowledge of them. When Grandfather Milne died, and the verdict of the current neighbourhood was passed on him: 'The poor will miss him,' nothing was said as to the feelings of the very poorest of the poor, his own family. They missed him, no doubt; but who can say whether it was with relief or regret that Grandmother Milne realized that he was now in a place where goodness was taken for granted? It may have been as heartbreaking to live without him as with him.

Whatever her feelings, she could trust herself safely to her son John, now *de jure* as for years he had been *de facto* head of the house. John was twenty-eight. Hovering between duke and dustman, he had been clerk in the counting-house of a biscuit factory, apprentice in an engineering firm, usher in various schools, nurse to his younger brothers, and mouthpiece for a distracted wife. ('You *must* talk to your father, John. Do you know what he's done *now?*') He had not reacted, as so many sons might have reacted, from the religious atmosphere of his home; he kept throughout his life the simple implicit faith of his father. But his religion was not a selfish religion, suited only to his personal use in the next world. It met the needs equally of his family and of those who had business dealings with him. I asked him once, when I was of an age not to be sent to bed for asking silly questions, whether goodness was so much God's concern that He was unable to distinguish between Aristophanes and Mark Twain as humorists, or between Grace and Shrewsbury as cricketers. Was Grace only the better man of the two if he went to church more regularly? I never got the answer and don't know it now. But I feel, and my grandmother would agree with me, that even in a Heaven for which goodness was the only qualification John would be entitled to a higher place than his unworldly father.

For years now John's over-mastering concern had been with education: the education of himself and of others. After twelve hours in the engineering shop, he would walk back to his room, spend an hour getting clean, and then settle down to the real work of the day, the achievement of a degree. B.A. (London) was his goal. It might seem that that first hour was being wasted: one can read Latin and Greek as well with dirty hands as with clean; but to him the daily struggle to rid himself of the filth of the machines was a ritual which symbolized his approaching escape from the world of manual toil into the more gracious world of the intellect. If he lost the integrity of his hands, he would lose the integrity of his mind. It was too late to be a duke, but he was damned, he would indeed be damned, if he were a dustman.

He escaped from the machines, and began to teach what little he had learnt, keeping always a chapter ahead of his class. He discovered that he really had the gift of

teaching for which he had longed, and with it the gift of
preserving discipline among boys bigger, and little
younger, than himself. No doubt it was to mark that
difference of age that he grew, as soon as he could, a
beard. He must have looked very small and lonely without it. But in the rough schools to which his lack of
academic qualification condemned him a beard was not
enough; he needed, and had, the two great qualities,
courage and a sense of humour.

Let me give one example from his later period of the
way in which his sense of humour served him. He has
reached at last the prosperity of a successful preparatory
school in Thanet. The boys are having their dinner.
'J. V.,' as they call him privately, sits at a separate table
with any of the family who may happen to be at home;
the boys are at four long tables under his eye, with an
assistant-master or a governess at each end. Outside, in a
recess between the kitchens and the dining-room, my
mother carves. She carves, as she does everything, better
than anybody else in the house, and, like a true artist,
insists therefore on doing it. When my father points out
that it would be much nicer for her to have her lunch
with him, before the smell of food has sickened her of it,
she says, 'Yes, and then who'd do the carving?' When he
offers, with a twinkle, to get the head-carver from Simp-
son's down for a term's trial, she says, 'What rubbish, as
if I'd let him.' This conversation has been circling on for
years. My mother continues to carve. The matron stands
beside her, helping vegetables in an obviously inferior
manner. She has just sent one of the boys upstairs to fetch
something for her. The boy comes into the dining-room.

'Henry,' says my father, 'you're late again.'

'Yes, sir. Please, sir, it wasn't my fault——'

'No excuses, Henry. You must put your chair away and
stand.'

So Henry eats his first course standing.

'All right, Henry, you may take your chair now.'

'Yes, sir, thank you, sir. Please, sir, Matron sent me upstairs for her spectacles just as I was coming in.'

Awed silence. 'Sucks for J. V.,' the boys are thinking, 'he'll have to apologize.' The younger assistant-masters look up anxiously. Do schoolmasters ever apologize? Isn't it bad for discipline?

'Then in that case,' says my father, wishing to get it quite clear, 'it wasn't your fault you were late?'

'Please, sir, no, sir.'

'Oh!' (Everybody is waiting.) 'Oh, well, then, you'd better take two chairs.'

And everybody laughs and is happy.

6

At the time of my grandfather's death, J. V. had passed the Intermediate, and was working for his Final B.A. He was also looking for a job. Two were suggested to him by the agents; assistant-master in a school at Wellington, Shropshire, and tutor in a private family at Tottenham. He would have preferred the former, for he was now beginning to feel at home in the rough-and-tumble of a school, but, for safety, he applied for both. The Tottenham reply came first, inviting him to lunch with the family for the purpose of mutual inspection. Unwilling to lose his chance of the Wellington post, he sent a reply-paid telegram to the headmaster, as from the Tottenham address, to say, 'What about it?'—or more politely, 'Has my application been successful?' The interview at Tottenham was satisfactory. He liked the family, and the family liked him. Over the luncheon-table he was offered the tutorship. Should he take it or was there still a chance of hearing favourably from Wellington? He put off an answer as long as he could; talked feverishly of the weather and Mr. Gladstone's Government; upset his glass of claret, and spent another five minutes apologizing. And then, in the last moment of delay, in came the maid with a telegram. His application to the school had been accepted.

A trivial business anyway. The salary in either post was only £100 a year, and the tutor might have become a schoolmaster again, or the schoolmaster a tutor. But he never thought it was trivial. To him it was the decisive moment of his life.

And, you might almost say, of mine.

For at Wellington, Shropshire, he met my mother.

Chapter Two

1

MY MOTHER came, as novelists say, of 'good yeoman stock,' or, more simply, was a farmer's daughter. At least, I think she was, but I am as uncertain of the farmer as of the stone-mason. When my father met her, she was keeping a School for Young Ladies. This piece of family history, which we picked up as children, never seemed authentic; for it was part of our creed that Papa knew everything, and Mama knew nothing. She didn't even know that *mensâ* meant 'by, with or from a table' until we told her, and our daily triumphs over Euclid aroused an enthusiasm unrelated, only too obviously, to the proportions of the victory. This, which we were learning, was Knowledge; this was what was taught in schools. Mama teaching! How funny.

But I see now that it is what clever women teach in girls' schools which is funny. My mother's girls were taught to be good wives to hard-working men, and there was never anybody so good as she at that. She could do everything better than the people whom so reluctantly she came to employ: cook better than the cook, dust better than the parlourmaid, make a bed better than the housemaid, mend better than the sewing-maid, wash clothes better than the laundress, bandage better than the matron. She was simple, she was unemotional, she was common-sensible. Nothing upset her. At one of those inevitable end-of-term entertainments Father would be twittering like a sparrow with nervousness, wondering if the claret-cup would go round, and whether he would remember Tommy Tucker's parents, whom last term he had mistaken for Peter Piper's; and Mother would be completely calm, knowing that if there weren't enough claret-cup, it was all they were going to get, and that if she mistook Mrs Tucker for Mrs Piper, as she always did, it wouldn't matter, as she would probably call them both Mrs Hogbin. She was a great believer in the name of Hogbin, and often offered it to Father as a solution of the difficulties which a bad memory brought him. Somewhere, at some time, I suppose, she had met a Mr Hogbin, and was always expecting to hear of him again; or of some of his family; or of the village, Hogbin, from which he derived. We nearly traced him once: 'a man with a funny moustache who used to come about the gas.' But on going into the matter we discovered that this man's name was Pedder, and he was clean-shaven. 'Well, I know I used to *call* him Mr Hogbin,' insisted Mother, to show that there was a good deal to be said for her side of the argument. There always was. Once, at dinner, when Father was telling us proudly, as if partly responsible for it, that Light travelled at the rate of 150,000 miles a second, our awed silence was broken by Mother's simple announcement from the other end of the dinner-table: 'I don't believe it.' What the answer to that is I don't know, nor did Father ever discover it.

They had musical evenings at Mother's school, and that nice, shy Mr Milne, the new master at the boys' school, was a great addition to the parties, for not only was he religious-minded (which meant something in those days) but he played accompaniments on the flute. And when he had got over his shyness, he talked a lot of nonsense which made the ladies laugh, and you felt somehow that you could trust him. And he was brave. Because one Sunday the Headmaster had preached a sermon to the boys, in which he told them that they were all going straight to Hell, or anyhow the boys who hadn't attended in class last week, and he described Hell in words which would terrify anybody who knew that he was going there. And that nice little Mr Milne got permission to preach to the boys on the next Sunday, and he told them that there was no such place as Hell, and no such thing as Everlasting Fire, but that they would all be very silly if they didn't work now, when work was made easy for them, because it would mean that they would have to work much harder later on, when it wouldn't be so interesting. And then he had offered the Headmaster his resignation, but the Headmaster wouldn't hear of it, and said that he was sorry, and that perhaps there wasn't Everlasting Fire after all. So that nice Mr Milne would be there next Thursday as usual, with his flute.

He was there, and when he said good-night to Mother, he left a note in her hand, asking her to marry him. For he was still very shy.

It was only after my mother's death that I knew she had said 'No,' and had gone on saying 'No' for more than a year to Father's insistent wooing. How hard to realize that one's father, that elderly Olympian, may also have endured the agonies and ecstasies of love, as we have endured them! How hard to believe that one's mother, one's own mother, could have inspired those agonies and ecstasies, and have failed to respond to them, because she too had suffered them on another man's behalf! Father and Mother—who knew nothing of these things!

At the last she accepted him; at the last, perhaps, fell in love with him. Did she? I don't know. I don't think I ever really knew her. When I was a child I neither experienced, nor felt the need of, that mother-love of which one reads so much, and over which I am supposed (so mistakenly) to have sentimentalized. I learnt no prayers at my mother's knee, as so many children seem to have done. It was Papa who told us about God, and we who told the governess. No doubt Mama felt that Papa was so good at it that she oughtn't to interfere. She may also have felt that Papa was so good at playing with a child, and amusing a child, and making a child love him, that she oughtn't to interfere there either. Certainly as a child I gave my heart to my father. If he were there, all was well; if he were away, I asked Mama when he was coming back. Later on, when I formed the opinion that, even if Father knew everything, he knew most of it wrong, it was with my mother that I was happier. She didn't argue; she didn't drive the moral home. She was simple; she was wise; she was affectionate. She was restfully aloof.

2

They married, and came to Henley House. This had been some sort of unsuccessful school before, and Father, being unexpectedly lent a hundred pounds by his unofficial godfather, Mr Vine, bought the 'goodwill'; which amounted to a twenty or thirty inky desks, and half-a-dozen inky boys whose parents had been too lazy to find a better school for them.

No echoes of that struggle to live came down to us. Whenever I took Papa by the hand and showed him the way to the Bank, kindly men would count out for him as many golden sovereigns as he wanted, shovelling them out from an inexhaustible store. Silver they didn't even bother to count, but gave to him in bags. And if my own income was no more than a penny a week, this was only because too many sweets were bad for children, or because Ken and I would have all the money we wanted when we grew up, if we worked at our lessons now. Meanwhile we had all the food we wanted, and all the fun we wanted, and never knew that we were poor.

We must have been very poor. Mama's sewing-machine never stopped working. She made her own clothes, she made our clothes, she would have made Papa's clothes if she hadn't been so busy making the curtains. Not only did she save money by making things, but she saved it by preventing Father from spending. It was not until her death that I realized what he was like when left to himself. He never could resist a good advertisement. The discovery that he could buy a new theodolite (in leather-finished case) which definitely superseded the old theodolite which he had never bought, convinced him that a theodolite was what of all things he needed. He only started smoking because a cigar-merchant wrote to him what seemed like a personal, and was certainly a very friendly, appeal to buy a sample cabinet of twenty different cigars between the lengths of three inches and thirteen. The price was nominal, owing to the fact that it was Father's future custom on which they were relying, and they did not rely in vain. In her heyday Mother would never have allowed this, but, even then, there would have been times when she had her eye off him; and the arrival of a first-born to Mrs Milne may have coincided with the arrival of a gymnasium to her husband. It is difficult to say which would be the more surprised to find that 'that was what they looked like.'

With this childlike belief in the sincerity of advertisement and the value of a bargain, with a generosity as ample as his father's, he combined the strictest integrity in money matters, and an adequate respect for the laws of addition and subtraction. He kept elaborate accounts, in a blue-black ink such as was familiar to us on our fingers, and a red ink to which we might not hope to attain until we had grown up. I felt then, I still feel now, that I could write more beautifully in red ink; and I still wonder why there are so many things in the world (like red ink and toast) which are automatically denied to children. Luckily as a child one does not wonder for long. Papa says it, and he has the backing of God or Dr Morton, and in a moment we shall be wondering about something else. So Papa kept his accounts, and pursued every penny into its right column, and at the end of the year we were all still alive and he owed no man anything. And next year he would be able to afford a holiday or a new suit or perhaps even another gymnasium. For the school was growing. And it was his own.

He was the best man I have ever known: by which I mean the most truly good, the most completely to be trusted, the most incapable of wrong. He differed from our conception of God only because he was shy, which one imagined God not to be, and was funny, which one knew God was not. His shyness became apparent to us when we went out walking together and met an acquaintance. As soon as the acquaintance was sighted Papa would cut short his conversation, or ours, and prepare for the ordeal. The funny story, the explanation of the Force of Gravity, our answer to a catch-question had to wait. . . . He let my hand go, and put his own up to his hat. 'Good morning, Mr Roberts, good morning to you, good morning.' Mr Roberts had returned the greeting and passed, but Papa's greeting went on. His hand still went up and down to his hat in nervous movements, he still muttered 'Good morning to you.' We waited. We turned the corner. 'Well, now then,' he would say, 'what's the answer? A goose weighs seven pounds and half its own weight. How much does it weigh? Now *think*.' Coming out of church on Christmas morning must have been agony to him. A merry Christmas to you

—thank you, thank you—the same to you: there was so much to say, so much to murmur to oneself afterwards, so much to make one doubt if one had said it in the right order. Or was it no agony to him, with whom it was now an unconscious trick, but only an embarrassment for his family? Poor Papa. It seemed such a funny way to be shy. We were tongue-tied and awkward before strangers, but we looked up brightly at people we knew, and waited to have our heads patted.

We 'sat under' Dr Monro Gibson at the Presbyterian Church in Marlborough Road. We were seated in the extreme right-hand corner, farthest from the door, and as Dr Gibson gave a hitch to his gown in readiness for the sermon, the three of us clambered out of our pew and toddled sturdily for home, the envy and admiration of all. 'The darlings,' thought all the mothers. 'Lucky little devils,' thought the fathers. So much feeling did we arouse that Papa was asked to change his pew for one next to the door. Even so envious heads came round for a moment. In spite of this, Papa rose to be an elder, and was recurrently to be seen (but not by us) standing at the door with the plate, as the rest of the congregation came out. Luckily he was not required to say 'Good morning' or 'Thank you' to them. He also sang what he called 'seconds' in a resolute way which linked him up unofficially with the mixed choir in the gallery. It seemed to me then rather an easy way of singing, Papa, particularly in the anthems, allowing himself a certain independence both of words and music. 'The lions do lack and suffer hunger' dropped melodiously to us from above, and Papa, in a deep voice reminiscent of a lion, lacked and suffered hunger on two notes for the rest of the anthem. He did it with such conviction that one could not doubt the need of it. Deep down inside him there was a great musical artist struggling to be free: one

41

to whom the flute was not enough. After Mother's death, he used to write to the B.B.C. and tell it where it went wrong—the privilege throughout the ages of the unfreed artist.

3

Papa looked proudly at his hands, on which there was no axle-grease, and told himself that he was a B.A. (Lond.) and an elder of the Church. Ken looked at him, and said a little scornfully: 'When *I'm* a man, I'm going to have *M.A.* after my name, and put it on a brass plate for *everyone* to see.' On another occasion Ken told him that he wasn't solemn enough for a schoolmaster. 'Oh, but I'm *very* solemn,' said Father, making the appropriate face; 'in fact, I'm Solomon.' Ken shook his head sadly. 'Solomon,' he said, 'was a *wise* man.' Many years later I used to get letters at the *Punch* Office, beginning: 'My little boy, aged six, said rather an amusing thing the other day, which I have been advised to send to you'; indeed, I still get letters like that, being supposed to have some special interest in the quaint things which children say. Possibly these two remarks of Ken's, generally regarded as his masterpieces, were offered to the public; possibly not; but they were in private circulation for years. My own contributions at this tender age to the Family Bible were not so good, were, in fact, not funny at all; but they seem to have made a great impression on my father, and he never tired (as we did) of recapturing them. 'It bored me hellishly to write the *Emigrant*,' said Stevenson; 'well, it's going to bore others to read it: that's only fair.' And I think it is only fair, after listening to it so often, that I should now tell the world exactly what I said in '84.

Barry was getting on for five, and it was time he learned to read. Ken was three, and inclined to be naughty. If

the nurse-governess were teaching Barry to read, what
would Ken be doing? Something bad. Hadn't Ken better
learn to read too—it would keep him out of mischief? So
it came about that large sight-reading sheets were hung
over a blackboard in the nursery, and Barry and Ken and
the governess got to work; while Baby Alan, good as
gold, sucked his thumb in the corner and played with his
toys. And one day Papa came up to the nursery to see
how the young readers were getting on. Just as they were
going to begin, Baby Alan, playing with a piece of string
in his corner, said to anyone who was listening, 'I can do
it.' Papa told him not to talk now, there was a darling,
because they were busy. Alan tied another knot in his
string, and said, 'I can do it.' Papa said, 'S'sh, darling,'
picked up the pointer, pointed to a word on the sheet,
and said, 'What's that?' Barry and Ken frowned at it. It
was on the tip of their tongues. Bat or Mat? And from
Alan's corner a complacent little voice said, 'Cat.' As it
was.

I can see that that has the makings of a good story,
when told of the right person. 'I can do it'—said by Abra-
ham Lincoln at the age of two. Nowadays, when I refuse
to do any of the intolerable things which for some reason
are expected of writers: lecture, open bazaars, make
speeches, go to Hollywood: I am told, a little unfairly, I
think, that I am spoilt. 'You never do anything you don't
want to do.' Which is true. But alas! it would not be true
to say that I can do the things which I do want to do. My
first recorded remark should have been 'I won't do it'
not 'I can do it.'

Well, anyway, I could read before I was three, and I
was not much older when I made my second contribution
to the Family Bible. I have never set much store by this
myself, but to my father, on the numerous occasions later
when he recalled it to us, it became the token by which

he realized that his youngest son was Destined (under Providence) for Great Things; or, as I suppose he meant, was not after all, a half-wit. We were walking along Priory Road, when a coal-cart stopped in front of us, and the coal-man staggered through the gate of a house with a sack on his shoulders. I said, 'Why do they both?' Nobody knew what I was talking about, and nobody ever did know, and nobody knows now. But Papa, hammering away at it, decided that what I meant was: Why do you have to employ both a man *and* a horse? Why shouldn't the *horse* deliver the coal, or the *man* pull the cart? 'Isn't that what you mean, darling?' Having a lot of other questions to ask, naturally I said, 'Yeth'; whereupon Papa gave me a lecture on the Economics of Co-operation. In after years he got to think that I had given him the lecture; and that, since I was only three at the time, I must have been pretty well advanced for my age. However it was, 'Why do they both?' joined 'I can do it' in what one might call the family *incunabula*. It seemed to Papa that the future of his youngest son was assured.

We went to Torquay that summer, and Ken on his fourth birthday was given his first real book *Reynard the Fox*. We both read it. When, forty years later, I wrote a book called *Winnie-the-Pooh*, and saw Shepard's drawing of Pooh, the bear, standing on the branch of a tree outside Owl's house, I remembered all that *Reynard the Fox* and *Uncle Remus* and the animal stories in *Aunt Judy's Magazine* had meant to us. Even if none of their magic had descended on me, at least it had inspired my collaborator; and I had the happy feeling that here was a magic which children, from generation to generation, have been unable to resist. *Uncle Remus* was read aloud to us by Papa, a chapter a night. One night he had to go away. Little knowing what we were doing we handed the sacred book to our governess, and told her to go on from there.

44

Some such experience, no doubt, caused the first man to coin the phrase that he 'could not believe his ears'. Terrible things were happening all round us. Was this Uncle Remus? Was this our own beloved Bee? One of our idols had to go. Stumbling painfully through the dialect, Bee got to the bottom of the page and asked if she should go on. We said not. It wasn't very interesting, she thought. We thought not too. Should she read another book, or should we play a game? We played a game. Next night we found the place for Papa. Three lines in that lovely understanding voice, and Uncle Remus was saved. But Bee never read aloud again. She was a darling; I still loved her; but I was glad that I was marrying Molly.

Papa also read *The Pilgrim's Progress* to us, or, as we always called it, *Bunyan's Pilgrim's Progress:* I can see the book now, in a dirty yellow binding. We longed for it, we were thrilled by it, as we should neither have longed nor been thrilled had it been read to us on a week-day. But we were Presbyterians; Sunday was reserved for religion, and Papa had somehow got it into his head that *Bunyan's Pilgrim's Progress* was a religious book. We didn't tell him the truth. We listened, rapt, and hoped that he would never find out. For it was the only excitement of Sunday, apart from the possibility, on the way back from church, of finding a religious-minded caterpillar out for a walk. The other permitted books were bound volumes of *The Quiver*, and a series of works which began with *Line upon Line,* went on, a little un-originally, to *Verse upon Verse* and *Chapter upon Chapter,* and ended, the author now completely in the grip of his theme, with *Testament upon Testament.*

I have mentioned *Aunt Judy's Magazine.* I hope that she means something to some of my contemporaries, for she meant Heaven to us. We had all the bound volumes; but I never knew, nor know now, whether the components were still in circulation. Was Mrs Ewing Aunt Judy? Who were the other contributors? Any poor laurels which I have won as a writer for children I strip from my head and distribute apologetically, leaf by leaf, to those of them who have remained unknown. To us the volumes of *Aunt Judy's Magazine* were friends as familiar and as well-loved as were (in this more practical age) the volumes of the *Children's Encyclopaedia* to my own child. Aunt Judy was not practical. She entranced us, but never told us how to make a tricycle.

4

Henley House was two houses. On the Family Side you entered the front door, and found yourself in a small lobby. Opening the coloured-glass door of the lobby you came into the 'hall,' a hall no bigger than was determined by the junction of a broad staircase with the passage. From the right-hand wall depended the horns of a buffalo, a looped lasso and a pair of Mexican spurs; so that every time one slid down the banisters, one slid through Kilburn into a romantic world of which one's imagination was the only master. To-day complete synthetic Mexicans ride down complete synthetic buffaloes in continuous performance, and imagination can take the modern child no further than Hollywood has left him. But we roamed prairies such as were never seen (as Papa, we supposed at first, had once roamed them), wearing spurs as big as saucers, lassoing buffaloes as big as elephants, stamping rattle-snakes into the ground with our big, high boots, sliding under the belly of our horse when Indians went by, and then regretfully leaving all this and sliding down the banisters again. It was some Old Boy, we discovered later, who had given us these trophies of a life in Mexico for which Papa's Algebra lessons may or may not have prepared him; a boy called Nuñez. Mama remembered him too, but still thought that the bit of buffalo between the horns would collect the moth, and as for the spurs, they would just have to get rusty, that was all. With her permission they did.

On a little table, opposite Mexico, was an aquarium, stocked with samples of all the animal life which the Leg of Mutton pond at Hampstead could show. A piece of coral stood in the middle, and the little fishes and the newts swam through it and around it in a pleasing manner, and sometimes a frog would climb to the top and sit there, half in, half out of the water, and wait, the lid being off, and we watching to see that he did not escape, for flies to come within his jump. The aquarium was emptied each week with a siphon. Papa explained, in his delightfully interesting way, *why* the water continued to rush up one bend of the pipe and down the other, when once you had started it by suction; and we all took turns at starting it by suction; and if anybody sucked too long, and found himself with a mouthful of dirty water and a small left-over newt, it was probably poor old Ken. No doubt Papa went on to tell us, while he was there, all about the Principle of Archimedes, and for days afterwards we would go about shouting 'Eureka' (preferably with nothing on) and at first frightening and then boring our governess.

The first door on the left of the passage led into the drawing-room. The drawing-room had a gas-fire, which was a novelty in those days, and made us wonder whether anybody else in Kilburn had a gas-fire. This was my first acquaintance with asbestos (not that it has ever come into my life very much), and Papa explained asbestos to us; but without any great conviction, being perhaps a little uncertain of it himself. However, as the drawing-room was only used when visitors called, it was convenient to have a gas-fire in it. It was said from time to time in our hearing that Mama had the most beautiful drawing-room in Kilburn. I remember asking a governess once if it were *really* beautiful, or if Mama only thought it was, and she assured me that it really was. Ten years later, when the school had moved to Thanet, and I was at Cambridge (and it was identically the same drawing-room), I asked the matron if *she* really thought it was beautiful. She said she did. So I left it at that. To-day, if the curtain rose on it in the First Act of a period play, it would be received with a round of applause, and Motley or Mr Rex Whistler would walk away with the notices. For it was perfect: it had everything. But I am certain that it meant nothing to my mother. Having seen, in other people's houses, enamelled drain-pipes (for bulrushes), poker-work bellows (for blowing out the gas-fire?) and velvet-embroidered frames (for hand-tinted family groups), she would say scornfully to Father: 'I could make a better one myself,' and prove it. Only one sample of her work remains with me. It is almost her earliest work. Hanging on the wall of the room in which I write is a tapestry reproduction of Leonardo's 'The Last Supper'—three feet by two, as they say in catalogues. In her farm in Derbyshire little Sarah Maria sat stitching, stitching, stitching; and on the snows of the Crimea men lay dying, dying, dying; and in a thousand churches over Europe the Christ to whom little Sarah Maria was paying her childish tribute was pledged in aid of the appropriate artillery. Only Sarah Maria's work has survived. It is always better to be an artist, however little.

The next door led into the sitting-room, and through a door opposite we went into the big schoolroom which was the corresponding drawing-room and sitting-room thrown into one. An iron bar beneath the ceiling marked the old division between the two rooms, and with dependent curtains could make the division again, but it was never so used. Indeed, its only use was an unofficial one which we found for it in the holidays, jumping on to it from a convenient desk and swinging off it on to a more distant one. The first that Papa heard of this was a loud crash one evening, followed by a curious groaning noise. He rushed in to find his Benjamin on the floor, badly winded and quite unable to explain that there was nothing the matter with him except that, being winded, he couldn't explain that there was nothing the matter with him. I was carried up to bed—Mama looking up from her sewing-machine to say 'Better send for Dr Morton, dear, tell Hummerston to go'—and the doctor was sent for; I might have been Royalty. In later years Father would refer to this as the great crisis of my life, and say gravely 'At first we feared for his spine'; and in still later years, when Ken and I did a little amateur rock-climbing, and I slipped, and grazed a shin, Ken would say, 'Hurt?' and then shake his head and say gravely—well, he would hardly need to say it, for it had become a catch-phrase with us.

To return (as I did, in the arms of Papa) to our own side of the house. At the end of the passage were two little rooms. One we needn't bother about. The other was called the music-room, having a piano in it. A Mr Howard came in from time to time, to find out which boys were making a mistake in trying to learn the piano, and under his tuition Ken and I practised a duet for the school concert. I remember this as a wild, romantic piece, full of grace-notes and arpeggios, in the course of which our hands crossed from time to time (intentionally, I mean), and our feet fought vainly for the loud pedal. On referring to it in the school magazine I find that it was called quite simply 'Melodious Exercises,' and the name of the composer is not given. Perhaps I am confusing it with a later appearance at the Town Hall, when the school held what it was pleased to call a Conversazione. On this occasion Ken and I gave a stirring rendition of 'Duet in D,' also anonymous, like the cheaper wines, but obviously in a different class from Melodious Exercises. We also sang a song called 'Tommy and the Apples,' after which it was decided that I had better be something else.

Mr Howard was of French extraction, and had fought in the Franco-German war. Indeed he was said still to have a German bullet in his head, but I may be confusing him with a later acquaintance, a French master at Westminster who was said still to have a German bullet in his behind. They both had bullets, but they may have had them the other way round; and, in one case (since both, I am sure, were brave men), it must have been an accidental French bullet. No doubt all the foreign masters of those days were so credited. There was another one at Henley House who had been engaged for years on an invention to render the tops of omnibuses waterproof. It took the comparatively simple form of a large umbrella in the middle of the floor, but there were technical difficulties about opening and shutting it, which I never understood, and which Mr Steinhardt (if that was his name) never properly surmounted. Perhaps he was a little before his time.

We now open a door on the right, and fall down some stairs into the basement. Beneath the drawing-room was the kitchen, where Davis the cook, and Hummerston, the butler, reigned. I used to think that they were married, but they weren't, which accounts for their having different names. They were as essential a part of Henley House as the buffalo horns, with, in Davis' case, much of their rugged quality. When (some years later) my son was born, our cook, who had been allowed an early pre-view, came down excitedly to tell me that he was 'tall, like mistress.' No doubt Davis, who must have been in at the birth of all of us, gave Hummerston some such rapid summary of the new presentation: 'short, like mistress,' or 'ugly, like the devil.' Of me she probably said: 'Don't tell the master, but it may be an albinium, it's that fair.' Outside the kitchen-door Davis kept a large bin of oatmeal; and when Ken and I got up at five o'clock in the morning, as for various purposes of our own we often did, we would take out a handful of oatmeal from time to time, and stick our tongues into it, thus keeping ourselves alive until the breakfast porridge. Davis made perfect porridge, which was one of the reasons why she stayed with us so long. Papa, being a generation nearer to Scotland than we, never had sugar on his, and was a source of amazement to us, who never had enough. He seemed to have wasted the whole business of growing-up.

Beneath the sitting-room was what the rest of the school called The Kids' Room. Here we ate, lived, worked, played with our governess, until we had left Miss Budd's, and here, when we were part of the school, was still our home from home.

Chapter Three

1

WE WERE undoubtedly part of the school, but we still had long hair, and one foot in the Family Side of the house. A kindly old gentleman, whose function it was to preside over the annual examination set by the College of Preceptors, came across me in the sitting-room on his first arrival, and was so carried away by my nursery charm that he turned up next morning with a toy butcher's-shop for the little one. It was a good shop in its small way, the joints of meat being realistically coloured and hung on hooks, but in the interval, under his not too invigilating eye, I had been dealing with the Algebra paper, and, as appeared later, had got ninety-five marks out of a hundred. Mama said, 'Well, he didn't know, darling,' and Papa said that it was really very kind of him, and I must write him a letter, and I wrote him a letter: reluctantly: feeling that, if only I could have my hair cut, the need for these letters would not arise. Only a few days before, owing to the fact that, by some mismanagement, it was my hair-washing night, I had nearly missed a meeting of the school Debating Society at which we pledged ourselves to give Lord Salisbury's foreign policy our support. When women complain to me now of the time they have to spend at the hairdresser's, and the subsequent appointments for which they are late, and the bother it all is, I smile to myself in a superior way. They're telling me. Me!

The only occasion on which I spoke in the Debating

Society was at what was called an 'Impromptu Debate.'
The names of the members were put into one hat, the
subjects for speech into another. In an agony of nervousness I waited for my name to be called. It came at last,
'Milne Three.' Milne III tottered up and drew his fate;
not that it mattered, for one subject was as fatal to him as
another. He tottered back to his desk and opened the
paper. The subject on which he had to speak was 'Gymnastics.'

I stood there dumbly. I could think of nothing. The
boy next to me, misapprehending the meaning of the
word 'impromptu,' whispered to me: 'Gymnastics
strengthens the muscles.' I swallowed and said, 'Gym-
nathticth thtrengthenth the muthelth.' Then I sat down.
This is the shortest speech I have ever made, and possibly, for that reason, the best. A little later I came out
top in the Gymnastics Competition (Junior Division),
and won a prize . . . and (presumably) strengthened the
muscles. I also boxed a boy called Harris; we were the
only competitors. No doubt I made some use of my hair
for covering-up purposes, such as would not be allowed
in the ring to-day. The result was declared a draw, 'Harris using his right with good effect, but Milne III dodging
well,' or so the magazine chronicled. Probably I ran away
and he couldn't catch me.

And what was Ken doing all this time? No prizes or
showings-off for him. And equally no grudges against
me. School meant little to either of us compared with
the life we lived together, a life into which competition
did not come.

We had two day-dreams. The first was of a life on the
sea. This was the result of reading that great book *The
Three Midshipmen*. We three (for Barry was in this for
a moment) would be three midshipmen, and capture
Arab dhows, knife sharks, and swim through the heaving

waters with a rope in our teeth. After talking the matter over carefully, we went up to the sitting-room to announce our decision. We went solemnly in, closed the door behind us (as requested) and spoke by the mouth of the eldest.

'We have come to tell you that we all three want to be sailors.'

It must have been a little surprising to Papa, coming for no apparent reason at no particular moment, but he took it well. He just said, 'Well, you'll have to work, you know. There will be examinations to pass.' This was the moment when Barry decided not to be a sailor. Ken and I, however, continued to prepare ourselves for a life on the sea. We used to go for long walks, taking care to keep in step all the time, for we felt that the ability of two sailors to march in step for long periods must count in a naval career. We also tried chewing tobacco. This is said to allay the pangs of hunger, and is obviously more useful when shipwrecked than when aboard a well-found vessel. In the sense that we were not hungry for a long time afterwards we did allay the pangs of hunger, but the experiment was not really a success, and we decided that, if any ship we were in should find herself piled up on a coral-reef, we would remain on board with the captain. It was only when Ken accidentally got a scholarship at Westminster that my love for the sea left me, for I knew then that I could not be happy until I had got a scholarship too. As I have said, I did this when I was eleven, and a year or so later the Headmaster wrote in my report: 'Have you ever thought of the Navy as a profession for him? I think it would be the making of him. Or is he too good for that?' That was as near as I got to the Navy: my father thought that I was too good for it. I like telling sailors this story. They laugh breezily, but you can see that they are affected by it.

Our other dream must have been with us earlier, for if it had become reality, there would have been no Navy to join. Our dream was, quite simply, that we should wake up one morning and find that everybody else in the world was dead.

This sounds callous, but it was really no more than a variation of the desert-island dream which every small boy has. It just didn't seem possible to get to a desert island, Kilburn being where it was. The problem bristled with difficulties. The adventure couldn't begin until we were on some sort of schooner, and how would Papa, who could never get us off by train to Sevenoaks in the summer without arriving an hour too soon at Victoria, and saying, 'Thank you, thank you, thank you. Good morning to you, a happy Christmas,' to every porter of whom he took directions, how would Papa ever get us on to a schooner? And it was as unimaginable that he should let us go without him, as it was that we should go without permission. Almost as babies we were allowed to go walks by ourselves anywhere, in London or in the country, but we kept to the rules, and he knew that he could trust us. Schooners were out. A desert island was an impossibility.

But it *was* conceivable that God, who had done something on these lines more than once, should destroy everybody in the world but Ken and me. And even if He were not doing it directly, or with any great enthusiasm, yet (as it were, in spite of Him) disasters did happen, a plague might fall upon the people, and everybody might die. (Except Ken and me.) One could imagine it. Papa doesn't have to take tickets for anywhere first. He just dies like the rest of them . . . 'and leaves the world to dear old Ken and me.'

Yes, it sounds horrible put like that. For we loved him dearly; we loved Mama too, though not so dearly; we loved Bee—and, more fitfully, Davis and Hummerston. We also loved a succession of animals. We were not unloving children, and of course we should keep the animals anyhow. It was just that we wanted to be alone, and free. In a week, perhaps: perhaps less if one of us hurt himself badly: in a week we should wish them all alive again. But oh! to wake up one morning and find that everybody was dead—except Ken and me.

It was the freedom of the sweet-shops which we wanted most. Never to have to pass a sweet-shop again, but to be able to step in confidently over the body of the dead proprietor—that was Heaven. All up the High Road, darting from side to side as the fancy took us, across to West End Lane where they had those particularly good marzipan potatoes, over the footbridge to the Finchley Road (jumbles), and then up Fitzjohn's Avenue to the Heath, stopping at that little shop on the right for ices, ices, ices: this was our immediate programme, this was how we planned it out in bed. Afterwards we might put on a Mexican spur each, and see if we could lasso something, and there was probably a good deal to be done in Wastnage's Cycle Shop where Maida Vale began. And could one drive a 'bus? When one sat on the box seat and talked to the driver, he didn't seem to be doing much. Well, now we would know. So many things to eat, so many things to try!

As a fact we were given more freedom than most children. We had a habit of getting up early, and it seemed to be understood, at any rate by us, that, if we got up early, we could do what we liked, so long as we did not wake Papa and Mama. At one time we had a passion for hoops; not the slow wooden hoop, which is hit intermittently with a wooden stick until it falls lifeless into the gutter, but the fiery iron hoop spurred by a hooked iron prong from which it can never escape. Even now I can recapture the authentic thrill of those early-morning raids on London, as we drove our hoops through little, blinded streets, clean and empty and unaware of us; never tiring as we should have tired with no magic circle of iron to lure us on; lured now into a remote world of tall, silent houses, pillared like temples, behind whose doors strange, unreal lives were lived; until at last we burst into the Bayswater Road, and wondered if anybody had ever run before from Kilburn to the Bayswater Road, and what Papa would say when we told him. Then back to breakfast, with pauses now for breath, and chatter, and challenges to each other, back to Davis' porridge, back to the most divine meal of the day, the only meal which could never be a disappointment.

There came into the house one day two bamboo poles, twelve feet long. Papa had cousins in Jamaica, had indeed been born there, though whether this was to our glory or our shame, a fact to be circulated or suppressed, we could never be sure. On the one hand, very few boys could say that their fathers had been born in Jamaica; on the other, most of those who could had woolly hair. Somehow it seemed to leave Papa not quite an Englishman, and us, in consequence, a little suspect. Well, anyhow, there were the two bamboos, sent over by an optimistic relation, who hoped that Cousin John and Cousin Maria would find them interesting. Cousin Maria looked them over, and finding that they were as good as poker-worked already, that they couldn't be enamelled, and that even if cut into lengths, they were serviceable only for firewood, disavowed interest; but Cousin John, a little on the defensive and feeling that he owed it to the West Indies, attached them, as a rowing-man his oars, to the wall over the aquarium.

At five-thirty next morning Ken and I slid down the banisters, turned our backs on Mexico, climbed on to the aquarium table and removed the trophies. We found them interesting. At the moment he was Robin Hood and I was Will Scarlett, but we might change round later; the important thing was that here at last were those 'quarterstaffs' for which we had been looking so long, and with which a 'bout' was so long overdue. We would go into the playground and have a bout.

At six o'clock an angry head looked out of an upper window. We had forgotten about him. It was one of the masters, and he said very loudly and clearly: 'What the deuce do you think you're doing?' We could have told him that Little John was now having a bout with Friar Tuck, and that, as far as could be seen, neither was having an advantage over the other, but by this time we were as tired of the business as he was. It had sounded so wonderful in bed the night before, talking it over, but the wonder had gone, our arms were aching, and it would be more fun to empty the aquarium and fill it again. There was a finality about complete emptiness which neither of us (it seemed) could hope to achieve with a quarterstaff. We trailed in, replaced the oars, had a handful of oatmeal before Davis came down, took a suck at the syphon and thought perhaps not, went a quick walk round Mortimer Road and Greville Place, crossed the gymnasium on our stomachs, kicked a stone across the playground hopping on one foot (very difficult, we would get up really early one morning and do it properly), and were in our places for 'prep' at seven o'clock. The school day was beginning.

2

In a current number of the school magazine there was an analysis by 'J. V. M.' of the characters of certain boys, for whose names letters of the alphabet were substituted.

Since in my case (I was 'D') the author was not only schoolmaster but father, he may be assumed to have been speaking with authority—in so far as the old can speak with authority for the young, or, indeed, for anybody but themselves.

D. He does not like French—does not see that you prove anything when you have done. Thinks mathematics grand. He leaves his books about; loses his pen; can't imagine what he did with this, and where he put that, but is convinced that it is somewhere. Clears his brain when asked a question by spurting out some nonsense, and then immediately after gives a sensible reply. Can speak 556 words per minute, and writes more in three minutes than his instructor can read in thirty. Finds this a very interesting world, and would like to learn physiology, botany, geology, astronomy and everything else. Wishes to make collections of beetles, bones, butterflies, etc., and cannot determine whether Algebra is better than football or Euclid than a sponge-cake.

It is the portrait of an enthusiast.

Many years later, when I was myself the father of a boy of D's age, I was a guest at a dinner of Preparatory Schoolmasters. They all, so it seemed, made speeches; two Public School Headmasters made speeches; and the burden of all their specches was the obstructiveness of the Parent to their beneficent labours. I had disclaimed any desire to make a speech, but by this time I wanted to. That very evening, offered the alternatives of a proposition of Euclid's or a chapter of *Treasure Island* as a bedtime story my own boy had chosen Euclid: it was 'so much more fun.' All children, I said (perhaps rashly), are like that. There is nothing that they are not eager to learn. 'And then we send them to your schools, and in two years, three years, four years, you have killed all their enthusiasm. At fifteen their only eagerness is to escape learning anything. No wonder you don't want to meet us.' It was not a popular speech. 'Gymnastics strengthens the muscles' would have gone better. But afterwards a Headmaster came up to me and said: 'It was absolutely true what you were saying, but why is it? What do we do? I've often wondered.'

So if at this time I was still an enthusiast, it was because I was still at my father's school, and he was an enthusiast. And if I disliked French, and thought mathematics grand, it was because he, who could teach, taught me mathematics, and did not teach me French. As I said once to a Headmaster, a school report cuts both ways; it is a report on the teacher as well as on the taught. 'Seems completely uninterested in this subject' may mean no more than that the master is completely uninteresting. In Papa's house it was natural to be interested, it was easy to be clever.

We 'collected' everything. We collected 'minerals.' We bought a 'geological hammer,' whose head was like a chisel at one end and a marlinspike at the other. With this on one Easter holiday we attacked the cliffs of Ramsgate for ammonites, stalactites, stalagmites and fossilized remains of prehistoric animals. We got no more than a piece out of poor old Ken's leg, with the chisel end. Nevertheless our collection grew. It included Iceland spar, Blue-John spar and various other exciting crystals. In those days I knew that granite was composed of 'mica, feldspar and quartz.' Perhaps it still is. We spent many a Sunday afternoon in the neighbourhood of Finchley Road looking for a stray piece of feldspar which had got separated from its quartz. Every night our collection was taken from its drawer in the dressing-table and laid out on Ken's bed.

On one proud afternoon we set out to show our collection to the Curator of the Geological Museum in Jermyn

Street. He hadn't invited us, we just thought that as fellow-workers in the same field we ought to meet. Papa gave us the 'bus money to Oxford Circus, and made us promise not to cross Piccadilly without a policeman. We went. We still looked like Shirley Temple, and we had our collection tied up in a fairly clean handkerchief of Ken's. The Curator was a little surprised at first, thinking that we were offering it to the nation; but when we explained that we only wanted one or two things identified, he was very helpful, identifying one ammonite as an old date-stone, and telling us all about Blue-John Spar. In return we told him all about mica-feldspar-and-quartz. And now we had to cross Piccadilly Circus again. The first time had been easy. There was the policeman, there the traffic. The one held the other up, and we crossed royally. But now, as it happened, Piccadilly was entirely empty. We could have played leap-frog across it, we could have stopped in the middle of the street and spread out our collection again. Yet we had promised Papa; and without (I think) being prigs, we did believe that a promise was a promise. So, after a little discussion on the pavement, we waved to a policeman. He came across to us majestically, and, not understanding about promises, was extremely annoyed when we asked if we could go back with him. He strode away with great dignity and we followed with an air of being in the party.

We had twopence of our own to spend. Half of it went on a box of fusees. Fusees, I should explain, were very, *very* much more exciting than ordinary matches, and we proposed to strike one every night after the lights were out. In this way a box would last for several weeks. The other penny was to be spent at Callard and Bowser's in Regent Street. We were looking wistfully in at the window, wondering how best to lay the money out, and wishing it were more, when we attracted the notice of a

61

passer-by. He may have had a dear little girl just like us, or he may have wished he had, but for whatever reason he stopped, put a shilling on the top of the matchbox which I was holding, and hurried on. We could now, we felt, buy the shop.

But we didn't. Not for a moment did it seem possible to keep the money. We had promised never to take money from strangers. It shows how completely Ken and I were one (and perhaps how completely Papa had our love and our confidence) that we didn't even argue about it. We spent our penny, giving the shilling in payment. Sixpence went into a missionary-box on the counter, Ken being anxious to do something definite for the Chinese, about whom he had been reading lately; threepence went to a crossing sweeper at the next corner; the remaining three pennies were taken home and put in the dressing-table drawer with the 'collection.' After all, they were 'minerals' too.

Were we too good, too Shirley Temple? If so, we made up for it later; as regards finance, no later than in our schooldays at Westminster. In any case, I am (oddly enough) more ashamed of the bad things I have done than of the good things I have done, of the promises broken than of the promises kept. I like to think of that threepence in the drawer, *tabu* even in the darkest days before the Saturday pocket-money.

Pocket-money began by being a penny a week, and was then increased to threepence on condition that we didn't drink tea. Later we seemed to be drinking tea and still having threepence, so I suppose there was a time-limit to the condition. I remember going with one of the boys to see his aunt (don't ask me why), and as we left, she pressed a coin into my hand. The aunt of a Henley House boy was obviously not a stranger, and a ha'penny was a ha'penny, but when we were safely away and good manners allowed me to open my hand, it was a shilling. I can remember my utter incredulity, my certainty that a mistake had been made, until the nephew showed me his own florin. Being a good deal bigger than I, and it being *his* aunt, he might well have claimed my shilling too, but he contented himself with sending me into a chemist's shop to buy him twopennyworth of pigeon's milk. This was a great joke of those days, but unfortunately for him I knew it. Poor old Ken had bought it a few days before.

3

In our walks abroad, looking for feldspar and caterpillars, and qualifying for the Navy, we were accompanied by a Gordon setter called Brownie. Brownie attached himself to the family at Sevenoaks, where we had taken a house for the summer. If I couldn't remember dates any other way (and I am not remembering them very well) I should always know that I was seven at Sevenoaks. Brownie was gun-shy, and a clap of thunder would send him under the table, so I suppose that he had been shown the door of whatever lordly kennels he had been disgracing. He came to our house, collarless and unhappy; in less than a week it was clear that he was ours and we were his. He was beautiful and faithful and loving, and, with the possible exception of Papa, the most admirable character in the family. We took him back to Henley House. He was ours.

It was on a damp and misty Sunday afternoon that Brownie first proved his real value as a sporting dog. The rejected of Knole became the hero of Finchley. In a field off the Finchley Road he began to dig; our excitement grew with his; and when a mouse scurried out, no ordinary domestic mouse, but a live field-mouse, we felt one with Bevis, Masterman Ready and the Swiss Family

Robinson. We were real country boys who had caught a real country mouse with a real sporting dog. All the secrets of the wild were ours; put us on a desert island and we should be for ever at home. Mice in themselves were nothing to us. We had bought mice, we had swapped mice. But to catch your own wild mouse, there was glory for you.

At the moment, however, we hadn't caught it, nor, it seemed, would. But Brownie was still at his hole, and another mouse might come out. We prayed (it was Sunday afternoon) that another mouse might come out; another mouse did; and this time we were ready. We took it home and built a special cage for it. The mouse lived long enough to enjoy it, but died soon after, and was buried in the front garden amid the geraniums, the lobelias and the calceolarias. The little town, as Lord Tennyson had been saying, had never known a costlier funeral.

It was at this time, while still feeling countryish, that we found a toad and decided to stuff it. We began by trying to climb a tree, and when I had got a little way up, I fell out of it. Luckily nobody feared for my spine; but two little girls, who were playing with their mother in the same field, came running up to us. They stood hand-in-hand, very shy, and one said to the other, '*You* ask him,' and the other said, 'No, *you*,' and the first said, 'Let's bofe,' so together they said, 'Have you hurt yourself?' and I said, 'No,' and they ran back to their mother. From then on, whenever Ken and I wanted to do a thing together we said, 'Let's bofe,' and giggled. Well, now we were on the ground, and bofe looking, with Brownie's help, for anything we could find, and there was this toad, and it seemed suddenly of enormous importance that we should have a stuffed toad to live with us. Was it already dead, or did we kill it? I cannot remember. But there and then, the little girls and their mother having gone home to tea, we cut it open and removed its inside. It was astonishing how little, and how little like a toad, the remnant was. However, we took it home and put it in the mineral drawer, where gradually it dried, looking less and less like a toad each time we considered it. But a secret so terrific, a deed so bloody, had to be formulated. The initial formula was Raw Toad (as you would have believed, if you had seen what we saw). Raw Toad was R.T., which was 'arte,' and Latin for 'by with or from art.' Artus was a limb (or wasn't it?) and the first and last letters of limb were L.B. Lb. was pound; you talked about a 'pig in a pound'; pig was P.G. and (Greek now, Ken has just begun Greek) πηγη was fountain. So, ranging lightly over several languages, we had reached our mystic formula—'FN.' Thumbs on the same hymn-book in Dr Gibson's church, we would whisper 'FN,' to each other and know that life was not all Sunday; side by side in the drawing-room, hair newly brushed for visitors and in those damnable starched sailor suits, we would look 'FN' at each other and be comforted. And though, within six months (the toad still unstuffed and crumbled into dust), we were sharing some entirely different secret, yet, forty years later, the magic letters had power to raise sudden memories in two middle-aged men, smoking their pipes, and wondering what to do with their sons.

4

Papa had a great friend called Dr Willis, and in our hearing never called him anything else; but I suppose that, when we were not there, they relaxed and called each other Milne and Willis. Very few Victorians were on Christian name terms with each other; Holmes, after twenty years of intimacy, was still calling his colleague Watson. Dr Willis lived in West End Lane. He was in

some sort of partnership with our own Dr Morton, whose
wife spoke always of Mr Willis, since her husband was
an M.D. and Dr Willis was only a M.R.C.S. He was a
man of great enthusiasms, a man, I should say, of great
charm to a contemporary; in appearance a little like
Trilby's friend Taffy, and with the same passion for
exercise. By an ingenious arrangement of his own invention, he could fix up a horizontal bar in his study, and
on Saturday nights a few friends would drop in, say good-
evening to Mrs Willis, and follow their host in astonishing 'up-starts' and long arm balances. He had a theory,
or had made the discovery, that most toadstools, cooked
the right way, were good to eat, and in his spare moments
would lead expeditions to search for the right ones. A
particularly loathsome-looking growth was called 'inky,'
though not, I suppose, by botanists. It is fair to say that
he would never risk the lives of his guests with inky, but
only those of his own family.

It was Dr Willis who taught Papa to ride a bicycle.
They discussed life on long bicycle rides together. 'I
remember Dr Willis saying to me once when we were
out cycling'—how many times in his old age Father would
begin like this; and Ken and I, if we were both there,
would catch each other's eye, and wonder which of the
historic sayings this would be. Sometimes Father was the
author: 'I remember saying to Dr Willis.' One day Dr
Willis must have said to Papa, 'More people ought to
eat toadstools,' or Papa must have said to Dr Willis, 'Isn't
Nature wonderful?'—however it was, in a little while Dr
Willis had heard of, or was organizing, a series of Botan-
ical Lectures. About twenty very earnest people attended
them, as did Papa, Ken and myself. We all met at the
appointed place, which might be Edgware or Rickmans-
worth or Highgate Woods, and trailed after the lecturer,
Ken and I trying, whenever possible, to trail at the end.

There was one tremendous afternoon when we got into the wrong train, or mistook the meeting-place, or the day, or something, and sat happily on the bank of a river, just the three of us, and played and talked, and never heard a word about pistils or stamens; and, after that, since it was now proved possible, we prayed every Thursday that we might miss the party again. Heaven, however, only managed it once more—on a day, as it happened, when Papa couldn't come. The rendezvous was Highgate Woods, a place in which anybody, even if interested in botany, might get lost, and we lay on our stomachs in a ride, and raced caterpillars across it, until the approaching voice of the lecturer warned us that we must move along, quickly, and look for him in some more distant part of the wood.

It would seem from this that I was not so eager to learn botany as my character-reading suggested. Let us put it down to the dullness of the lecturer. A little later I had another opportunity, for there came to Henley House a young Science Master, the first it had ever had. As he has told in his own autobiography, this was H. G. Wells, no less. On the publication of that great work, a newspaper rang me up to ask if I remembered Wells as a schoolmaster, and if he had taught me anything. I said that he had taught me all the botany I never learnt. ' "Yes," said Mr Milne, "he taught me all the botany I know" ' was how it appeared in the paper next morning, as if between us we had exhausted the subject. H. G. is a great writer, and a great friend, and I am indebted to him for many things, most of all for the affection which he always felt for my father; but he was not a great schoolmaster. He was too clever and too impatient. He had the complete attention of his class once when vivisecting a frog (kindly provided by a day-boy), but school-life was not lived at that level, and on the lower slopes we lost him. Fortunately we met him again in the school magazine; in which for a year or two he kicked and stretched himself, before jumping, fully waked, into the world of letters.

Chapter Four

1

THE best of our life was lived in the summer holidays, and it is only by them that I remember dates. 'That,' I think, 'was the Limpsfield year; it was the Seaford year that I had my hair cut.'

The first holiday which I remember clearly was the one at Cobham in Kent: Mr. Pickwick's Cobham—or, if you prefer it, Lord Darnley's. It was in 1888. I was six.

As a child I had a habit of little illnesses, which meant nothing, but kept me out of school; I suspect that they were due either to over-eating or to the fact that I was the Headmaster's Benjamin. Probably Papa and Mama were only too glad of an excuse to stop me working. I can see myself now, propped in Mama's big bed, and waiting in great embarrassment for Ken to kiss me good-night. He had no desire at all to do this, nor I that he should, but he had been told to 'say good-night to Alan and run along,' and we had realized with a simultaneous horror that a kiss was expected. We delayed it up to the very last second, but there was no escaping. In an agony of unhappiness we kissed; Ken ran out of the room; and an unsuspecting mother took my temperature. It had gone up alarmingly.

But in 1888 I had been more definitely ill. I had what was to me a lump, but to Dr Morton a glandular swelling on my neck, and I was sent to Margate with Bee in search of fresh air. Whether anything more was intended at the time I don't know; regardless of his doom the little victim played on the sands; and a fortnight later Papa came down and took me to see Dr Treves, brother of the great Sir Frederick. He decided to operate next morning.

It may interest other parents to hear that

1. For all Papa's and Bee's innocence I *knew* on that first morning that something dreadful was going to happen, and I was terrified while waiting to see the doctor.

2. Though now I knew what was going to happen, the rest of the day, picnicking with Papa and Bee on the sands, and going over the North Foreland lighthouse, was (though for Papa, no doubt, complete misery) for me complete happiness.

3. Next morning I waited, and went into the operating-room, quite unfrightened.

4. On the following morning I was terrified again, but didn't cry when the dressings were taken off; and thereafter was quite happy, and extremely cocky about the whole thing.

It was now August, and as soon as we could say good-bye to Dr Treves, Bee and I joined the family at Cobham. Barry and Ken were very excited to see me, because they had discovered a wonderful walk which the three of us were to take early next morning. At six o'clock we started off, I very proud and stolid in my bandage, and Barry and Ken running round me in circles, telling me of the wonderful thing we were going to see. It was a castle, and to-morrow we should go into the castle, but to-day we could only look at it from the outside. Even though I had been inside a lighthouse (and they hadn't) I was thrilled at the idea of seeing this castle from the outside. Was it far away? Yes, a good long way, we should have a long walk first; and Ken looked down suddenly and said that he had swallowed a fly, but it really sounded more like a laugh than a cough, which made me think that perhaps it wasn't so far away after all. I was wrong. We walked, and we walked, and we walked. . . .

At last we came to the castle.

'There!' they said proudly. 'Isn't that lovely?'

It had a grey stone tower. It was lovely.

'Couldn't we go in now?' I asked.

'Well, we *could,* but as we're all going to-morrow, I think we'd better wait.'

'Oh, all right,' I said.

Ken looked at Barry, and said: 'I'm rather hungry, aren't *you,* Alan?'

I was always hungry.

'Let's go into that house and ask them to give us some milk.'

'Don't let's,' I said quickly. (How *could* we?)

'*I'm* not afraid,' said Barry. 'Are *you* afraid, Ken?'

Ken, to my surprise, wasn't.

'Oh, all right,' I said.

We knocked at the door. (How *silly* of them both.) The door opened.

'There you are, darlings,' said Davis. 'Just in time for breakfast.'

This is the most completely successful joke which has ever been played on me. Next day, being Sunday, we all went to the 'castle.' I was only six, remember.

Ken was eight on the 1st of September. One of his presents was a bow and arrows. It was no good putting an apple on my head and expecting me to stand still, I was eating the apple long before they had got to the shooting-mark. So we all shot arrows in the air, they fell we knew not where. In a little while Ken's birthday-present was dissipated. He was unlucky in that his birth-day, coming in the summer holidays, brought useful, out-door presents which we could all share. It was really a communal birthday. But he was always unlucky. At the

71

school Sports in 1892 (its only Sports meeting) he was second in the open Half Mile Handicap (190 yards) and won the useful present of a whisky-flask. He let me look at it on the way home, I dropped it, and that was the end of Ken's flask. I offered him my useful aneroid barometer (first prize, also from the 190-yard mark), but he wouldn't take it. However, as you can't keep an aneroid barometer private, it was really as much his as mine. Later on, Barry sold my bicycle for a pound, and gave the pound to Ken, so matters even themselves out in the end. We bore no grudges about that sort of thing.

Our house was next to what used to be The Leather Bottle and was now The Pickwick Inn. Papa explained to us about that, and we agreed with him that it was a great pity. At the church opposite we had our first sight of a surplice, which was very exciting, and kept our interest until it was time to miss the sermon. Most of our weekdays were spent with Bee in Cobham Park, and, more particularly, at the top of a high wooden erection called The Crow's Nest, from which there was a wonderful view of the Medway and the Thames. One day, while we were camped there, Lord Darnley brought a friend to admire the view, and seeing from the bottom that there was no room at the top, sent Papa a message through the Vicar, to say that he was delighted for us to use The Crow's Nest as long as he could use it himself sometimes too, and would we mind not nesting there. We were all very sorry; and an uncle who was staying with us, and who spent half the day swimming in one of the ponds in Cobham Woods, went off quickly to Paris to see the Paris Exhibition; but whether from remorse or because he wanted to see the Paris Exhibition, I don't know.

It was not until Limpsfield (1890) that Ken and I really found our walking form, but we did go out alone one

early morning—he just eight, I six—and walked and
walked until we came to the outskirts of Gravesend. We
got a little frightened then, and wondered if a press-gang
would kidnap us and send us down the river in a sea-
going merchantman; and we turned back and talked very
quickly about breakfast, to hide, each from the other,
that just for a moment something had happened. It never
happened again. Together we had no fears of anybody
or anything, nor were ever given cause for them.

2

Sevenoaks seems now to have granted us our least
happy holiday; I don't know why; perhaps because it was
so definitely not a village. We played in Knole Park (but
were careful not to camp in the best bedroom); we played
in the chalk-pit at Dunton Green, and we found Brownie.
The Heaven-sent gift of Brownie may have driven every
lesser happiness from my memory. But I remember
Penshurst Place.

Philip Sydney was born at Penshurst Place. Having
written this, I thought that I would make sure of it, for
very often people are not born in the places expected of
them. So I looked for my *Life of Philip Sydney,* and on
the front page I read, in my father's writing, 'Alan A.
Milne, gymnastics. Under 14.' I was talking about this in
the last chapter, but I had forgotten what the prize was,
or that I still had it. In some odd way it gives me the impression (as I hope it gives the reader) that this autobiography is going to be more truthful than most. At
any rate we haven't gone wrong over gymnastics. Well,
in 1889 I hadn't seen a real gymnasium, so we didn't
know much about Philip Sydney, but we did know about
the glass of water; and when we heard that we were going

to see his house, we shouldn't have been surprised if next day we had driven in some other direction and seen Hector's house, or Hereward the Wake's.

At Penshurst Place we had arranged to meet an Old Henley House Boy, called Alfred Harmsworth. It was he who had started the *Henley House School Magazine* in 1881, and he was now starting *Answers*. This was the first time I met him. The next time, as will be told if I get as far as that, was in 1903, when he was Sir Alfred of the *Daily Mail* and the Amalgamated Press, and I was just beginning to be (as I hoped) a 'writer.' My one vivid memory of him on this occasion was, naturally, concerned with food. We had been over Penshurst Place, we had lunched and, for whatever reason, the grown-ups now wanted to get rid of the children. So we were sent into the village to buy ourselves sweets. And Harmsworth pulled out a great handful of pennies, just as if he had been selling *Answers* personally round the corner, and poured them into our pockets with an ease of manner which convinced us that he was already the millionaire which afterwards he was to become. 'Isn't he rich?' we said to each other. 'I *say!*'

3

It is time to introduce Ken as the writer of the family. We were at Limpsfield in 1890, Ken was just ten, I was eight-and-a-half. He wrote an article for the school magazine called 'My Holidays,' and I wrote one called 'My Three Days' Walking Tour.' I was all that younger than he, and it is natural that my article should seem childish compared with his. But I am now forty-seven years older than he was then, and I still do not see how, for all the million words I have written, I am to better his description of one of our walks. Here, then, is Ken's contribution to this book.

CHILD

A few days afterwards Alan and myself went for a walk. We started about 10.30 a.m. It was a lovely day, and very hot. Nothing occurred until we reached Godstone Church, about three and three-quarter miles. Here we asked for a glass of water which refreshed us and made us ready to start again. Here our adventures began. We started, and when we had gone on a little way we asked a baker's boy how we could get to a little village called Tandridge, about four miles distant. His answer was this: 'Go along the road until you pass the gentleman's house, then you'll see a stile leading across a field, go along it, round the pond, over a bridge, through the wood, and you will find yourself on the Tandridge High Street.' Well, we happened to remember this; but we could not carry it out, for when we saw the gentleman's house we actually went through his garden, and along his paths. Soon we found where we were, and hastening out, we went over the stile, which led to three magnificent ponds, and a gentleman was fishing there. Thinking that it was no use carrying out the baker's boy's orders, we asked this gentleman the way to Tandridge. After he had given his answer, we failed to remember it, and we said that we would toss up for it, and it came that we had to find our own way, as there was no one about. We passed through some hop-fields, and came into a potato-field. Here we asked a labourer the way to Tandridge. Luckily, he said that if we went straight along this path we would find ourselves in Tandridge; and we did. Here we felt the heat terribly, and taking off our coats and rolling up our shirt-sleeves we set out. After a great deal of wandering we found ourselves on the Godstone road. Now, if we had liked, we could have gone straight home; but as we were not tired, we thought we would take a longer way; and reading the sign-post, we found that we would get to Limpsfield, only in a longer direction. Here we found the time was one o'clock; and hastening back, we reached home at two o'clock. It was a very enjoyable walk, about twelve miles.

He was ten when he wrote that—and I was eight when I walked it.

AUTOBIOGRAPHY

Limpsfield (to quote Ken again) 'was a pretty village, small, and with a few shops. We lived about the middle of the village (which was on a slope).' Later on, in an account of a cycle ride, he says: 'We pushed our machines up Limpsfield Hill (a very steep hill, and not worth while riding up) and then mounted them.' Now the parenthesis may make you smile, as you think to yourself: 'I know that sort of hill that is "not worth while" riding up; I know many things which are "not worth while" doing, as soon as one finds that one can't do them.' But Ken also may have had an ironical smile as he closed his brackets, for in fact we did ride up Limpsfield Hill once, and found that it was not so much worth while as we had hoped.

We had a tandem tricycle. Ken sat behind, and had the steering, the bell and the brake under his control; I sat in front and had the accident. Sharing a bed is really nothing compared with sharing a tandem tricycle. Bent double against a head-wind or a hill, the one in front feels, with every labouring breath, more and more certain that the one behind is hanging his feet over the handle-bars and looking at the scenery; and the one behind (according to Ken, but I doubt it) is just as convinced that he is doing all the work himself, and that the one in front is merely going through the motions of an entirely unfounded exhaustion. However, though we quarrelled about it, we remained inseparable. Now, that same uncle who was with us for a little at Cobham before going to the Paris Exhibition, was with us for a little at Limpsfield (before going, I suppose, to the Paris Exhibition); and he had promised us that, if ever we rode the whole way up Limpsfield Hill, he would give us sixpence each. So early one morning, after a period of training, we started out to win this great reward. Even to-day it must be a fairly steep hill, but to us then it seemed almost unscaleable. There were times when we were in danger of going backwards, and Ken had to jam on the brake and give us a moment's easy; times when we had to stand on the pedals in order to force them round. Slowly we went up, not straight but in serpentine fashion, crossing and re-crossing the road, puffing and blowing, resting again with the brake on (but of course not dismounting), and then putting all of our strength into 'twenty good ones,' so as to work up a little momentum for the extra steep corner that was coming. . . . And we did it. We lay on the common at the top of the hill, still panting but profoundly happy, and made plans to spend our shilling. A whole shilling; what a day! What an uncle! Luxuriously we coasted back to the house, put the tricycle away, and went triumphantly into breakfast. *'We've done it!'*

And we were disqualified. The uncle said that we had stopped on the way. Well, of course we had, we'd just told him. But that wasn't fair. What d'you mean, not fair? Well, suppose it had been a hill-climbing competition for bicycles, then you *couldn't* stop and rest. But this wasn't bicycles, it was tricycles. Yes, but you weren't allowed to stop, that was the rule. Well, why hadn't he made the rules for us before we began? Naturally, he thought we knew; everybody knew that you couldn't stop and *rest*. But we'd *told* him, we'd have gone *backwards* if we hadn't put the brake on. Well, there we were, we hadn't done it.

We looked at him, entirely bewildered. Such a thing had never happened to us before.

'Do you mean——'

'Get on with your porridge now, dear,' said Mama. 'We can talk about it afterwards.'

'Do you mean,' said Ken slowly, picking up his porridge spoon with a trembling hand, 'that we don't get the money?'

'Of course you don't. You didn't do it.'

We got on with our porridge. For the first time in our lives porridge brought us no satisfaction. Civilization had crashed. Say not the struggle nought availeth, the labour and the wounds are vain; but that was how it seemed to be at the moment. We finished our breakfast in silence, we separated, each of us afraid, perhaps, that the other might want to cry and would rather do it alone. It was Papa who found me, and said: 'Rules are rules, darling, but I think you deserve a consolation prize,' and left a small tin of sweets in my hand; Mama who found Ken and said: 'Never mind, dear, your uncle *is* like that sometimes, and I think it was wonderful that you did it at all,'—comforting words when accompanied by threepence. We joined each other more cheerfully, a cheerfulness which was doubled when we found that the other had got something too; we trotted down the village to our favourite shop.

Now here was Providence's great chance of doing something spectacular. Providence, however, is rarely tempted by the spectacular, seeming in fact quite lackadaisical about what she is doing. She does not trouble to choose the exact moment, neither for her favours nor her frowns. There was a large, flat, circular chocolate-cream to be bought at this shop, whose extraordinary virtue was that its slightly hollow inside *might* contain a sixpenny-bit. We bought twelve. Assuming that Papa and Mama had given us equal presents, we were exactly sixpence short. We had never yet bitten into one of the lucky chocolates. Surely to-day, with twelve chances and being owed sixpence anyway—— No. Providence remained stolid. And, as far as uncles were concerned,

Limpsfield Hill remained 'a very steep hill, not worth while riding up.'

I shall now introduce myself as a writer, on my first appearance in print:

We walked to Edenbridge, six miles, and drank out of a pump—and while we were drinking a girl came to us and told us we were drinking river-water, so we went into a shop and bought some ginger-beer. After we had had a good drink we walked to Hever. . . . When we got to Hever, a distance of nine miles, we had a good dinner. While we were waiting for dinner we went over Hever Church and Castle, where Queen Anne Boleyn was born. We then had a lovely dinner of ham and eggs. Afterwards we went two miles across some fields, and ate some lovely nuts, and then into a road which led to Chiding Stone. When we got there we bought some biscuits and some ginger-beer, and we went on the Stone and ate them. Then we walked to Cowden. On the road we met a gentleman who showed us the way (he himself was going to the Isle of Wight). He left us at Cowden Station, which was a mile from the town. We then walked to Cowden, and here we hoped to have a rest. When we got there, we found there was no room at the inn! We then hurried away to the station a mile off, and took train to Tunbridge Wells. Here we found a lovely hotel called 'Carlton Hotel'; we had a tremendous tea of ham and eggs, after a grand wash, and then went to bed. It was nineteen miles' walk that day altogether.

I like the opening of this: 'We walked to Edenbridge, six miles, and drank out of a pump'; as if we thought nothing of walking six miles for a drink. And I shall insist again that I was eight years old; and I will add, because it has just occurred to me, that I was carrying a knapsack. If any other eight-year-old has walked nineteen miles in a day carrying a knapsack, let him write to his local paper about it.

The three days' walking tour did not quite live up to its name. On the first day it rained so continuously that, after an interrupted fourteen miles, we made for the nearest station and splashed home. We started again two days later. The first day now was the one which I have described. On the second day we had done eleven miles by lunch-time. Now it will have been noted, perhaps, that on that first day we had not only 'a lovely dinner of ham and eggs,' but also a 'tremendous tea of ham and eggs.' Undoubtedly, as was natural, a terrific breakfast of ham and eggs had preceded the one and followed the other. I could have gone on doing this for years, but Ken lacked something of my feeling for ham and eggs, and when at Mayfield on that second day there was nothing to be had for our mid-day meal but—— Well, as soon as he heard the unlovely words, he was (as I kindly put it) 'bilious.' So we had to go home. But since we had always said that we would have a three days' walking tour, and since that was to be the title of my great holiday article, we had to make it so by adding in that abortive day in the rain.

Ken says that we did 'a lot of cricketing.' I don't remember this, but I remember Strawberry, the local fast bowler (and butcher), and a never-ending family of Leveson-Gowers, who all played cricket on the common. We watched their matches with a condescending interest, having been brought up on Grace, Stoddart, Shrewsbury and Gunn; Stoddart had played as a boy against Henley House, and I should have put his name first.

For the rest, as Ken says, 'Alan and I often used to get up at five o'clock and go out, and walk about five or eight miles, but towards the close of the holidays we did not.' I don't know why.

CHILD

4

On a day towards the end of July 1891 Ken and I were photographed together—for the first and last time. We are wearing rather tight brown knicker-bocker suits with lace collars. Ken is holding an open book, which the two of us are reading, I with my head resting lovingly on his shoulder. The photograph commemorates an occasion of great happiness to him, of great unhappiness to me. Ken, for the first time in his life, is leaving me. He is going to have his hair cut.

It shows how completely I had identified myself with him that I had always assumed our hair to be one and indivisible. We couldn't start algebra together, share a bed and a tandem, fall off the same bicycle, be the only living members of the FN Society, and one of us have long hair and the other short. It didn't make sense. If we are waiting until Queen Victoria dies or we go into the Navy, all right; if we are waiting for that beastly cousin to come over from Jamaica, all right. We will wait together.

But no. Ken was too old now for long hair; and I, who thought of myself always as his contemporary, must bear my burden alone. A last photograph of the Little Lords Fauntleroy.

I have a particular reason for remembering that photograph. In the dressing-room the usual last-minute combings and curlings and twistings round the finger were going on. Ken was finished first and ran off into the studio. He came running back excitedly to say that there was a suit of armour there. 'Quick, Alan, come and look.' I couldn't. A governess was holding me firmly by the hair, and trying to disentangle her comb.

'Just a moment, darling.'

'I say, can't I—*ow!*'

She has got her comb back, and starts on another lock. 'Just a moment, darling.'

It is the first day of the holidays. Time cannot go too slowly for me; not a minute now that is not precious. To-morrow we are riding down (the tandem's last season) to Stanford-in-the-Vale. Six glorious weeks; there they are waiting for us; nothing can shake them. However troublesome my hair, Stanford will still be in the vale, waiting; the armour, as immovable, in the studio. There is no hurry.

But there was. I can remember thinking, and it must have been my first philosophical reflection: 'It may be a little time, it may be a long time, but some time I shall see that armour. And when I have seen it, I have seen it, and it is over. And the holidays will be over; and I shall wish that I hadn't seen that armour, and that I still had it to see, and that I were here, having my hair pulled, with everything in front of me, armour and holidays. And one day I shall be old, and it won't matter how long she took over my hair, because I shall be old, and it will all be over. But oh! I want to see that armour *now!*'

I saw it. It was a little disappointing.

Stanford was in Berkshire, a new country to us. We rode down on the tandem. If Ken had been in front, I shouldn't have recognized him. We sat on a bank, and dangled our legs, and Papa asked a passer-by if we were right for Stanford.

'That's right,' said the farmer. 'About another six mile.'

We continued to dangle. Another cart came past.

'How far is it to Stanford?' asked Ken, and we both giggled.

'About four and a 'arf mile.'

'Good,' said Papa. 'We're getting on. Your turn next, Alan.'

'We can't keep *on* asking,' I protested.

'Yes, we can,' said Ken.

A boy came out of a cottage, and looked down the road. Ken nudged me.

'Can you tell me how far——'

'He can't hear you,' said Ken. 'Shout.'

I rolled off the bank and ran over to him.

'Well?' they asked, when I came back.

'Just three miles,' I reported.

'What would you like to do?' said Papa. 'Wait here until it comes, or go and meet it?'

We went and met it.

There was great excitement that night in Stanford-in-the-Vale. The most notorious character in the village was being 'burnt in effigy.' Papa explained to us what this meant, and, as discreetly as he could, why it was being done. It was because he was a very bad man, who had run away from his wife. But if he was a very bad man, I said, wasn't it a good thing for his wife if—— Ken interrupted to say that he had got somebody into trouble. What sort of trouble? 'Just trouble,' Davis said. 'I suppose he sneaked on somebody.' Papa interrupted to say that we couldn't know the truth of it, but evidently the village felt very strongly about it. Ken hoped that *he* would never be burnt in effigy. I hoped I wouldn't either. Papa thought we probably shouldn't if we told the truth, and worked hard. So we decided to go on doing this.

Meanwhile, noses pressed against an upper window, we watched the village's retribution on the sinner. Three times they paraded his effigy round the green, the men banging pans and kettles, the women screaming, the boys making every sort of noise they could. Then they turned on to the grass, and gathered round into a circle as if for prayer; and there was a moment's silence; and suddenly a flame shot up to heaven. . . . 'Coo!' we said to each other.

It must have been great fun, and I should have thought that the opportunity for it would occur more often.

We did very little walking at Stanford. With the loss of Ken's hair something had gone out of our lives: our love of adventure, our habit of getting up early, even our desire to be alone together. Ken moved a little up to Barry and I clung on as best I could, so that now we were all three playing lawn-tennis for the first time, and watching an ox being pole-axed, and messing about by the river with village boys. Of course we had to keep friendly with Barry anyhow, because he was the only one of us who had a bicycle; but later, when Papa took us into Faringdon and hired bicycles for us, I seem to remember that Ken and I were drawn together again, even getting up early in order to practise six different ways of mounting, and riding without hands, and standing on the saddle, and other tricks which would give us the chance of calling proudly to Mama: 'Look at *me!*'

However, we did start another three days' walking tour, Papa, Ken and I, but something happened to it. We walked over Lambourn Downs, and on the second day were lunching in Savernake Forest. For some reason Papa suddenly thought it would be fun to take train to Southampton. Anything was fun to us, and we agreed happily. We slept at Southampton, and next morning Papa thought it would be fun to take a boat round the Isle of Wight. I thought so too. But Ken, who had once been sick on the ornamental waters of Regent's Park and rightly felt that he could be sick anywhere, wasn't so sure. However, after a little persuasion, he said that he didn't mind practising. So we went round the Isle of Wight. Ken wasn't ill, but he left his knapsack on board. As the boat was now going round the Isle of Wight again, time slipped by, and eventually, so as not to miss church on Sunday, we went home by train. It was not quite the walk it should have been.

5

At Seaford I had my hair cut. The cousin from Jamaica landed in England, came down to Seaford, took one glance at my beautiful hair, and went on telling Mama about her troubles with black servants in Jamaica. There's gratitude, I thought bitterly. After all I've done for her.

The next day saw the last of Shirley Temple. As Ken and I came back from the barber's, carrying the precious locks in a paper-bag for Mama, we re-passed a little group of locals. They knew us by sight, for they had often seen us chasing butterflies on the cliffs here. They whistled 'Get your hair cut.' It is odd that this, the first moment of my emancipation, was the only time when I had 'Get your hair cut' whistled at me.

Seaford brought us two blessings: butterflies and the sea; of the two we probably got greater pleasure from the butterflies. The first article which I wrote for the public press was written at this time. It was severely practical, being entitled 'How to make a Butterfly-net.' We hoped a lot from this; and I can only suppose that the reason why Ken wasn't writing it was because he was busy on an article 'Common Butterflies and their Haunts.' My article was sent to *Chums*, Ken's to the *Boys' Own Paper*. That was the last we heard of them. Seaford in those days was full of butterflies. When, as periodically happens, some enthusiast writes to *The Times* to say that he has seen six Clouded Yellows simultaneously at Lower Beeding, and is followed by an authority who says that every seventh year brings a visitation of Clouded Yellows from the Continent, I count in sevens from 1892 to see if either of them knows what he is talking about. 1892 was the peak year for Clouded Yellows. Ken and I would go out together with our nets, find a suitable camping-place, and then separate. In half-an-hour we would meet again. Nothing was to be said, but the position of the butterfly-net on the return to camp would indicate to the other the nature of the bag. Net at the trail in the right hand, nothing better than a small Tortoiseshell; in the left hand, Brimstone or Red Admiral; at the slope on the right shoulder, Peacock or Painted Lady; on the left shoulder, Clouded Yellow; over the head, anything special.

Ken had been given Morris' *British Butterflies* for a birthday present, and we knew it by heart. The kings and queens of the British butterfly world were, and I suppose still are, the Swallow-Tail, the Purple Emperor and the Camberwell Beauty. A few Swallow-Tails were to be found in Norfolk, where we never went; a few Purple Emperors at the tops of oak-trees (where we never went); a few Camberwell Beauties, no doubt, at Camberwell— where, also, we never went. We realized that these great butterflies were not for us. One day, while we were at breakfast, Papa called to us to come into the garden and see something. We went . . . and there on the flagstones just outside the garden-door was, incredibly, a Swallow-Tail. Left to ourselves Ken and I could have caught it, but the competition was too severe. Barry rushed for a net, anybody's net. The Jamaica cousin's son, who de-rided our English butterflies, and told us stories of West Indian butterflies like eagles, thought that he might start a collection with a Swallow-Tail, and dashed for his hat. Even Ken and I, each secretly longing to be the captor, however certainly we shared the spoil, got into each other's way. It was all too much for the butterfly, which

86

went back to Norfolk. I am still hoping that one day I shall read a letter in *The Times* asking if the Swallow-Tail has ever been seen as far south as Sittingbourne. 'Sir,' I shall write.

I had been taught to swim at the Hampstead Baths, part of the teaching taking the simple form of pushing me in at the deep end and fishing for me with a hooked pole when I came to the surface. It was a relief to discover that nobody could push me into anything at Seaford. When the sea was rough (as it nearly always was), we bathed at the end of a long rope whose other end was held by Papa. Like many Victorians he couldn't swim; unlike, I imagine, anybody else who couldn't swim, he could float. At the Hampstead Baths he would lower himself carefully into the water and cross the bath on his back, with an impressive dignity which left you feeling that he would have done it on his front if he had been in a hurry. We wondered sometimes if it was just that he didn't want to get his beard wet. In any case a rough sea was no good to him. Realizing that he wouldn't be able to save us if we were in danger, he insisted on the rope. We resented it, but I expect he was right. Waves, like everything else are not what they were. In those days they were terrific, and we came out of the water blue, black and red all over.

We had a book called *Common Objects of the Sea Shore*, but there were not many to be found at Seaford. Ken had taken temporarily to spectacles. He would remove these before bathing, and put them on a breakwater. Next day, when the tide had gone down, we would look for them. They were about all we ever found.

Chapter Five

1

THE Johnstons were very old friends of the family. David Johnston had been a colleague of Father's at Wellington, his wife had been a mistress at Mother's school, his brother, Jim, was a master at Henley House. The brothers had adorable Scottish accents and an adorable Scots twinkle in the eye; David could do conjuring tricks; and Jim was very nearly a first-class cricketer. We felt that Papa had done surprisingly well in choosing them as friends. I can see Jim's burly back now, next to mine. It is the first day of the Christmas holidays, and we are kneeling side by side at after-breakfast prayers. All through this long last prayer I have been eyeing that back through my fingers. I have a great joke in mind. 'Amen,' says, with great solemnity, Papa; 'Amen,' echoes my neighbour reverently; 'Amen,' I flash, and jump on Uncle Jim's broad back with a merry laugh. The joke goes about as well in the Milne family as it would have gone in the Swiss Family Robinson. I am a very naughty little boy.

Uncle Jim often spent a few days of the holidays at Henley House, and in term-time he spent a good many hours with us in the Kids' Room. We remained unsuspecting, however; and it was a great shock to us when we heard that he, not Barry, was marrying our belovèd Bee. They went off together to South Africa, leaving us, as near as might be, orphans.

David Johnston had a school in Buxton, and at Buxton

we spent one delightful Christmas holiday. 'It is not the object of this work to give a description of Derbyshire,' as a greater writer has said. 'A small part of Derbyshire is all the present concern.' Nowadays winter-sport is almost an obligatory subject in a child's education, but to a Victorian child who only knew of Switzerland as a good subject for map-drawing if a brown pencil were available for mountains, Buxton gave all the sport in winter which seemed possible. There was no pretence in those days of keeping roads open for traffic. The Manchester road was handed over without any fuss to the tobogganists. I suppose I have never been happier than I used to be on the Manchester road. For at Buxton one never lacked for seasonable weather. It was here that we learnt to skate—and, as far as I was concerned, stopped learning to skate. I was speeding along with Ken in pursuit, and very skilfully (as I thought) stopped dead, so that he should shoot past me. When I came round, I was lying on the bank with an anxious Papa hanging over me, a sensible Mama telling him that there was nothing to worry about, and an embarrassed Ken longing to be assured that I should live, and, as a consequence, that he could go on skating. I lived, but still have the scar on my chin, token of the perfect knock-out. Luckily it was a Saturday, which made it easy to postpone a complete recovery until Sunday morning—after the others had gone to church.

The long, unlovely hours we laboured through in church, the golden hours we wasted. What were we doing there? Even if men believe that the Incomprehensible Being which created this incomprehensible universe is morbidly anxious that little atoms on one of his million worlds should praise him for it in set phrases on every seventh day, is it likely that he should wish them to do so in words which reach no higher than a child's mind? And if the words are beyond a child's mind, what is the child doing there? How were Papa's soul and mine to be uplifted, our spiritual difficulties to be resolved, by the same teaching? The lovely hours which were torn from us that we might be told not to covet our neighbour's wife. God (and we stopped skating to hear the good news) was not three incomprehensibles, but one incomprehensible. It still left him something a little less than friend.

There was a Sunday in Buxton when even Papa, if told not to covet his neighbour's daughter, would have thought the command unnecessary. Rose, the youngest Johnston, was about our age. We were on our way to church in our stiffest and best clothes. Papa bent down to tie up his lace, and Rose, with no desire but to amuse, put a handful of snow down his back. There were really no words for the situation: Sunday—the threshold of the church—his host's little daughter—the quickly melting snow. There were no words to say, and he said none. In silence we entered the church, Ken and I looking back at Rose and her tight-lipped father, and wondering if girls ever got spanked, and if so where. Papa went on to his knees, forgetting, in that moment, everything but his God. But when he rose from them, and sat back, then he must have remembered his host's little daughter again. Bless her.

This was Christmas 1891. I date it, a little uncertainly, by the Duke of Clarence's death. I know that we were at Buxton when he died, but he may not have died when I think he did. What I remember very well is the Limpsfield uncle telling us (many months earlier) that the Duke of Clarence would never come to the throne, because there would be a revolution if he did. When the news of the death came to us, and the church-bells were tolled, and everybody was very sorry, Ken and I shared a secret solemnity which meant, 'If only Buxton knew.' The

Limpsfield uncle was very much more a man-about-town than Papa. He had a velvet smoking-jacket, and had been (as I may have said) to the Paris Exhibition. He could be relied upon in these matters.

Normally we spent the Christmas holidays in London. We didn't hang up stockings on Christmas Eve. Somebody—at first supposed to be Father Christmas, but at a very early age identified with Papa—came into our room at night, and put our presents at the foot of the bed. It was exciting waking up in the morning and seeing what treasures we had got; it was maddening to know that we should not be able to enjoy them properly until we had come back from church. Was it really supposed that a child, with all his Christmas presents waiting for him, could give his mind to the herald angels?

> *Hark the herald angels sing*
> *(I've never had a paint-box with tubes in before)*
> *Glory to the new-born King*
> *(I'll paint a little cottage with a green front door)*
> *Peace on earth and mercy mild*
> *(My knife's a jolly good one, they've marked it Sheffield steel)*
> *God and sinners reconciled*
> *(I've got it in my pocket, I can feel it when I feel)*
> *Hark the herald angels sing*
> *(I wish it were tomorrow, I must sail my boat)*
> *Glory to the new-born King*
> *(I'll take it to the bathroom and just watch it float)*

One Christmas we decided to put on a play. We had a boy, name of Charles, staying with us. If anybody read the last chapter and thought: 'What was the other brother doing all this time, when Ken and Alan were so busy? Did he play by himself?' the answer is that nearly always there was somebody left over from school whose parents were in India. On this occasion it was Charles, whose mother was in America. The three of us (for Charles was illiterate) had just read one of those threepenny novels (Forget-me-not Library) called *The Golden Key*. It was the most completely moving and exciting story which we had ever read. It was about a poor but lovely governess at Marchmont Towers, who was wooed by young Lord Marchmont (or as he was sometimes called, Lord Robert Marchmont) in spite of relentless opposition of old Lord Marchmont (or, as he was sometimes called, the Duke of Marchmont) and old Lady Marchmont, the Duchess. But the young couple won through in the end, for Love, as perhaps you have guessed, is The Golden Key which unlocks all gates. It was such a beautiful story that we were impelled to dramatize it. We divided the story into suitable scenes, but left the actual dialogue to the invention of the moment, indicating the lines on which it was to be conducted.

I was the wistful young governess, and I put my hair up for the occasion. For the first and last time in my life I wore a bustle, this being the mode. I looked sweet. Charles was the hero, for it was thought that he could get more passion into the proposal scene than could either of my brothers. We explained to him, since he had not our wide experience of literature, the proper method of proposing to a lady: that on no account must she be shocked by a blunt 'I love you,' until some preliminary trial had been made of the gentle creature's feelings. He must lead delicately up to the great moment; a little drawing-room conversation, enlivened, perhaps, by a touch of badinage, then the sounding of a deeper note, then the proposal. Charles promises to give us all of it. Everything seems simple to him now that he is assured of having a burnt-cork moustache. My own part is easier. It is for Lord Marchmont to lead, for me to follow. Any awkwardness which I show, any first-night nervousness, will be in keeping with the character.

Observe us, then, on the night. The great moment is here. I am seated in the arbour in maiden meditation, yet not unaware, for my womanly intuition so tells me, that I have won his love. Lord Marchmont is announced (thus we preserve the forms at Marchmont Towers), and enters, top-hat in hand. 'Lord Marchmont?' I cry, affecting surprise. 'Pray be seated.' He sits down. After a pregnant silence a voice is wafted across the arbour from behind a bank of holly. It says, 'Go *on*, you fool.'

The exhilaration of the burnt-cork has worn off, and Charles is dumb. He closes his eyes in an agony of thought. I wait. It is all a woman can do.

'Do you like apples?' says Charles, coming to life suddenly.

'Yes,' I say wistfully.

There is another pregnant silence. Charles wrestles with his hat, and looks imploringly at the ceiling for inspiration. Inspiration comes.

'Do you like pears?' he asks, sounding a deeper note.

'Yes,' I murmur shyly.

Charles feels that he can now give way to his emotions.

'Will you marry me?' he asks, dropping his top-hat and picking it up again.

'Yes,' I breathe.

Charles nods triumphantly to himself. He has done it. He puts his top-hat on, and goes passionately out. The curtain comes down.

2

There was something a little mysterious about Cousin Annie. She was plump, and cheery, and I suppose, but children never know ages, about twenty-six. She worked in a shop in South Audley Street and lived in the flat above it. To-day nothing could be more delightful, but in those days the social degradation of the one was as regrettable as the moral degradation of the other. Cousin Annie, we felt, was full of secrets which only Mama knew. She was Mama's cousin, not Papa's; and in some way we had the impression that Papa often pointed this out.

Cousin Annie was introduced to us a little late in life. One ought to know the full tale of relations from the beginning, so that even if one's Cousin Annie doesn't come to the house until one is eight, one can at least think to oneself after meeting her, 'So *that's* Cousin Annie.' We had always supposed that we had just the two cousins, boys of much our own age at Henley House, and here was an unheard-of person, too young to be Mama's cousin, too old to be ours, and she was to be called Cousin Annie in future—most mysterious. However, we accepted her. We had tea at her flat one Sunday afternoon. I seem to remember that there was somebody else there, and that he was explained to us as the gentleman who owned the shop; as no doubt he did. We tried not to think about the shop, but only about the tea. With the help of a very good tea this was easy.

We went to Ramsgate one Easter holiday, the three of us, in charge of this new cousin, who had now become a sort of temporary governess. Whether this was a way of finding a more respectable job for Annie, or a way of getting us out of the house, or a way of giving us a little fresh air, was none of our business. On Ramsgate beach we were in the full centre of the music-hall world. We listened, rapt, to 'Hi-tiddly-hi-ti,' 'The Brick came Down,' and 'I asked Johnny Jones, and I know now.'

> *Rolling round the town,*
> *Knocking people down,*
> *Having a jolly good time, you bet,*
> *Tasting every kind of wet——*

Nearly fifty years later the beautiful words sing themselves again into my memory. But what was The Brick? I seem to remember 'The brick came down, we had our half-a-day,' which doesn't lead us anywhere; yet this, or some assonance of phrase, made us shriek with laughter. We also watched, entranced, the Ally Sloper family: including the beautiful young girl with the painted face, who gave me at times a strange choked feeling of happiness, until Benefit Night revealed him as a man. Cousin Annie was right in thinking that none of this would do us any harm; right also in thinking, if she did think so, that we got just as much enjoyment an hour later from Punch and Judy. But she was wrong, perhaps, to make the beach so exclusively a social entertainment; starfish meant nothing to her.

However, she took us for a sail in the *Skylark* once. Ken, of course, was sick as soon as we started. Barry survived the voyage out, but gave up at the turn. I landed intact, but unhappy; another wave would have seen the finish; and even now. . . . Again Cousin Annie was wise. She took us straight to a chemist, and gave us all a dose of brandy. It was, she assured us, and how right she was, purely medicinal, but we needn't tell Papa. We came out feeling grand.

And then, one morning, the three of us went out for a walk by ourselves. Why weren't we on the beach listening to 'Hi-tiddly-hi-ti'? I can only suppose because it was Sunday. Why, then, weren't we in church? I can only suppose because wise Cousin Annie thought that a walk would do us more good—or, perhaps, that a novel would do her more good. There were some low hurdles by the side of the road along which we were walking. We started jumping them. Barry was in front, I came second, poor old Ken was last. We looked back at him just in time to see him fall. We had to stop and laugh. A doleful voice came from the ground: 'I've broken my arm!' We laughed more loudly. He struggled up. His right arm was a shape which we had never seen in an arm before. We made a sling for him with his lace collar and mine, and brought him back to an overwhelmed Annie. She hurried him to the doctor. He didn't cry at all. But was it a Sunday, or wasn't it? I wish I could remember, for it seems important.

3

When we first knew Papa he rode a tricycle. It had one large wheel on the right and two little ones, joined by a bar, on the left. Sometimes, when he was riding madly to the Bank, or to see Dr Willis, one of us would sit on the bar, legs dangling, and observe the left-hand pavement. Like pillion-riding, this was neither comfortable nor instructive, but its insecurity made it fun. In those days the only bicycle was the 'ordinary' or 'dangerous,' and it was not until some time after the 'safety' bicycle came in that Papa abandoned his tricycle. His first bicycle had pneumatic tyres; it was as if he were waiting for Dunlop to invent something like this before deciding that bicycles were worth his attention. When he got a puncture, he wheeled his machine to the nearest station and went home by train. Mending a '91 tyre was a day's job.

By 1892 we were all keen bicyclists. In those famous sports when Ken won (and lost) a whisky-flask, there was an Under 14 One Mile Bicycle Handicap. The other competitors had solid tyres, but by some chicanery of argument I managed to persuade Thom III to lend me his new birthday bicycle, the apple of his eye (with which he slept at night), a bicycle with 'cushion' tyres. This took me about three weeks, for it was difficult to meet his objection that if one were so callous as to risk a bicycle like that in the hurly-burly of a race, one would ride it oneself. The result was: '1. Milne I (100 yards); 2. Milne III (200 yards); 3. Milne II (160 yards),' which leaves the racing-value of the cushion tyre uncertain but the handicap-value of being the Headmaster's son beyond dispute. We were thrilled to be riding on the famous track of the Paddington Recreation Ground, where so often we had watched 'ordinary' bicycle races. The competitors of those days seemed to belong exclusively to the Catford B.C. or the Polytechnic B.C. Our hearts were with Catford, and in particular with the champion of Catford, Osmond. Osmond was my only hero. I wondered what he was like when he stopped flashing past you on a bicycle, and you really got to know him; I longed to be Osmond. 'Osmond, Osmond!' we shrieked as the bell rang for the last lap of the race, and the mad struggle began which left half a dozen competitors spread-eagled on the ground, but never Osmond. He had a rival in the Polytechnic, whose claims Barry and Ken never ceased to urge on me, wanting Osmond to themselves; a dark unlovely man, soured by the knowledge that he could not be Osmond, and that Osmond would always beat him. Osmond—a beautiful name. I think that as A. A. Osmond I should have written much more dashingly.

At the end of 1892 the first detachable pneumatic tyre appeared, and a boy could now mend his own puncture by the wayside. Papa took advantage of the occasion to make the most splendid benefaction in history: he gave each of us a new Dunlop-tyred bicycle. There may have been other boys with such bicycles in England, but in our journeys we never came across them. No boy at Henley House could boast one. No boy-driven pneumatic tyre ever met us, ever passed us, on the road. We lived on those bicycles in the holidays. All the early morning streets knew them, which had once known our hoops. We rode behind buses up Park Lane, ringing our bell impatiently and then swinging magnificently past them; we darted between hansom cabs; 'Look at *us!* look at *us!* Did you ever see bicycles like this?' Two years later they were to become the fashion of the fashionable squares through which as gods we drove our contemptuous way.

That Easter we all rode down to Hastings to show our new bicycles to the Limpsfield uncle, for by this time we had forgiven him. It was always our ambition to ride a hundred miles in a day; by 'ours' I mean Ken's and mine, Papa had no ambitions that way. We did not achieve it until 1897. We were living in Thanet then, and spending our summer holiday in North Wales. Father gave us the train fare from Dolgelly to Westgate-on-Sea, which must have been over fifty shillings for the two of us, and told us that we could ride home if we liked. Even if we took four days we could still show a profit, but secretly we hoped to do it in three. Unfortunately we took a road over the mountains which no cartographer should have included in any map, and along which for nearly ten miles we could do no more than push our bicycles. By the time we reached Llwymllpllwgh, if that is what it was called, we were sick of the whole business. An early lunch revived us; an enormous tea, and the discovery that it was two hours earlier than we had guessed it to be, revived us still more; and at ten o'clock that night, tired but happy, we came into Hereford. Over a cup of coffee and a sausage-roll we followed our journey on the map. We had ridden (and pushed) our bicycles ninety-six miles. Only four miles more for the hundred! Such a chance might never come again. We said good-bye to Hereford and rode eastward into the night. At eleven o'clock we reached the fourth milestone. There was no house within sight, no village within miles, and we were certainly not going back to Hereford. We wheeled our bicycles into a field and lay down. The grass was very wet, but we were very tired. I lay there, and thought how lucky Ken was to have fallen asleep so quickly. At two in the morning Ken said, 'Are you awake too?' I said, 'Yes.' He said, 'Haven't you slept at all either?' I said, 'No.' I said, 'I'm sick of it, aren't you?' He said, 'Yes.' We mounted our bicycles and rode on. The dawn came, but we couldn't give our minds to it. The birds began to sing, but we weren't really listening. At six o'clock we struggled into Cirencester. We rode through the silent town. We came to its last public-house. It was no good, we could not, we dare not, leave it behind. We sat on a heap of stones outside, and waited for it to open its doors to breakfast. . . . Then we went home by train.

This was in 1897. It was in the previous summer, when I was fourteen, that we first found our own lodging for the night. We were riding from Westgate to Weymouth, and came into Brighton at about six o'clock. Brighton has never lacked hotels, but most of them suited neither our pockets nor our clothes. We went into a fruit-shop, made a small purchase of plums by way of introduction, and asked the proprietress if she knew of anybody who could put us up. 'Well now,' she said. 'I wonder. I should think my friend Mrs Green could just do you nicely. George, take these young gentlemen round to Mrs Green. She'll look after you nicely, it's only just round the corner.' We followed George, pushing our bicycles. We turned the corner. We read: 'H. Green, Chimney Sweep.' We didn't hesitate. Stammering that we had left our luggage at the station, we jumped on our bicycles, and rode madly away. We ended up at a pastrycook's, where we had high tea, bed and breakfast for three shillings each. That was our usual price. Those were the days.

4

In June 1892 Ken went in for the Challenge at Westminster, as the examination for election into College is called. Unfortunately he wore knicker-bockers, which may not have affected the result, but gave all the trousered little boys from the preparatory schools a good deal of amusement. There was never the least hope or intention that he should get a scholarship. He went in for 'practice.' In the following January there was a by-election into College for four vacancies, and Ken, profiting by his practice, wore trousers. He got the last place. It was a surprise, and something of a shock, to his family. It was a surprise to Ken, and would have been more of a shock if he had been given time to think about it. But there were only two days in which to turn him into a complete public schoolboy. Inventory in hand, Mama rushes him from tailor to hatter, from hatter to bootmaker, from bootmaker to hosier, from hosier to trunk-maker. They end up at the photographer's. Here, in cap and gown and spectacles, and still about three hours behind it all, Ken is clamped into a chair. The photographer, seeing at once that the property telescope is not going to be right this time, is inspired to put a book in his hands. The moment chosen for the photograph is that when Ken looks up from his book and says to the camera: 'Personally I think Plotinus is wrong in his major assumption.' Unfortunately Ken is wrong too. He is wearing, naturally enough, his Eton collar outside his coat, little knowing, as he will know tomorrow, that Queen's Scholars at Westminster wear their collars inside. The photographs are wasted, we can never circulate them now. But one copy is preserved in the family album.

Poor old Ken. If only it could go on like this: being exciting, and going into shops with Mama, and having telegrams, and showing Alan his gown, and trying on the new trousers, and reading his name in the papers again. But now to-morrow is here. No Alan with him on this new adventure. He has never left home before, he has never known a school which was not also a home, he has never been by himself. He feels very small and lonely. 'Good-bye,' he gulps. 'Good-bye. I say, thanks awfully. Good-bye. Yes, I hope so, I mean I expect so, I mean I'm sure to. Good-bye.' And he is alone in the dark four-wheeler with Papa, and desperately unhappy. Oh, if it could be yesterday again, and always yesterday: in those bright shops with Mama, dear Mama, so warm, so friendly and so safe.

Poor old Ken.

5

We realized now how lucky we were that Ken had got into College at a by-election, for this meant that he would be only two terms away from me. There was never the least doubt in my mind about the June Challenge. Even if I had known then that I should have to be the youngest scholar ever elected, I should still have taken it for granted that it would happen. If ever in my life I said, 'I can do it,' I said it then. I worked in those next five months as I have only worked (over any length of time) twice in my life since.

Meanwhile Ken came home at week-ends. Under his tuition I learnt all the rules and customs of College, all the strange words. 'Bag' was milk and 'beggar' was sugar, and 'blick' was ball: and the coat you wore up-Fields, whether it was a house blazer or just an ordinary coat, was a 'shag'; and you always said 'up' for everything— up-Fields and up-School and up-Sutts (Sutts was the food shop), and you were a Junior your first year, and then a Second Election and then a Third Election and then a

Senior, and they didn't call 'Fag!' as they did in *Tom Brown,* they called 'Lec!' which was short for election, and if you forgot anything, you got 'tanned,' which was four with a very thick cane as hard as they could hit, but he hadn't forgotten anything yet, only there was such an *awful* lot to remember. Oh, and Juniors weren't allowed to wear gowns in College, and Second Elections had to, and Third Elections could get leave from Seniors not to, and Seniors did what they liked. And when the Headmaster crossed the Yard to go up-School in the afternoon, you had to be standing outside College door, if it was your turn, and then shout 'Rutherford's coming' down College, spreading it out as long as you could, like this, and you had to remember when it was your turn, because if you forgot you got tanned. And then in the morning——

Nothing about work 'up-School'; nothing about games 'up-Fields'; only this meaningless, artificial life in College in which all morality was convention. Never 'That *must* be wrong because it's silly'; always 'That *must* be right, because people have been doing it for three hundred years.'

✓ Poor old Ken with all this to learn. Lucky young Alan, who knew it all before he got there; and thought it must be right because Ken had been doing it for six months.

He came home on Saturday afternoon. He got a shilling a week pocket-money now, given to him on Saturday morning. Somehow my weekly threepence had to be made into a shilling by Saturday so that I could keep on equal terms with him. Somehow it was. Perhaps a penny wheedled out of Davis, perhaps tuppence for holding wool for Mama to wind, perhaps sixpence from Papa for a problem in trigonometry which he had been certain I couldn't do. Each of us had his shilling, and together we would go up the High Road to that shop on the right-hand side just before you get to Brondesbury. And there would we sit and eat ices and more ices, while Ken went on telling me about Westminster; which meant, only and always about College: where I would be in September. It was the one utterly certain thing in the world.

6

There was once a young man who went in for a Divinity Examination. Having heard that the examiners were likely to be interested in the Kings of Israel and Judah, he made a list of the Kings of Israel and Judah and committed it to memory. He now felt confident of answering one question anyhow. However, when he got into the examination room he was horrified to discover that there was absolutely no demand for the only information which he could supply. Luckily Question 8 asked: 'Who were the Minor Prophets?' He replied with dignity: 'Far be it from me to make invidious distinctions among the prophets. Rather let us turn to the Kings of Israel and Judah. As follows.'

I was mathematical. I knew, as I have disclosed, the Greek for fountain. That was about all the Greek I did know. There was nothing about fountains in the Greek Composition; no running water at all. I searched the Greek Unseen for πηγή, but in vain. Well, one can but do one's best. I contented myself with turning all the Καις into 'ands,' and leaving blanks in between; so that an extract from Xenophon looked like this ' . . . and . . . and . . . and . . .,' while a more intricate passage from Herodotus looked like this ' . . . and . . . and . . . and . . . and . . .' In the Greek Composition I put the 'ands' back into Καις. This, I always think, is more difficult. However, I did it.

At Latin I fancied myself rather more. I had actually

begun Latin Verse. I have written a good deal of English Verse since, and some of it has been published and paid for. It is time that my Latin verse was published. I can only remember one line of it, but I shall publish that now. A pentameter, no less.

Persephone clamant; nonne pericla times?

As one sees, a perfectly straightforward statement of a question (expecting the answer 'Yes') addressed to Persephone. But *poetry*.

This question of Greek and Latin Verse has always interested me. At school and at Cambridge one would hear of a 'marvellous set of Latin Verses' by which Snooks had won a scholarship, and the 'brilliant Greek epigram' with which Crooks had won a gold medal; and one knew Snooks and Crooks, those 'brilliant' Classical scholars; and one knew that Snooks hadn't a line of poetry in him, and that Crooks was utterly devoid of wit. In their own language they make no stir; but with the help of a dictionary Snooks teaches himself to sing and build the lofty rhyme, and with the help of a lexicon Crooks beats his pate and fancies wit will come. Bless thee, Bottom, bless thee, thou art translated!

What would an ancient Roman have thought of Snooks' scholarship verses? Would they have been good enough for the school magazine? Perhaps. And Crooks' prize epigram? An end-of-term house-rag? Possibly. It's all very strange to a professional writer and a mathematician. Let us go back to the Challenge.

I was eleven, and I had 'done' Algebra, Euclid, Trigonometry, Geometrical Conics, Analytical Conics, Statics and Dynamics. When I say I had done them, I mean I had begun them, and got sufficiently far to answer all the questions on them in the Higher Mathematics paper. I mention this without any complacence, because I had now nearly reached my zenith as a mathematician. When I was twelve, everybody thought I was going to be a Senior Wrangler. But at twelve I stopped working. I no longer thought mathematics grand.

I was by myself in the playground when the result came out. Afternoon school was engaging the attention of everyone else, but I was free; for from now on, said Papa, I was to do just as much or as little work as I liked. He meant this to apply to the rest of the summer term, but it really applied to the rest of my life. I was half-way up the gymnasium rope when they waved a telegram at me from the sitting-room window. 'Good,' I thought to myself, 'now we're all right,' and slid down.

7

We are now to say good-bye to Papa and Mama. Public-schoolboys do not have papas and mamas, they have fathers and mothers. It is a little awkward making the change, but if you write for a whole term to 'Dearest Father,' and end up with 'Give my love to darling Mother,' then by the holidays you are almost ready for it. Papas and mamas are dying out anyhow. They sink into the Victorian sunset as period pieces, to rise brightly with the new century as real daddies and mummies. Meanwhile the youngest Queen's scholar in history (or so they say) writes twice a week to his dearest father. And, when he wants some more food, to his darling mother.

We are also to say good-bye to Henley House. At the end of my first term at Westminster we moved, leaving the mineral-collection, the remains of the toad, three-pence, the gymnasium and the goodwill of the school to Papa's successor. Papa (for he shall not make the great change until the next chapter) had been uneasy about

Kilburn for some years. The 'neighbourhood' was 'going down.' Moreover, he was becoming convinced that there was no future for his sort of private school. The only privately-owned school which could now succeed was the preparatory school for boys under fourteen. For the last year or two he had been looking about for a suitable house in the country. He generally took me with him on these excursions. Wishing to be unhampered in his preliminary conversations and negotiations with the railway company, he would deposit me in the waiting-room of some strange station in some strange part of London, and then leave me, for, I suppose, a few minutes, but minutes which seemed like hours. The only unreasoning fear I can remember feeling as a child came over me on these occasions. I knew that Papa would not wilfully abandon me; I was almost sure (but not quite) that he wouldn't forget about me; I had no certainty at all that he wouldn't have an accident, and be unable to return to me. Two together are so much braver than twice one. Ken and I would have been completely happy in those waiting-rooms, hoping against hope that Papa wouldn't come back, and that we should have to do something exciting about it. What we did would not be his brave action, nor my brilliant plan, but an intimacy of collaboration which could not go wrong. Alone I felt lost. Papa never had the least suspicion of my fears, but I begged Mama once to ask him to let Ken come next time. She said that he couldn't afford to take more than one of us. I think that this was my first realization that we were poor: so poor that, for want of a few shillings, I had to endure these agonies.

Papa found the house at Westgate-on-Sea. It was an old house and a long unlived-in house; it had seven acres of grounds, and the rent was £350 a year. Papa had his thousand-pound legacy. When the day-boys were gone, and the boarders over the age of fourteen discarded, he had ten boys left. Thanet was full of prosperous and fashionable schools, whose headmasters, if not, as often, Blues or Firsts, were at least Oxford or Cambridge. Papa (B.A.Lond.) having nothing to guide him in the conduct of a preparatory school but his own good sense and genius for teaching, took his ten boys to Streete Court, and made enquiries as to the best tradesmen. The best tradesmen, who had already made enquiries about him, gave him three years. In three years Streete Court would be empty again. . . .

Farewell, Papa, with your brave, shy heart and your funny little ways: with your humour and your wisdom and your never-failing goodness: from now on we shall begin to grow out of each other. I shall be impatient, but you will be patient with me; unloving, but you will not cease to love me. 'Well,' you will tell yourself, 'it lasted until he was twelve; they grow up and resent our care for them, they form their own ideas, and think ours old-fashioned. It is natural. But oh, to have that little boy again, whom I used to throw up to the sky, his face laughing down into mine——' And once, when he did this, his elbow, which he had put out at cricket, went out as he threw, and he had to catch me with one arm, and he told us the story, how often, and Ken and I would nudge each other, how often, and feel mocking and superior, as if *we* had never told a story more than once. But still, you had me until I was twelve, Papa, and if there was anything which you ever liked in me or of which you came to be proud, it was yours. Thank you, dear.

SCHOOLBOY

1893–1900

Chapter Six

1

In the summer holidays of 1893 I read Prescott's *Conquest of Mexico,* and learnt by heart a poem of William Allingham's. (Yes, that one.) This, I had discovered, was the holiday-task for the Upper Remove at Westminster. Ken had spent his first term in the Upper Remove, therefore I should; so I reasoned; and I proposed to endear myself to my form-master by learning a holiday-task which made no official claim on me whatever. I discovered at once that voluntary work got you nowhere. Nobody asked me to recite, nobody wanted to share my knowledge of Mexico. But I was not discouraged. Nothing could discourage me until I had got on level terms with Ken.

Ken was in the form above me, the Under Fifth. The Upper Remove was the top form of the Lower School, so that, until I was out of it, I couldn't even share a mathematical set with him. I doubled to and fro among the Classics; Ken marked time; and in January I joined him.

As far as work was concerned, I was now to spend my happiest term at Westminster. I was in the Upper School, and in the top mathematical set. For the first time in my life (perhaps because we were doing Martial, a much more amusing writer than Caesar, if not such a good general) I really enjoyed Latin. Even in Greek I was adding happily to my knowledge of fountains. Possibly the weather was good too: I can't remember. But there was a sunny air about that form-room in the spring of 1894.

The air seemed still sunnier at the end of the term

when we both got removes. In those days the only report of his son's progress which came through to a parent was the Headmaster's brief summing-up. Mine said 'Keen, intelligent and improving fast,' and I don't see how anybody could say fairer than that. Ken's said, in effect, 'About time too,' but said it in a nice sort of way. Father, who took our reports seriously, being himself a headmaster, had his happiest holiday. We bicycled gaily up and down Kent.

I can't remember what Ken's next report said, but I know it must have been worse than mine, because it always was. This was accepted by both of us as bearing no sort of relation to our respective labours or relaxations from labour. Ken's report in the summer of 1894 was definitely worse than mine, and mine said: 'Has done ill, showing little or no ambition, even in mathematics.' When he read this, Father turned his face to the wall, and abandoned hope. I, on the other hand, turned my face to the lighter side of life, and abandoned work.

For (I would point out) I was twelve. I was in the top mathematical set of the school, and in the term's examinations I had come out top of that set. Nobody could specialize in mathematics until he reached the Sixth, at which point he diverged into the Mathematical Sixth. At this time there were three boys in the Mathematical Sixth. With the exception of those three boys, aged 16 to 18, I was top of the school in mathematics, at the age of twelve. And I was told that I had 'done ill.'

I can remember that report busting into our happy summer holiday, and Mother's anxiety at sight of the envelope in case poor old Ken had got another one, and Ken's reassurance that his wouldn't be too bad, and my own certainty that mine would be so good that it would be good enough for the two of us . . . and then Father's stern, set face, as he began to read. I can remember being rather annoyed by mine; an annoyance which changed to bewildered indignation when I discovered that it was not, as I had assumed on a first reading, '*except* in mathematics,' but '*even* in mathematics.' It was useless to point out to Father that the report was written before the result of the examinations was known, and that the examinations proved that the report was ridiculously wrong. Headmasters' reports *couldn't* be wrong. If Dr Rutherford said I had done ill, I had done ill.

Well, that was that. There seemed to be nothing left to work for. In my own subject I had beaten everybody I could beat; I was now permanently with Ken; and Father's happiness appeared to depend, not on my own efforts, but on an entirely haphazard interpretation of them. I stopped working. It is clear to me now that I never was a mathematical genius, but just a clever little boy who could learn anything which an enthusiast taught him; a mixture of ambition and carelessness; who liked learning chiefly for the victories it brought him. There were neither enthusiasts nor victories in sight. Only Ken. Together we settled down happily to idleness. My 'education' had begun.

2

It went on. In my French set at this time I had my first experience of 'cheating.' To the average boy there are two kinds of cheating: that which gives you the advantage of another boy, and that which enables you to hold your own against a master. The first is 'not done'; the second may have to be done. The master in charge of this set had the longest and most beautiful pair of moustaches (one could only think of them as a pair) which I have seen. He was also, as I discovered later, one of the most delightful of men. But he over-estimated the capacity of his form for absorbing French. At every lesson he would dictate twenty-four questions to which we had to write down the answers. Anybody who got less than twenty correct answers was 'sent up-School'—which meant that he had to work in the afternoon instead of playing games. To be sent up-School more than fifteen times in a term brought you in danger of a public 'handing' (with birch) by the Headmaster. For a Queen's Scholar to be sent up-School even once a term was considered disgraceful.

When we had written down our answers, we changed papers with the boy next to us, so that each boy was correcting somebody else's paper. This, which was supposed to prevent cheating, made cheating more certain, for one was now doing it with an easy conscience on another boy's behalf. We sat alphabetically, and I was next to a boy called Moon. Leonard Moon was almost then, and was to become, the hero of every Westminster boy. He was just getting into the school elevens; he became a double Blue, made a century against the Australians, played cricket for Middlesex, played football for Corinthians and the South of England, was extraordinarily good-looking, and was, with it all, an extremely modest, charming person. Could I let this paragon, who was even worse at French than I, go up-School? Of course not. Could I, as a loyal Westminster, handicap the school by denying him his cricket and football practice? Unthinkable. When his name was read out, I said 'Twenty-one' firmly. And when my own name was read out, and he said 'Twenty-two,' it was equally unthinkable that I should rise in my place and say, 'Sir, I suspect this charming boy on my left of uttering falsehoods. I doubt very much if I got more than seven answers right. I insist on a re-count.' Instead I looked modestly down my nose. In a few weeks I had settled down happily to a life of deception.

What I could never settle down happily to was the food. Even now, after forty years, I cannot think of College meals without disgust and indignation. After an hour's work from 7 to 8 we had breakfast. Breakfast consisted of tea, bread and butter. The bread was, to me, the dullest form of bread, the butter the one uneatable sort of butter; otherwise I should have liked it, for I like bread and butter. Tea was tea, and I was never fussy about tea, but the milk had been boiled, and great lumps of skin floated about on the top of it. It made me almost sick to look at that milk, to smell that milk, to think of that milk; it makes me almost sick now to remember it. Well, that was breakfast, 'the most divine meal of the day, the only meal which could never be a disappointment.' At one o'clock we had the usual 'joint and two veg,' followed by pudding. The plates of meat had been carved well in advance, and brought to the right degree of tepidity in some sort of gas-cooler. If it were the fruit season, we had rhubarb. Not liking luke-warm slabs of beef (or rhubarb), I made no sort of contact with the midday meal. There was one terrible occasion when Rutherford came into Hall, and, observing my lack of interest in the meat, ordered me a glass of 'milk.' I managed to get my lips to it without being sick, and prayed earnestly to Heaven that he should move away before the shameful catastrophe happened. He moved; and thereafter I made a great show of business with knife and fork whenever he came into sight. The last meal was tea at 6.15. Tea was breakfast over again, with a few of the slabs of meat, now officially cold, for anybody who wanted them. Very few people did.

We were allowed to supplement breakfast and tea with such cold food as we cared to buy or bring from home:

sardines, tongues, jam, potted meat and so on. The home supply gave out quickly, and the problem then was how to lay out one's money so as to make the school food most edible for the longest time. One found that a 7-lb. tin of marmalade would see one through quite a lot of bread, and that a 2-lb. jar of pickles would make the evening meat almost palatable. Even so, one was left with an inordinate craving for food. I lay awake every night thinking about food; I fell asleep and dreamed about food. In all my years at Westminster I never ceased to be hungry.

As a schoolmaster, Father was unable to take our complaints about the food seriously. All boys complained about their food, it was part of the school routine. And Alan was notoriously fussy about what he ate. Why, there was even a time when he didn't like new potatoes! But even if he had believed us, there was little that he could do. We lived in College at the expense of the authorities, and our scholarships entitled us to no more than they chose to give us. We were left to keep ourselves alive.

Which we did. There were various expenses each term which demanded ready money: College subscriptions, entrance fees for competitions, hair-cuts, journey-money if we went out at the week-end, perhaps a wedding-present for a master who was getting married, or a wreath for a Canon who was being buried. To meet these expenses Father was accustomed to advance us three or four pounds at the beginning of the term, for which we had to account to him afterwards, handing him back the balance. We soon got into the habit of regarding this as our own money. We put by a small balance to take home to him, and spent the rest 'up-Sutts,' on the biscuits and sweets for which our neglected stomachs shrieked. The 'accounting' was child's play. Father couldn't know if a master had been married that term, and wouldn't know if a Canon, minor Canon or What-not had died that term; nor could he be dogmatic about the subscription likely to be demanded from each boy on these glad or sad occasions. 'Wreaths 15s., wedding presents 17s. 6d.' looked reasonable. Ken called our system the double-entry system, because we entered every expense twice, and he said that all accountants used it because it was a very good and well-tried system. Whether this was so or not, it served our purpose. Our most anxious moment was at one Easter, when Father suddenly demanded an account for £5 which we had hoped he wouldn't be thinking about again. The trouble was that on this occasion we had no change left at all. Now it was extremely unlikely that, in giving us £5, he had estimated exactly to the last penny the sum which we should want; it was still more unlikely that, if he had under-estimated it, we should not have applied to him for more. Obviously, then, we must show *some* small balance in his favour. Yet we had not one penny in our pockets. Ken put the crisis by for the moment while he went out to look for his dog who had gone off on some private business. He didn't find the dog, but he did find a shilling in the road. He spent a penny ha'-penny, and nobody would grudge it to him, on a ginger-beer, and came back triumphantly with the change. That night we presented Father with our account. There had been an exceptional mortality among the higher clergy of the Abbey (it had been a nasty cold winter) and a rather surprising outburst of matrimony in an unpromising-looking staff (but it had been a very tender spring), and what with one thing and another, there was a balance this term of no more than tenpence ha'penny. 'Have *you* got it, Alan?' I had. We handed it over.

Little Lord Fauntleroy seemed very far away.

4

School ended at 5. From 5.15 to 6.15 came 'Occupations.' The most usual occupation was going up-Library; alternatively you could join the Glee Society, learn drawing or go up-Gym. Starting my life at Westminster as an enthusiast, I went to Glee Soc. on Monday and drawing on Tuesday, leaving Wednesday, Thursday and Friday for Library. There is a story of a man about to be shot who was asked on the fatal morning if he had any last request to make, any last favour which he would wish to be granted. He said: 'Well, what about learning the violin?' In some such spirit I said, 'Well, what about learning to sing?' I couldn't sing, I can't sing, but I was prepared to try. As long as we were all rollicking together in 'Oh, who will o'er the downs with me,' I was grand. Even when Ranalow (the music-master, and father of MacHeath) said, 'Somebody is singing flat,' I could look indignantly at the boy next to me, and get away with it. But when he went seriously into this question of flatness, and discovered that, as long as I wasn't singing, nobody was singing flat, but that when I *was* singing, then *somebody* was singing flat, there was nothing for it but to swallow my bull's-eye and try to sing more sharply. Apparently I was not always successful. I persevered— or, more correctly, Ranalow persevered—but he was clearly happier when I was resting. This made progress difficult. I left Glee Soc. feeling that the others were keeping me back.

I thought it would be nice to be able to draw. I spent a year drawing a cast of Dante's head. Little had Dante realized that I was going to do this. At the end of a year I had acquired the perspective of Dante's head, the perspective of the drawing-master's head, and the best way of sharpening pencils. It was not enough. I tried Gym, and qualified for some sort of competition or display, but found on the night that everybody was wearing white flannel trousers except me. I had white flannel shorts. This disheartened me. I realized that I was doing none of these things because I wanted to do them, but only because I felt that I ought to improve myself. Starting next term, I would stop improving myself and spend every evening happily up-Library.

Occupation up-Library merely meant that you read for an hour. You could read *Coral Island* or *A Study in Scarlet* or *Wuthering Heights* or *Sordello* or *The Athanasian Creed Explained*. Nobody asked you what you were reading, or minded what you read, but the books were there, and you were there, and there was the Librarian; and at 6.15 he would dismiss you. Of all Westminster institutions this seems to me to have been the best. In no other way could a Junior (subject to fagging) be assured of an hour's undisturbed reading every day. It was wonderfully reassuring to feel through the darkest hours of school that David Copperfield or Becky Sharp or Mr Bennet was waiting for you round the corner, and that nothing could endanger the meeting. Books were not allowed to be taken from the Library, but it was possible to slip David up the waistcoat on a Friday evening, spend a happy week-end with him, and return together on the Monday.

The week-end was happy anyway. One could get leave to go home, or to stay with approved friends, and most of the boys did this, so that there were not more than a dozen of us remaining in College. Save for two compulsory attendances in Abbey on Sunday we were our own masters from Saturday's lunch until Monday's breakfast. College discipline relaxed. Whatever our individual standing, the few of us there were drawn together, as survivors of unequal rank on a desert island would be.

We were always the same happy few, and we affected to
despise the weaklings who must needs rush home at every
opportunity—as we should have done if home had not
been so far away. The high light of the Saturday was
football in the evening down the long stone corridor of
College; played with a tennis-ball, four or five a side: real
Henley House playground stuff, with a touch of the Eton
Wall Game thrown in. It was almost an advantage to be
little, so narrow was the passage, so confined the openings
between a broad defender and the wall. One felt the
equal of anybody, even of such heroes as were in the
school XI or near it.

And then Sunday. Now for the first time it was to
become a happy day. Having got up at a few minutes
before seven all the week, we got up at a few minutes
before nine. Breakfast, alas! was the same cold parody
of a meal, but one didn't feel quite so hungry for it.
Morning service in the Abbey was bearable. We sat next
to the choir, were probably mistaken for the choir, being
in surplices, and took a condescending interest in the
choir. During the inaudible sermon we tried to keep
awake. At the afternoon service we didn't even try; the
thing was clearly impossible. In the recitation of the
Creed everybody turned to the East and bowed, except
Ken and me. We were Nonconformists, and did not hold
with these Popish practices. We gazed stolidly in front of
us, giving the boy next to us a good view of our martyred
profiles. For a few weeks we felt heroic. Then Ken decided that it didn't matter either way, and turned to the
right. Firm in the belief that I was making a stand for
something, though I didn't know what, I continued to
face north. My mood was such that for twopence I would
have turned to the west and surprised everybody. After
the morning service we took the river air on the terrace of
the House of Commons. Since Queen's Scholars were the

only boys in the world who were allowed to do this, it seemed a duty to exercise the privilege; after a year or two we preferred to exercise the privilege of being the only boys in the world who were bored by it. Refreshed by the afternoon service we returned to College and 'messed about' happily until bed-time. No master had spoken to us all day.

5

There was no bullying in College. Big boys were not encouraged to take either a sadistic or a sentimental interest in small boys. It was an offence, punishable by tanning, for Junior and Third Elections to go about together. In any case Juniors were so busy that they really had no time in which to be bullied; and since each boy slept in a separate, and entirely sacred, cubicle in the long dormitory, they were equally safe when the labours of the day were over. But they were never safe from the threat of tanning.

It is often assumed, a little too confidently, by magistrates and members of Parliament that the fact that they themselves were thrashed at school is in some way a vindication of corporal punishment. To their opponents it seems, rather, a condemnation, as accounting for a stupidity and insensitiveness otherwise inexplicable. The curious, but not infrequent, boast: 'Thrashing never did *me* any harm,' invites the retort: 'Then what did?'

'Justice' in College was administered by monitors to Juniors and Second Elections under a show of legality. The slamming of Seniors' Room door was the signal for a 'case,' or, as one might call it, a sessions. The captain and the three other monitors sat in council within; the Under Elections, all potential victims, clustered together without. The chosen victim was summoned. He entered nervously, shuffled along the wall, step by step, until he faced his judges. The dialogue might go like this:

Captain: You were ragging up-Fields to-day.

Junior (swallowing): No, I wasn't.

Captain (negligently): Have you any other excuse to make?

Junior (at a loss): No.

Captain (formally and without interest): Do you wish to appeal to the Headmaster?

Junior (wishing to): No.

The Captain hands the cane to the monitor whose turn it is. The monitor takes off his coat, and judging his distance points to the place of execution. The Junior bends down and gets four. He shuffles out with an air of indifference, hurries into 'prayer-room' (the Under Elections' common-room), and rushes round in circles rubbing himself. The 'offence' and the names of victim and executioner are entered by the Captain in the Black Book.

Sometimes a more impartial justice was administered. When the interval after the last 'case' had grown tedious, the summons would come for 'all people talking up-Library.' It was an offence for Under Elections to talk up-Library as it is an offence for old gentlemen to snore in the Club reading-rooms, and equally beyond control. On any particular evening any of those gathered outside the door might or might not have offended. The custom was for four volunteers to take over the company's liabilities. A hearty Second Election, who was already beginning to sustain himself with the thought that this sort of thing made the Empire what it was: another who felt that it was coming round to his turn again anyway: a Junior who had been reading school-stories, and was determined, at whatever cost, to be popular: another who was pushed in at the last moment because he explained

too volubly that he didn't go up-Library on Tuesdays:
four went in, and three came out, to wait at the door and
wonder, in the few moments left for wonder, who their
executioner would be. Not, they hoped, Parkinson. The
four would meet again in prayer-room, the one who had
drawn Parkinson more subdued for the moment, if more
voluble later, than the others.

It is as difficult now, as it was difficult then, to feel any
enthusiasm for the practice of tanning. On the other
hand, I am not roused to an extreme of indignation at
the thought of it. I don't suppose it did much harm,
either to those that gave or those that took. It was not
the actual pain but the perpetual fear of it which seems
to me now to have been such an unnecessary hardship.
Every evening after tea, as one walked back through
Cloisters from Hall to College, one was aware that within
five minutes the door might slam and a case be called; in
which event one's only guarantee of immunity from tanning would be the fact that one had been tanned earlier
in the week; *mens conscia recti* was of no value. It seems
to me now a pity that a small boy's enthusiasm for life
should have had this arbitrary shadow cast over it.

I was talking the other day to one who bears some degree of responsibility for the good name of that famous
school X——. He said: 'Your boy's at Stowe, isn't he? Is it
really a fact that new boys are happy at Stowe?' Something in the tone of his voice made me add a note of
apology to mine as I admitted that they were. 'They
aren't happy at X——' he said. For a moment I misunder-
stood him again, thinking that he was claiming this as one
of the assets of his great School. But it was not so. He
was genuinely anxious to discover Stowe's secret. One
obvious explanation was that at Stowe (as, I suppose, at
any good modern school) the rules of conduct are based
on reason, not custom. The *tabus* are the *tabus* of the

preparatory school and the home, already learnt. No shock of apprehension clutches at the new boy's heart as he realizes that he has turned up his right trouser instead of his left. He goes about his business unconstrained by any artificial code of manners. That is surely to the good. The business of growing-up is complicated enough without adding to it these arbitrary embarrassments.

6

There were no baths in College; it was enough that it was built by Christopher Wren. One cannot have everything; probably there are no baths in St Paul's Cathedral. There was no hot water in College; but in every cubicle (or 'house,' as it was called) there was a shallow tin bath, in which one could make cold splashing noises every morning. These noises were about all that Juniors did towards keeping clean. After a muddy game of football in the afternoon, one had a quarter of an hour in which to get the mud off with cold water, and change back into a stiff white shirt, Eton collar and white bow-tie. If it was one's turn to shout 'Rutherford's coming' one had five minutes less. It can be imagined how white and well-tied the ties were. On the rare occasions when Ken and I went out for the week-end, our kind hostess (fore-warned by Mother) led us straight to the bathroom, and left us there to soak. We soaked: more out of kindness to her, and in return for the enormous meals we proposed to eat, than from any personal itch for it. Small boys can assimilate comfortably quite a lot of dirt. Luckily, when we were bigger and more ready for it, hot water had reached College. There were still no baths, but there was a divinely hot (if you wanted it hot, and cold if you wanted it cold) spray-and-shower. To-day, so quickly do our old schools move with the times, there are real baths in College. The argument that Warren Hastings did without one (and look at him) is no longer valid.

It will be seen that life in College was hard, but it was not unhealthy. In my seven years there I was never once 'out of school' for illness. On the whole we were as happy as one could expect to be at school. Happiness at school is relative. A boy is happier at his public school than he was at his private school, or happier this term than last. Only at one period was I positively happy, waking up in the morning and saying, 'Hooray, another day beginning.' I must have been a Third Election by then, with no College cares and apprehensions; I must have been in the Mathematical Sixth, and free to work or slack as I chose; and I was, as I remember, just beginning to find myself at football, so that, in fact, I was waking up and saying, 'Hooray, I'm going to play football this afternoon.' For a Third Election, keen on games, untroubled by work, with a little money (his own or his father's) in his pocket, College was as good a home from home as could be found.

As a Third Election I was certainly untroubled by work. My decision at the age of twelve not to be Senior Wrangler was to save me a great deal of anxiety, for Westminster in those days lived only for the Classics. No ardent mathematician could have breathed happily in that atmosphere. The young Newton sat in the corner of a form-room whose natural inhabitants were wrestling with factors or the first book of Euclid, and only when the clamour of these legitimists had been silenced for a moment by the awful shape of an isosceles triangle on the blackboard, was the master free to stroll across to the rebel in the corner, and say, 'Well, Newton, how are *you* getting on?'

One of the pleasant privileges of Westminster, dating,

as most of them did, from an earlier Queen Elizabeth, was the disposal to deserving scholars of Maundy money. A complete set of Maundy money consists of a silver penny, a silver twopenny-piece, a silver threepenny-piece and a silver fourpenny-piece. These were distributed, a coin at a time, to the boys who had come out top of their forms or sets over a certain period. The correct marking of our mathematical set in our last year there presented difficulties. If it were the Algebra hour, Ken and I, sitting together, might be doing Indeterminate Equations, the boy next to us The Theory of Probability, and half a dozen others might be no farther on than the Binomial Theorem. Moreover, some of us might be spending the hour on Hall and Knight's exposition of the theory, and the others, having already studied it, might now be solving problems for themselves. Nevertheless, at the end of the hour each boy would be asked for the record of his work, so that it could be entered up in the mark-book. Half-a-dozen boys doing problems on the Binomial Theorem might be distinguished by the number of problems which each had solved, but it was not easy to see how 'Six, sir' from one of these boys could be compared with 'Two and book-work, sir' from Ken or me. I didn't complain of this system of marking, because, whatever the master's method of reducing us to a common denominator, I always came out top; but it didn't seem fair to Ken, who was doing the same work as I and the same amount of it. So, for a term, we arranged that he should win the Maundy money. When I said 'Two and book-work,' he said 'Three and book-work,' when I said 'Six,' he said 'Seven.' It was no good, I continued to come out top. As soon as I had collected the complete set of Maundy money, I made a point of asking for threepenny bits. These, being just like ordinary threepenny bits, could be shared by us up-Sutts.

SCHOOLBOY

At the end of my third year we had reached the fringe of the Sixth, and were ready to become whole-time mathematicians. We said good-bye to Latin, French and Greek. With the English language we had never had any official dealings, and the only History we had learnt was the history of Greece and Rome. We now said farewell to Alcibiades and the mother of the Gracchi. We were in the Mathematical Sixth, and almost literally our own masters. I was fourteen.

Chapter Seven

1

STREETE COURT was 'an extremely desirable residence, Elizabethan in parts, and enclosed in its own ornamental grounds of upwards of seven acres in extent.' The main part of the house was L-shaped, but there was an irregular third side which included not only 'all the usual offices,' but such unusual ones as a laundry and dairy. We even kept, killed and turned into bacon our own pigs, the architect having provided 'facilities' for this which it seemed a pity not to use. There was 'excellent stabling,' which housed a pony; an excellent pony as willing to take us for a ride as it was to mow the cricket-field or fetch the luggage from the station. There were two tennis-lawns, a croquet-lawn, a woodland border full of birds'-nests, a kitchen-garden full of fruit, a duck-pond full of ducks and hives full of honey. We loved it all.

The family's living-room was now called the library; it seemed more in keeping with our new state. This must have been a billiard-room at one time. There was a high window-seat along one side from which one could look down upon the players; and on the glass borders of these windows were engraved such helpful aphorisms as 'Lookers-on see most of the game,' 'Nothing venture, nothing win.' The fireplace was Dutch-tiled, inside and out, with Biblical scenes not always easy to identify, one prophet in his beard being much like another; but the Whale returning Jonah was unmistakable, and the attention of visitors was always called to it. The big open fireplace in the hall was also Biblical, but more embarrassing. The prospective parent missed it as she was shown in by the maid, but saw it as she was conducted out by Father. 'Oh, look at all that carving,' she cried, '*isn't* that interesting, what *is* it?' She went a little closer, Father clearing his throat and saying that Thanet was noted for its invigorating air and that he was quite sure that Geoffrey—Gerald—that her boy—— She was now in no doubt. 'Oh, yes,' she said in a detached art-gallery voice, 'how interesting. *What* were you saying, Mr Milne?' Potiphar's wife, a woman of full figure, was telling Joseph that there was no hurry.

The broad staircase had the broadest rail for sliding down which I have ever felt, but it ended in a lamp, which made it necessary to take the rail side-saddle. Upstairs there was something which I have never seen before, nor have seen since, a bathroom with two baths in it, one big and one small, end to end. For a school of little boys, whose baths needed superintendence, this was just what was wanted: the matron could soap three at a time; but for ordinary folk one would have thought that two baths of normal size would have given the best combination of comfort and familiarity. However, here it was, one of the less Elizabethan features of the house. Tossing up for the big bath, Ken and I spent many happy hours there, throwing the soap at each other and catching it, with our heads still keeping the sponge in position at the back of the bath—one of the more important rules of the game. I forget what the record was, but at whatever cost to our feelings as loyal Westminsters we would have gone on soaking in those baths until we had achieved a hundred. We were always in pursuit of records at Streete Court. Father built a large play-room, called (how the word clung to him) the gymnasium, and we would spend hours in this, hitting a tennis-ball against one of the walls, until we had 'kept it up' more than six hundred times. We had an outdoor record against the stable-door, but there was too much glass in the neighbourhood for others to be as interested in it as we were, and it was not long before attempts to improve on it were forbidden. Luckily Father had also made a 'playground' of the Henley House type, and across this we punted and caught a football until we had 'done fifty.'

At the appropriate seasons we spent a good deal of time in the kitchen-garden. There was one summer *exeat* when we only left our encampment under the gooseberry bushes to come in to meals. The *exeat* would be in the middle of term: that is, somewhere about the fifteenth of June. It is an odd thing (showing how times change and the world is not what it was) that, though I have my own gooseberry bushes now, the middle of June never finds me beneath them. Every summer as the month reaches its fullness I say to myself, 'It must have been just about now that Ken and I made such pigs of ourselves,' and I go to see if there is any chance of recapturing, in a slightly more grown-up way, that first fine careless rapture. But no; the gooseberries are as hard and small as cherry-stones. I return to my deck-chair and meditate upon the legendary days when poetry was music, music was still cool, and gooseberries were ripe in June.

It was inevitable that we should start a collection of birds'-eggs. We collected the blowpipes, the special brad-awl for boring the single hole through which we sucked the egg's contents—(why were they not called suckpipes?) —the cabinet of shelves, divided into squares, for storing the eggs, Kearton's book for recognizing the eggs, the pink cotton-wool, the labels and the gum. Where we got the money for all this I cannot remember. We would spend Father's money on food, but would have been horrified at the thought of spending it on anything else.

Ken's September birthday was no good for Easter; my
January birthday was so close to our return to school that
its gleanings would certainly have gone up-Sutts; my first
Easter report might have been worth something to us,
but nothing was to be expected of the later ones. Yet
somehow we had the money, and with it obtained all that
was necessary for a really good collection. All but the
eggs. Blackbird, thrush, missel-thrush, starling, hedge-
sparrow and house-sparrow, we blew and labelled these
again and again, but got little further. No matter. We
were London boys, and to find any sort of nest with real
eggs in it was a thrill to us.

We discovered now that there were other flowers than
geranium, lobelia and calceolaria. Beneath our bedroom
windows there was a dahlia bed, whose glory synchronized so steadily with the summer holidays that dahlias
have made themselves a place for ever in my heart which
their gaiety alone would not have given them. The
flowers which Mother would send us through the summer
term brought with them a nostalgia almost unbearable,
whose sublimation dwelt in those sprays of wistaria which
lay, a little crushed, on the top of the box, and conveyed
somehow all that I felt, but could not express, of Home
and Beauty. Yes, I was happy at school, but only because
I had to be at school, and must get therefore what happiness I could out of it.

2

One way and another we got a good deal of happiness
out of it, if not always in the way expected of us. We sat
together now, never to be separated, in the Mathematical
Sixth, which meant that we occupied one corner of a
room in which some lowly mathematical set was being
taught. Since we could not talk without disturbing the

master-in-charge, we wrote letters to each other: long letters detailing our plans for the next holidays. Interest was added to these letters by our custom of omitting every other word, leaving blanks which the addressee had to fill in. Our minds were sufficiently in tune for this to be possible without being easy; one could get the general sense without being certain of the exact word. As in my old French set, we then changed papers and marked each other's mistakes. Sometimes our communications were in initial letters only. During 'second school,' for instance, it was certain that one of us would ask the other 'SWGUSIB?' This clearly meant 'Shall we go up-Sutts in break?' a question which expected the answer 'Yes' and got it. Ken would feel in his pockets and decide that, since we already owed Father 15/6, we might as well owe him sixteen shillings. We did.

Work, conducted on these lines, was pleasant enough. Games of any kind we always enjoyed, even when they were compulsory. College in those days did not take part in Senior House Matches, but had the honour of playing the rest of the school (Queen's Scholars *v.* Town boys). The honour stopped there, for, with only forty boys to choose from, we did not make much of a show at it. But it was clear that any Q.S. who was any good at all at games was compelled by duty, even when no longer by authority, to persevere with them. Under Elections, of course, had no choice. They had to do what they were told.

Games play such a large part in a schoolboy's life, and I have had so much pleasure from them one way and another, that I must make some mention of them here. But I realize that there is nothing so uninteresting to the athletic as the record of some other undistinguished performer's achievements; nothing so unintelligible to the unathletic. 'A bore is a man who insists on telling you about his last round when you want to tell him about

yours,' and he is still more of a bore if you are not quite
clear whether he is talking about hockey or water-polo.
So I shall be as little wearisome as possible.

We were small and active (I the smaller and the more
active) and we played football with enthusiasm, if without much distinction. When Ken left Westminster, which
was two years before I did, we were still without honour,
even in our own House. Then I began to grow; and in
the next year I got my College colours and my second
XI's. In my last year I got my 'pinks' or School colours.
At cricket Ken was definitely the better of the two; we
both had enthusiasm, but he had style. In those days the
young cricketer had to look after himself. Age and influence would take him into a 'House Net,' skill into a
'School Net'; otherwise he played in a succession of pick-
up games. Since on an ordinary day the time available
for cricket was, for the first game, 2 to 3, and, for a subsequent game, 5.30 to 7, it followed that a side never had
more than three-quarters of an hour's batting, and, in
consequence, that a member of it might go through a
whole term without ever getting to the wicket. Form-
matches on Wednesday afternoon gave him a little more
hope, but in our case only a little, since we were always
in a form of boys much bigger and older than ourselves.
But if we never became noticeable, we enjoyed what
little practice we did get, and could always look forward
to a net of our own in the holidays on the Streete Court
ground.

Then, in 1896, the Captain of Cricket hit upon the
brilliant idea of encouraging the young. Evening nets in
the charge of the school professional were thrown open
to 'promising young cricketers,' each house nominating
two boys. As between Ken and me, Ken had the obvious
claim; as between us and half-a-dozen others the College
captain had no exact knowledge to guide him. But be-

cause, I must suppose, I was so small and looked so young (and promising), because I ran about so actively at football and played so enthusiastically down the long corridor on Saturday evenings, there was a Milne chosen for the net, and it was I not Ken. At the end of that term I was only just outside the College XI—a particularly strong one, with six 'pinks' in it—and nearly got my 3rd XI colours. In the following year (Ken's last) he did get his 3rd XI's, while I got my College colours and 2nd XI's. In my last two years I had my 'pinks.' Which shows the value of coaching, even from a 'pro' who never said more than 'You should 'ave come out to that one, sir,' while indicating with a forward movement of the hands how this was to be done.

I must record again that Ken, once more outdistanced through no fault of his own, or merit of mine, remained sweet-tempered about it. All the rivalry between us came from me. As soon as we became competitors on anything like equal terms, I had to prove myself the better man of the two. Being given the chance at cricket, I took it. And when, in Junior House matches that year, I had gone in first and got out for twenty or thirty, and Ken, going in later, was approaching the twenties, I could bear to watch him no longer, but had to look away until he got out. He never knew this, he would never have suspected it of me, he could never show any such ungenerous feeling himself. He was, after all, 'the better man of the two.' I like to think now that one Wednesday afternoon in his last term, when I was playing in Big Game, and telling myself that this was something which Ken had never done, he, in a Form Match, was doing something which Alan had never done, nor was ever to do; he was making a century. Doubtless the opposition was not strong, but it was a hundred, and the only hundred the Milnes of Kilburn have ever made.

3

Ken, however, remained the writer of the family.

It is time that something was said about this business of writing. When I read other people's autobiographies, and learn that Miss Sylvia Marchpane has been scribbling since she was six, and had written half-a-dozen novels, mostly in exercise-books, before she left school: when I read that the thoughts of Mr John Merryweather were turned to the stage by the present of a toy-theatre on his fourth birthday, and that before *he* left school, he had written half-a-dozen plays, mostly on the backs of envelopes: then it is brought home to me, that whatever other sort of writer I am, I am not (alas!) a 'born writer.' It is comforting, but not conclusively so, to remember that probably Shakespeare wasn't either.

We did no English at Westminster. In my seven years there I never wrote so much as one essay for authority. There was a Literary Society in College to which I was admitted in my sixth year. It read the plays of Shakespeare on Friday evenings in the company of the Master of the Queen's Scholars and his wife. Owing to the presence of Mrs Raynor (who must have known much more about these things than we did) it was the custom of each reader to omit the more outspoken passages and elide the grosser words, a practice somewhat embarrassing, since the housemaster was following the text in his book to see what one did elide. Well, not following it for that purpose, of course, but sufficiently up with the field to wonder, at some surprising hiatus, whether Shakespeare could possibly have meant what Jenkins apparently thought he did. *Othello* offered the most difficult problem to our chivalry, and I doubt if we ever quite deceived Mrs Raynor as to what was going on.

My other official contact with the Dramatic world was

through the medium of the Latin Play. It is unlikely that a performance by schoolboys of Terence's *Adelphi* or *Andria*, from whichever side of the footlights seen, is going to give anybody a passion for the theatre. It certainly aroused no passion in me. I have described my first appearance on the stage. My second was in the topical Epilogue to the Latin Play. One of the affairs current in 1893 was an attempt by some French explorer to teach equatorial monkeys the French language. Ken and I represented two backward equatorial monkeys who had got no further on than small French noises. This could not properly be called a speaking part. The following year I came on (without Ken) as a paper-boy, calling *'Omnes victores.'* This part demanded the smallness of stature which I could provide rather than the histrionic ability which I could not. I then left the stage until 1899 when I got my first, and only, part in the Play itself. I was *Geta*, a slave. I rushed down to the footlights, pushing past the old gentleman who was to astonish me so much by his presence when I had finished soliloquizing, and burst out with the unforgettable words (for I am still unable to forget them): *'Nunc illud est, cum si omnia omnes sua consilia conferant, atque huic malo salutem quaerant, auxili nil adferant.'* I went on in this way for quite a time, pacing up and down in front of the footlights as if hungry and keeping my eyes firmly on the audience so as to build up to my start of surprise when it was time to see the old gentleman behind me; and the old gentleman, in my intervals for breath, called attention to his hiding-place in the middle of the stage by interpolating *'Hem!'* and *'Heus!'* until the great moment arrived. At last, with the Latin equivalent for 'Well, I suppose I had better be getting back,' I turned round. . . . It was what is so well called a 'dramatic' moment. *'Henry!'* I cried, *'you* here?'—no, this was Latin, his name may

have been *Sosia* or *Micio*, and I was only a slave at that
—I probably said, '*Hem, perii!*' meaning roughly 'We're
sunk!'—it is odd that I remember my entrance speech so
clearly, but forget the details of the big scene; is this, I
wonder, a common experience among actors? Well, there
we were. While I stood by exhibiting horror, *Micio* (or
Demea) indicated to the audience that, having accidentally overheard my private thoughts, he now had enough
new material to keep the next act going. He walked off
with dignity, and I followed him. I don't think I came on
again. There was no reason why I should. I had made the
play.

There was nothing in all this to arouse one's dramatic
instincts; nor were our contacts with the English theatre
numerous enough to give its glamour a firm setting. The
first play I saw was an Adelphi melodrama (William Ter-
riss and Jessie Milward) called *Boys Together*. Our very
own Dr Morton was putting up with us for the week-end,
and nobody could do it so understandingly as he. His
habit was to tell us the times of meals, to call attention
to the bathroom, and then to leave us entirely to ourselves in a room at the top of the house well provided
with books. On this occasion it was suggested that we
should also join the family in a visit to the theatre. We
had to confess that, at the ages of sixteen and fifteen, we
had never been to a theatre. Dr Morton was surprised
and doubtful. Would our father mind—it was quite a
nice play? We were sure he wouldn't mind. But writing
home on Sunday to break the news, Ken made it perfectly clear that though we had been extremely excited
by this play it had left no permanent mark upon our
characters. We were unsullied.

I went to the theatre three more times while I was at
Westminster. I saw *Florodora*, *The Greek Slave* (with
Marie Tempest and Letty Lind) and *The Rose of Persia*.

To the first two I was taken; to the last I went with another boy on a wet Wednesday afternoon. To avoid mis-
understanding we had asked for leave to go to an illustrated lecture at the Polytechnic Institute. When we got
back from *The Rose of Persia*, our housemaster asked us
what the lecture was about. We told him that it was
called (and it seems to me a very good title for a lecture)
'Our Navy To-day and Every Day.' Actually it was just
called 'Our Navy,' but the advertisement in the papers
had misled us.

4

No compulsory prose was extracted from us at school,
but an annual excursion into verse was demanded from
Under Elections. On the last Saturday of the summer-
term there was an entertainment (for Upper Elections)
known as 'D-clams'—I write it thus to ensure the correct
pronunciation. This took the form of a recitation of
declamatory verse on the leaving Seniors by those who
had suffered under them for the last year. Lolling
repletely at tables covered with the fruits (and fruit-
drinks) of the season, the Upper Elections take their ease
on the floor of Seniors' Room; high up beneath the ceiling, on a specially-constructed rostrum (table on table,
chair on chair) stands a trembling Junior. In his left
hand is a large candle, a tolley, in his right a packet of
verses. There is no other light in the room. Ready to the
hand of every boy beneath him is a plate of small, hard
ginger-nuts. To a Junior with a genius for invective this
would seem to offer the opportunity for revenge for
which he had been waiting all the year; but actually it
turned out to be a better opportunity for the Senior with
a genius for throwing ginger-nuts. After one's first experience of declamming a monitor more popular with his
contemporaries than one had supposed, one realized that

authorship had no further perils to offer. Professional critics might throw mud, amateur critics might throw eggs, but nobody would throw ginger-nuts again. It may have been this which decided me, sub-consciously, to be a dramatist.

D-clams have now been abolished. Somebody fell off the rostrum (and I wouldn't blame him), or had his eye put out with a ginger-nut, or set light to himself with the candle—I did hear, but have forgotten. Mothers will breathe more freely, and fathers will say that the world is getting soft. But I doubt if satiric poetry has suffered. The standards were the standards of scholarship Latin verse. Scansion was almost enough.

5

We wrote home every Sunday. As most of our experiences during the week had been shared, we made some sort of division of the available material, Ken, as it might be, taking the weather and I the Saturday match; but as we grew older, we became more literary, sacrificing facts to the exploitation of our personalities and enlivening our letters with such scraps of quotable poetry as had lately come our way. I warned Father one Sunday, but in what connection I cannot remember, that there were more things in Heaven and earth than were dreamed of in his philosophy; and he cannot have been more surprised than Mother was next Sunday, when I assured her that it was better to have loved and lost than never to have loved at all. If Ken was doing this too, he was doing it more allusively and more gracefully. Gradually it became accepted in the family that his letters, if not 'good enough for *Punch*,' were good enough for a boy very much older, and that in the words of Father, 'he might make something of it one day.' Not for a moment did

Father suppose that any son of his could make a living by it; as he said to me when the appropriate moment arrived, 'We can't all be Dickenses, you know'; but it was within his vision that a Ken, securely settled in the Civil Service or somewhere, 'might pick up an occasional guinea' with an essay in *The Spectator* to which casual reference could be made when showing a 'parent' the gymnasium.

Meanwhile it was time to find a real profession for Ken. It was now clear to Father that he would get no sort of scholarship at the University, and, more important, it was clear to Ken that in his last year at Westminster he would not be a monitor. This was too great a strain even on his humility. He would be the senior boy in College, in his seventh year, and still without authority. It was time he left.

But what to do? He had no ideas, no ambitions, and little more than average public-school qualifications. Barry was articled to a solicitor, and would be admitted next year. It took four years to become a solicitor; four long years in which you need not wonder what you were going to be, four long years before you had need to prove yourself. We were neither of us go-getters; we had discovered a talent for idleness; but I had a sort of jealous obstinacy, heritage of that childish 'I can do it' spirit, which he lacked. To him the four years' respite was attractive. Since he didn't mind what he was, he would be —what was it?—a solicitor.

6

Father and I took what he thought was going to be a pleasure-cruise to Norway that summer. I was sixteen, and just beginning to fancy myself at cricket. I was also just beginning to grow up. I was, in fact, unbearable.

There was a very attractive young woman on board who had all the men round her. I was on the outskirts of the crowd, hoping for, and sometimes getting, a smile. In my pink-and-white tie (second XI) and green and blue cap (College colours) I could probably have got a smile from anybody. When she sat swinging her legs on the deck rail, gaily holding her own against all our compliments, mine wordless but by far the most sincere; when at moments she caught my eye, or her eye caught my tie, and she gave me that warm, sudden smile which meant —that we two had some secret which the others did not share; then I felt that I could have died for her, or thrown my cap overboard (though I was more doubtful about this) if she had so desired it. Was I in love for the first time? I don't know. The sea moderated, her ladyship emerged from the cabin in which, solitary, she had been praying for death, and her ladyship's maid, that adorable creature, returned demurely to her duties. It was a great shock to all the men. They went about pretending that they had always known it, but had wanted the little thing to have a good time while she could. My distant adoration left me less compromised. Without any embarrassment I transferred my affections to the charms of deck-cricket and a girl called Ellen. Ellen was my own age. I remember her surname, but shall not mention it here in case she is no longer my own age; I also remember her face. Do you suppose she remembers *my* name or *my* face? Of course not. O faithless Ellen! I haven't given you a thought since 1898, but it seems that I can never quite forget.

At the end of the holidays I returned to Westminster, alone. I discovered now what delightful letters Ken wrote, but they did not make up for his absence. Without him there seemed to be nothing to do but work and play games. I did both. I was never within a hundred miles of being the hero of a school-story (or even of a single schoolboy), but I got as near to it at the end of the next summer-term as I could ever hope to get. I had just been given my 'pinks.' In the Town-boy match on the last day but one of term, I dislocated my thumb when fielding. Batting as near one-handed as might be, I then made top score of 39; and on the next day, left hand picturesquely in a sling, I collected with the other hand all the mathematical prizes which were available, and was installed as head monitor (under the Captain) for the coming year. I felt grand.

I felt less grand next term when I went in for an open scholarship at Trinity (Cambridge) and was completely unsuccessful. Not that it mattered very much. Westminster gave three scholarships to Christ Church, Oxford, every year, and I could be certain of one of these. The important thing now was to get my colours at football.

7

It was in the Christmas holidays of 1899 that I discovered the itch for writing which has never quite left me. I know how I discovered it, but I know not how it came to be there. The discovery was odd and accidental. It may not deserve, but it shall certainly be given, a new chapter.

Chapter Eight

1

In September 1899, the Boer War just about to begin, an Anglo-Indian brought his wife and family to Westgate. The two boys (twelve and eight) were sent to Streete Court, the two girls (fourteen and ten) to a neighbouring school; and it was arranged that Father should have the care of all the four children in holiday time. The parents then returned to India.

I knew nothing of this until the moment of my arrival home in December, when Mother happened to mention Geta—with a hard 'g.' I explained, being still full of it, that it was pronounced Geta, with a soft 'g'; *nunc illud est, cum si omnia omnes*—Mother interrupted me to say that she was talking about Ghita, the elder girl; the younger one was Irma. A few minutes later we were introduced.

They were nice children. Ken, articled to a Weymouth solicitor, came home for Christmas, and a good time was had by all. One day, after he had gone back to work, I came upon Ghita in the throes of composition. I supposed that she was doing some sort of holiday-task, probably in German, but it appeared that she was writing a letter to Ken. 'It isn't as difficult as that,' I said. 'What can't you spell?' She wiped some of the ink off her fingers, put her tongue back, and said that it was poetry. 'And oh, *do* help me, Alan, I *can't* get it right, it just *won't* rhyme when I want it to.'

I looked at what she had written. The theme, one of

143

cheerful insult, was good, but the execution was poor.
I took some of the bones out, moderated the scansion and
arranged for a few rhymes. The result was copied out by
Ghita and sent to Ken. In a few days he replied to her
with a set of verses which surprised me: verses in the real
Calverley tradition. I had had no idea that he could do it.
At the end of them he had written: 'All my own unaided
work—and I bet yours wasn't.'

So I wrote back to him and confessed that Ghita had
called me into collaboration. And just to show what I
could do on my own, I enclosed a set of disparaging odes
to all the four children.

Of these, my first attempt at light verse, I remember
only four lines. They were part of the ode to Irma, a
placidly grubby child whom we all loved.

> They say the Dutch prefer their ladies short
> And fat as fat can be, but not as clean as
> Is usual here. Out there, dear, you'd be thought
> A Venus.

Quite in the tradition, save for the Cockney rhyme.
But in those early days I was as little shocked by the
Cockney rhyme as our modern poets seem to be to-day.

Ken wrote back, in surprise equal to mine, 'Good
Heavens, you can do it too'; to which came the obvious
corollary, 'Let's bofe.' So for two years we wrote light
verse together.

2

Writing light verse in collaboration is easier than one
would think. I don't mean by 'easy' what our fellow
Westminster, Cowper, meant when he boasted of the
ease with which he wrote *John Gilpin*. To Cowper, who
knew nothing about it, light verse was merely verse which

was not serious, and which demanded, therefore, no application. What I mean is that light verse offers more scope for collaboration than at first thought seems possible. For a set of light verses, like a scene of stage dialogue, is never finished. One can go on and on and on, searching for the better word, the more natural phrase. There comes a time when one is in danger of losing all sense of values, and then one's collaborator steps in suddenly with what one sees at once is the perfect word.

Naturally I cannot remember now the details of all our collaborations, nor say which of any poem was Ken's inspiration or my last word, but I can give two instances of the way in which we supplemented each other. Even if they have no technical interest for the reader, they will show the sort of thing which we were writing.

The first is from a contribution to the Limpsfield uncle's school magazine. It began like this:

You ask for a poem, my ownest own editor—
  Don't be alarmed at the epithet, pray:
It occurs in Lord Tennyson's Maud—*have you read it?—a*
  Poem of merit authorities say.

Shall I write you a parody, smart and satirical,
  After the manner of Punch *and the rest—*
Or something in dialect, pretty and lyrical,
  Safe to remind you of Burns at his best?

Perhaps you would fancy an 'Ode to an Eider-duck'
  Telling his praises with never a pause:
How he was born a duck, lived—yes, and died a duck,
  Hampered by Nature's inscrutable laws.

Or a rapturous ode on the worth of some Lycidas—
  Blenkinsop Brown he was called when alive,
And reckoned as likely as not an explicit ass:
  Trivial facts not allowed to survive.

And so on. I was spending some of the holidays with Ken at Weymouth and we wrote this literally together; not, as more usually, by correspondence. The general idea, of course, was old and obvious. As I remember, Ken was responsible for the initiation of the first and fourth verses and I for the other two, but we worked them all out together. It is the third verse to which I invite your attention.

In the first 'final' version—as we thought a few days before it was finished—the last two lines were:

How he was born a duck, lived a duck, died a duck—
Fettered by Nature's miraculous laws.

I am still uncertain whether we improved the first of these lines, but I know that we argued about it for hours. There is a charming monotony about this earlier version, which echoes the monotony of a life from which no duck can escape; but I like the break in the rhythm of the other—(*'How he was born a duck, lived—yes, and died a duck'*)—and I like the hint of astonishment that even in death he was not divided from himself. I should say, though I cannot certainly remember, that Ken preferred the first version and I the second; modest Ken standing aside and letting the tragedy reveal itself, the more egotistic Alan intruding the writer's personality in comment on that tragedy. The comment had to come, in any case, in the fourth line:

Fettered by Nature's miraculous laws.

We thought this was very funny and ironic, until the more scholarly Ken pointed out that the one thing which Nature could not be was miraculous; it was a contradiction in terms. I agreed reluctantly, feeling that I ought to have seen this for myself, feeling it still more strongly when he suggested the perfect word 'inscruta-

146

ble.' Now it was my turn to assert myself. I said that we ought to improve 'fettered.' If you were fettered, you were without hope; you knew you couldn't escape, and you threw your hand in. It was much funnier to think of the duck continually trying to be a skylark, and continually being prevented, but always hoping. Some word like 'thwarted,' or 'obstructed' . . . or—Got it! *Hampered.* *'Hampered by Nature's inscrutable laws'*—we said it over and over to ourselves, loving it.

My other example is from a set of verses which we wrote in the *Granta* when I was at Cambridge. They described (in, as it happens, the same metre) the proposal of a cosmopolitan young gentleman to his love.

> *He called her (in Latin) his something in—issima,*
> *Hinted (in Greek) she was one of the best,*
> *Asked her politely in Spanish to kiss him, a*
> *Scandalous, scandalous thing to suggest.*

And more in that strain. The poem was Ken's idea, and he opened it with this verse:

> *An account of one Jones and the very last visit he*
> *Paid to the girl he first met at a dance.*
> *Now in languages Jones had a rare catholicity:*
> *Insular prejudice eyed him askance.*

I altered the last line to '*Jones had two Spanish-American aunts.*' A consideration of the two versions gives the clue to the separate qualities which each brought to the collaboration.

3

On January 18th I was eighteen. Ken sent me a pocket-book, and (since we were in that vein) a charming set of laudatory verses. I wish I could print them here, as a tribute not to myself but to him. Like many other things which I wish that I had kept, they are gone, even from my memory. I went back to school, almost, for the first time, happily.

We offered our services to *Punch* first, but *Punch* was unappreciative; so we turned to the school magazine, *The Elizabethan*. Over the initials A. K. M. we contributed verses and parodies. It was lucky for us that at this time an old Westminster of whose poetry we had no opinion was sending up 'serious' verse to the editor. Four lines of an ode which he wrote on the death of a distinguished contemporary so burned themselves into the memory that after one amazed reading we could quote them to each other ever afterwards. Even now . . . yes . . .

He than I was somewhat older, and no common tastes we
    had,
He was good at cricket, football, I was but a pensive lad.
He would sally forth to Vincent Square attired in flannels
    cool,
I would spend my leisure moments in the cloisters as a rule.

One began to wonder which of them was writing an ode to the other. If only Tennyson could have put as much of himself into the Wellington ode—

He would sally forth to Water-loo attired in spur and boot,
I remained at home, Euterpe's most industrious recruit.
He would interlard his speech with military 'Blast' and
    'Damn'—
I would spend my leisure moments writing In Memoriam.

We had great fun with this poet in *The Elizabethan*. The Captain of the school was *ex-officio* editor, and since we were both in College, and I was, as it were, his first lieutenant, I could make sure that all A. K. M.'s contributions were published. Indeed I could even persuade him to publish some rival's ridiculous doggerel in one number in order that we could parody it in the next.

All this was fun, but it never occurred to me that it might be a lifetime's occupation. I was going to be I was not sure what, but first I was going to Oxford or Cambridge, I was not sure which. Oxford looked like being more suited to my means, and (I was told) would suit better my particular mathematical talent, which, as far as it existed, was for 'pure,' not 'applied' mathematics. As against this I had always called myself Cambridge from childhood, and, having been to Cambridge for that scholarship, had got to think of myself as living there happily. Which should it be?

Then one day a copy of *The Granta* came to Westminster. *The Granta* used to call itself The Cambridge *Punch*, until it got the idea of calling *Punch* The London *Granta*. R. C. Lehmann had founded it, and all the Cambridge humorists, Barry Pain, E. F. Benson, F. Anstey, Owen Seaman, had written for it. My friend the Captain and I stood looking at this copy of *The Granta*, and suddenly he said, 'You ought to go to Cambridge and edit that.' So I said quite firmly, 'I will.' It has an heroic sound, but to anybody who has said 'I can do it' at the age of two, saying 'I will' at the age of eighteen is easy.

So it was to be Cambridge. I didn't tell Father why. His assumption was that I was going to a University in order to get a First. Having got a First, I was then going to come out top in the Civil Service examination, and turn (gradually) into one of those comparatively unrewarded but nearly always knighted gentlemen who are 'the real rulers of England.' He would have loved to think that I was going to follow him at Streete Court; but just as I had once deceived Rutherford into thinking that I was 'too good for the Navy,' so I was still deceiving Father into thinking that I was too good for a schoolmaster.

It was to be Cambridge, then, because I had set my heart on being Senior Wrangler, because the mathematical standards were higher there, because one could work there with less distraction. Cambridge—if Father could afford it.

He could. Streete Court had survived those first three years and was now flourishing.

4

Father and mother had always determined that there should be no favourites in their family. The three of us were to be treated alike: to be given equal affection and equal opportunities. In practice the affections are not so easily controlled. There was never any doubt that Barry was Mother's darling and that I was Father's, leaving poor old Ken to take second place in both their hearts, and first in mine and Barry's. But we were not to profit by these preferences. Nobody should say that our parents had favoured one of us at the expense of the other. At times this determination not to distinguish between us took rather an absurd form. Complimented by a visitor on the complexion, eyes, smile, hair or what not of one of us who had strayed accidentally into the drawing-room, Mother replied firmly and untruthfully '*All* my sons are good-looking.' A little later, when Ken, now in the Civil Service, had received official praise for the elegance of a report which he had drafted for his Minister, Father offered his congratulations in the words: 'I always said that all my sons could write.' Barry was then expressing himself in letters beginning 'Yours of even date to hand in reply to which we beg to call your attention,' and I was being funny on *Punch,* so that a Civil Servant got as little satisfaction from being compared with one as with the other. 'All my sons' became a catch-phrase with Ken and me, as it was becoming a habit with Father and Mother. We felt that, if one of us committed a murder, their first reaction would be a bland assent that all their sons ought to be hanged.

Meanwhile all their sons were to receive the same financial assistance. Consulting his beautifully-kept accounts, Father discovered that the cost of turning Barry into a solicitor, from the day he left school until the moment of admittance, had been just under a thousand pounds. A cheque for the balance was sent to Barry; Ken was told that he also would have a thousand pounds with which to turn into a solicitor; and when Alan left Westminster to educate himself in whatever way he wished for whatever profession he proposed to adopt, he could expect neither more nor less than his brothers had had. But it was to be understood, of course, that Ken and Alan drew the money in reasonable amounts to meet reasonable expenses.

It was a very fair, very generous settlement, and I was delighted with it. I could live comfortably at Cambridge on £300 a year, £70 a year of which would come from Westminster exhibitions. At the end of three years, I should be fitted in some mysterious way for some unconsidered mode of life, and earning, for some unspecified services, a substantial income; and all this with £300 in the pocket. Whose prospects could be brighter than mine?

However, I had still to get to Cambridge. In those days the Universities insisted on a smattering of Greek, even from the mathematical. The Little-Go, which I could have passed with ease at fourteen, seemed formidable to one who had done no Classics for years. It was necessary to spend an intensive term trying to recapture Greek: more particularly the Greek of Lucian and the New Testament.

Having told the story of the man who learnt by heart the Kings of Israel and Judah, I shall now tell the story of the man who learnt the gospels by heart. His knowledge of Greek was even less than mine, but he hoped that, in any passage from the Greek Testament which he was asked to turn into English, some simple phrase or key-word would translate itself, and thus give him the cue for the appropriate passage from the Authorized Version. If he could discover a starting-place and an ending place, all the middle could be left safely to his memory. In one passage the words 'Ho gegrapha gegrapha' caught his eye. I put it into English lettering thus, so that my lady-reader can understand it, and for her sake also I explain that they are the words of Pilate: 'What I have written, I have written.' This translation, however, was beyond our student; all he made of it was 'Ho' followed by the repetition of a much longer word. Searching in his memory, he suddenly identified the cue. The rest was easy. 'Oh, Jerusalem, Jerusalem,' he wrote, 'thou that killest the prophets. . . .'

I timed my translation better than this, but it didn't seem to be enough. An attempt to pass the Little-Go before I left school was unsuccessful, and it was not until I got to Cambridge in October that a second attempt gave me that standing as a Greek scholar which the University demanded. Having been a Westminster boy for far too long, I was now a Trinity man.

5

In seven years what had Westminster done for me, or failed to do? It is difficult to say. When I read that

Shelley was despised and persecuted at Eton, I reflect
that he still came out Shelley. When some superior
young intellectual attacks venomously not only his own
school but the whole public-school system, at least he
makes it clear that he remains well satisfied with himself; so well satisfied, indeed, that it is difficult to see
how any other school, or any other system, could have
made a better job of him. On the other hand, the fox-
hunting squire must feel that no system is sound which
turns out fellers like this Bloomsbury feller; who, in his
turn, is indicting the system as responsible for the fox-
hunting squire. It seems as if the public schools leave
us much as we were, fox-hunters remaining fox-hunters,
and prigs prigs.

So if I am to estimate my debt to Westminster, it is
not enough to reckon up my assets and liabilities on
leaving. As the landlady suggested when the lodger complained of the fleas, I may have brought them with me.
Even if I didn't, who can say that they were not due to
a normal expansion of capital? Seven years at any other
school might have left me neither richer nor poorer.
Moreover, in the end there remains the constant difficulty of life, the knowing which is asset and which is
liability.

That I was ruined as a mathematician was Westminster's doing. And which side of the count shall we put
that? Selfishly I have reason to be grateful; as Senior
Wrangler, or anything like it, I should have been 'too
good for writing.' Perched on the well-guarded heights
which Wranglers reach, I should never have known
those happy valleys where the unqualified may roam at
will. But is it to Westminster's credit that in my time
mathematicians were so neglected? She might reply that
it is her careless motherhood which has produced a Ben
Jonson and a Warren Hastings, a Gibbon and a Chris-

topher Wren. A true mathematician would have survived her treatment; anybody less than that was unworthy to survive, and must find some other means of
expression. It is an attractive argument which could
justify a good deal of indifferent teaching.

For the rest I was very much the conventional public-
school boy of those days, with conventional views (in as
far as I had any) on religion and politics, the conventional love of games and conventional ideas about 'good
form.' All that I have kept of that is the love of games.
But these conventional views were not forced on us. I
cannot remember anybody in College being on the unpopular side in the Boer War, but I feel that College
would have tolerated him if he had been. Certainly it
was possible to have no aptitude for, nor interest in,
games and yet be liked. I loved games, but was not
fanatical about them. *Stalky and Co.,* that record, as it
seemed to us, of incredible schoolboys at an incredible
school, had just come out; and I can remember defend-
ing it hotly against a completely incompetent games-
player on the ground that at least it justified the existence of the completely incompetent games-player. Why
he should have objected to this I don't know; perhaps
he thought that his existence didn't need justifying; but
we argued, on what seemed to be the wrong sides, with
great animation. As far as I remember, this was my only
lapse into unconventionality, unless a notorious distaste
for lavatory jokes was to be considered as one. In this
respect I only differed from my contemporaries by thinking that the first necessity of a joke was that it should be
funny; smuttiness was not enough. I still think so, and
I am still bored with nine-tenths of the smoking-room
stories which I hear, enjoying all the more the superb
tenth one. Nobody minded this aloofness at school, even
if nobody understood it. In fact, they were all rather

nice about it, apologizing if I were present, in the way that one would apologize for telling a story from Aberdeen in the presence of a Scotsman.

Looking back on it, I should say that tolerance was Westminster's great quality. Her ways were conventional, but you need not conform to them. If, after seven years of her mothering, you still had the orthodox religious and political views, it was because you hadn't bothered to think about religion and politics, in which case it didn't matter what your views were, but orthodoxy would make you less offensive to your own class. If, after seven years, you were no scholar, then scholarship had never meant much to you. It was for you to find yourself, and for her to let you find yourself. I didn't find much of myself, but perhaps at that time there wasn't very much to find.

UNDERGRADUATE

1900–1903

Chapter Nine

1

WHAT distinguishes Cambridge from Oxford, broadly speaking, is that nobody who has been to Cambridge feels impelled to write about it. If it is not quite true that everybody has at least one book inside him, it seems to be the fact that every Oxonian has at least one book about Oxford inside him, and generally gets it out. Oxford men will say that this shows what a much more inspiring place Oxford is, and Cambridge men will say that it shows how much less quickly Oxford men grow up, and we can leave it at that. But it explains why this chapter will have no particular interest for those particularly interested in Cambridge. Just as the practised public speaker singles out one man in the back of the audience and speaks solely to him, so I have singled out one hypothetical reader who is interested in me, and am writing solely for her. To-morrow, when she goes to the library, she can change this for a book about Oxford, and discover what University life is like.

One of the happy discoveries which I made was that I need not be hungry again. After seven years of starvation at Westminster it was delightful to be ordering one's own breakfast and lunch. Even when one dined in Hall and left oneself to the authorities, one was safe. On my first evening a waiter leaned over my shoulder and addressed a shy freshman opposite in the unusual words 'Capercailzie or beef, sir?' Capercailzie is pronounced like Cholmondeley and Cirencester—wrongly first time. The dialogue went like this:

Waiter: Capercailzie or beef, sir?
Freshman (startled): What?
Waiter: Capperkelly or beef, sir?
Freshman (very pink): Er—I didn't—er——
Waiter: Kepper——
Freshman: Beef, please.

The rest of us hit upon some standard pronunciation, I forget what, and avoided the beef. It is always difficult to know what to do about other people's pronunciations. I had to make arrangements with a mathematical coach, a Scotsman called Walker. I played football every afternoon, and didn't feel inclined to work immediately afterwards, so proposed to go to him in the mornings at some hour when I wasn't at a lecture. We discussed what subjects we should do together, and then he said, 'And will ye come in the for-r-r-noon or the affter-r-r-noon?' My three-quarter English blood boiled at the idea of saying 'for-r-r-noon,' politeness forbade me to say 'morning,' so I went to him in the afternoon, and never ceased to regret it. My previous coach, who had discovered that it was no good was E. W. Barnes. There we were, working away like anything at Differential Equations, and now he's the Bishop of Birmingham and I write plays. Somehow I never thought of him as a clergyman; probably he never thought of me as a dramatist. Certainly he never thought of me as a mathematician.

I did all the usual things in my first term. I bought two pipes, silver-bound, in a morocco case. I started a banking account, and established my cheque-signature as 'Alan A. Milne.' So it has remained: with the result that any letter addressed thus proclaims itself at once a bill, receipt or charitable appeal. This has been very

useful. I had breakfast with the Master of Trinity, the
famous Dr Butler. It was he who came into the break-
fast-room one wintry morning where half-a-dozen nervous freshmen were awaiting him, glanced out of the
window, and said genially: 'Well, well, we have a little
sun this morning' . . . and the most nervous freshman
who answered: 'I hope Mrs Butler is all right.' I kept
lectures, cut chapels, got up as late as I could, was called
on by strangers and, shyly, returned calls. I also played
outside-left in the Freshmen's match and a silent Greek
maiden in *Agamemnon*.

While this was going on, A. K. M. was sending in a
set of verses each week to *The Granta*, and receiving
them back again. It was not until the beginning of my
second term that we had our first contribution accepted.
Ken invented a nonsense verse, a little in the limerick
vein, which, once found, provided us with an easy
formula for humour. We hoped that the result would
come to be known as Milnicks, but it was not to be.
Here is an example:

> *He was a violoncello*
> *And she was a wedding-bell.*
> *He loved 'not wisely' (Othello)*
> *But she didn't love 'too well.'*
> *One day she addressed him as 'Fellow!'* . . .
> *And they buried him there where he fell.*

This was the first of half-a-dozen such tragedies, the
last of them having a more human note:

> *He was an ardent philosopher*
> *And she was a girl of physique.*
> *He said he was dying because of her,*
> *But she told him she couldn't stand cheek.*
> *Then he recklessly said it was cross of her* . . .
> *And he hopes to be well in a week.*

A day or two after these verses came out, Trinity, Cambridge, was playing football against Trinity, Oxford. On our way back from Oxford we stopped inevitably at Bletchley, and went into the refreshment-room for a drink. And while I was shyly drinking my ginger-beer, and wishing that I liked beer and whisky more than I liked rice-pudding, which was not at all, I heard no less a person than the Captain of the Side say to no less a person than one of the 'blues' in the side: 'Did you see those awfully good verses in *The Granta* this week—a new sort of limerick by somebody called A. K. M.?' I plunged a glowing face into the ginger-beer. This was authorship. If only Ken had been next to me, so that we could have nudged each other and grinned, and talked it over happily together afterwards. Well, I would write to him to-morrow.

It was unlucky for poor old Ken that our verses were appearing in *The Granta* and not in the *Weymouth Times*. As we went on contributing, it gradually became accepted that I alone was A. K. M., disguising myself under these alien initials, presumably from modesty. A few friends knew the truth, but to others a brother in Dorsetshire seemed as remote from reality as a Bunbury in Shropshire or the dog that you go to see a man about. Our contributions came out regularly now, and from time to time somebody would say 'I liked your last thing in *The Granta*,' of which a shy smile seemed the appropriate acknowledgement. To go on: 'Well, as it happens, I have a brother down in Dorsetshire' sounded like the beginning of a new and irrelevant anecdote desperately in need of an audience. With an apologetic nod the other hurried on his way.

Ken may have guessed that this was happening, though I don't think he would have resented it, but it made little difference; for, at the end of the summer term, he announced his withdrawal from the partnership. His reason was that I could do 'this sort of thing' just as well without him, and that he would prefer to try some other sort of thing without me. In short, his heart wasn't in frivolity, he wanted to be more serious. He put it, as he would, charmingly, making it seem that there had never really been a 'K' in A. K. M., making it seem that I had been generously carrying him on my back for two years. This was so completely untrue that I protested violently against any idea of separation; indeed, I felt miserable at the thought of it. It was in his second letter that he confessed to a wish to be alone.

Well, it was for him to say. If he wished it, he should write essays for *The Cornhill,* while I wrote nonsense for *The Granta.* And good luck to both of us.

The Granta was nominally the property of the editor, but in practice his rights did not extend much beyond the nomination of his successor. The printer managed the business side of it and told the editor what (if any) the profits were. When, as editor, I was told what the profits were, I looked forward eagerly to receiving my first literary earnings. After looking forward eagerly for some weeks I applied for the money; and was informed that, until all the advertisement revenue had been collected, I was heavily in debt to the printer, and that an immediate settlement could be made on these lines if I wished it. I replied coldly that I was 'putting the matter in the hands of my father's solicitors' (Barry), whereupon a cheque for my first literary earnings arrived. What the rights and wrongs of it were I don't know; but it seemed to me all against tradition that, as between Town and University, the University should be kept waiting for its money.

The editor at the beginning of my second year was a Trinity man whom I knew slightly. Under his auspices the initials of which I have since grown rather tired made a first appearance. The verses above them were not noticeably improved, nor, I think, weakened, by the substitution of a second A for the absent K. But there was, uniquely, a contribution in prose (of no great merit) such as would not have been made in collaboration. I wrote it rather diffidently, wondering if this were the way to write. While I was still wondering, I received a letter from the editor, not, as I expected, saying, 'Better stick to verse,' but making the incredible suggestion that I should take over the editorship in the following term.

This was almost the biggest surprise of my life. The most surprising thing was that he took twenty pages to elaborate his theme: the pleasure and profit to be derived from editorship and my supreme fitness for the job: when four words 'Will you be editor?' would have been enough. I suppose that I was the only possible person in sight, and he had to be sure of getting the paper off his hands somehow. It was a little disappointingly easy. There is no fun in saying 'I will' grandly, and then being as good as told that, willy-nilly, you've got to.

Well, anyway, I was editor.

2

A Cambridge friend had asked me to spend a few days with him after Christmas, and I had accepted his invitation cheerfully, even after hearing that the entertainment would include 'private theatricals.' I imagined myself, with the rest of the house-party, amusing a few friends in the drawing-room, my own part being one of those silent impersonations whose range, extending as it did now from a Greek maiden to a monkey, could embrace almost anything. More attractive was the thought that I might write the dialogue for the others to speak, or compose the lyrics for some home-made pantomime. At the least I should be helpful as prompter or scene-schifter. It was an appalling shock to find that we had taken the Ipswich Town Hall, and that in the one serious play in a triple bill I was to be the wounded hero.

Years later I wrote a series for *Punch* called 'Little Plays for Amateurs.' This might have been one of those. The hero can be (as you please) a Frenchman in the Franco-German war, a Roundhead in the Civil War or a Southerner in the War of Secession. Wounded after the appropriate battle, he drags himself to the house of his beloved, to find a German, a Cavalier or a Northerner billeted there; and not only billeted there, but making unacceptable advances to the heroine. One steps lightly into a play like this thinking that one is going to be the hero, only to discover in the big scene that it is the other man who is up-stage all the time, sacrificing duty and his own feelings to the call of an unrequited love. Personally I didn't mind being down-stage, if I couldn't be at home. Owing to the fact that I was wounded, the heroine and I had a passionate love-scene on the floor, with my head among the footlights; which was no position in which to remember a long speech describing my emotions during the Battle of Sedan. However I did my best. Only one line was unforgettable: *'All through that long night I thought of thee.'* She moved my head out of the footlights and stroked it; I wish I could remember what she looked like. I said again 'All through that long night I thought of you—thee,' wondering what came next. Fortunately it was the German colonel, a little early on his cue. Having informed me gruffly that I was his prisoner, and that escape was impossible, he left us. It was a desperate situation, but all was not lost: a secret passage in which the heroine and I had played as children offered a way out. She helped me to my feet, and we had an affecting farewell scene. 'All through that long night,' I said—but she was in a hurry. 'Quick, quick,' she cried, 'you must go!' She led me to the cunningly hidden door. 'Farewell, beloved,' I cried, and, opening the door, stepped into the arms of the Colonel who knew about it. He informed me briefly that I was still his prisoner and left us. The position now seemed hopeless, or would have seemed so in any other play. Fortunately we remembered that on the other side of the room there was a second secret door, leading to a second secret passage, where also we had played as children. We had another farewell scene which I took more gaily, realizing that in five minutes I should have left the stage for ever, and was editing *The Granta* next term. Flinging back the door, I cried, 'Good-bye, my love,' and stepped into the arms of the Colonel again. He seemed to know everything; it was very discouraging. I remembered suddenly, with a start of dismay which was effective, that there was another performance to-morrow night. The Colonel then took the centre of the stage and made his great speech of renunciation, giving me both little Renée and my freedom. All I wanted was to leave Ipswich.

But even at Ipswich one could get ready for next term. Alone in my bedroom, the Franco-German war forgotten for a few hours, I wrote a ballad. It began:

> *Oh Mary, my Mary, come over the sea!*
> *I am thinking of you, are you thinking of me?*
> *They are thinking of him, he is thinking of thee—*
> *(Oh Mary, my Mary, come over the sea).*

All through that long night I thought of Mary, and by morning I had written my first contribution for the new *Granta*. I submitted it to myself as editor, and accepted it. We had begun.

3

It was the custom for undergraduates to meet their Tutor on the first day of term, not to present but to receive an address of welcome, and to be informed of any new College or University regulations which might concern them. On the first day of Lent Term 1902 our Tutor so addressed us, and then added, 'Well, that's all, thank you, gentlemen. Mr. Milne will remain behind.' The others went out, wondering what I had done. So did I.

He told me. In effect the conversation went like this:

'I hear you are editing *The Granta* this term?'

'Yes.'

'Well, you can't.'

'Why not?'

'You had no business whatever to commit yourself to anything like that without consulting me.'

'Oh!' I decided to consult him. 'Well—may I?'

'If you had consulted me, as you ought to have done, I should have forbidden it.'

'But why?'

'You're a mathematician——'

'Well——'

'And the College pays you for being a mathematician——'

'Not very much.'

'And from what I hear you will have to work a great deal harder, even as it is, in order to get the degree that is expected of you. And this is the moment which you choose to take on other responsibilities——'

'I always meant to edit *The Granta*. I simply must.'

'I warn you that the College may decide to withdraw the money it pays you——'

'I simply must. I always meant to.'

There is a long pause. I am not looking heroic. I am looking sulky and stubborn and uncomfortable.

'I'd rather do it,' I mumble, 'than have the money.'

'And you think you can edit *The Granta* and do your legitimate work properly?'

'How many hours a day do you call properly?'

'I should expect at least six from anyone with any pretensions to be a scholar.'

'All right. Six.'

'Very well then. You will keep a record of your working hours, and show it to me every week.'

So there it was. It is funny to think that my 'working-hours' then were the stern laborious hours when I wasn't writing.

The constant weekly features of *The Granta* were the editorial, 'Motley Notes,' 'Those in Authority' (biographical sketches of the leading lights of Cambridge), Union Notes, Theatrical Notes, and comments on all the athletic activities of the term. The rest of the paper was filled with 'humorous' articles and verses.

The Union and Sporting Notes were written by Our Special Correspondents. There was a tradition that they were entitled to £2 a term for this, and another tradition that they never asked for it and never got it. Tradition was upheld in my time, save once by a football 'blue,' who was big enough to know better. I paid him as cheerfully as I could. Those in Authority chose their own biographers. An exception was made in the case of Edward VIIth, whom I put In Authority as Patron of the A.D.C. in the May Week number of *The Granta*.

Little or nothing is known of his early life [I wrote] but it is believed that even in this stage of his career he evinced that love for the drama which was destined to make him President, and afterwards Patron, of the A.D.C. Anyhow there is evidence to show that he frequently came on at Her Majesty's and the Court about this time, while the Princess of Wales first saw him in 1862 with the part of Leading Gentleman, a part to which he has always lived up.

I meant to send him a specially printed copy, but finance or laziness intervened.

One of the privileges of editorship was the possession of a free pass to the theatre. Even in those days I realized that dramatic criticism demanded no quality but enthusiasm, and that the man who saw *The Belle of New York* twice on his first Saturday at Cambridge could provide all the enthusiasm necessary. But it seemed that the Manager of the New Theatre wanted more than enthusiasm: he wanted a definite promise in advance that his productions would be treated with more tenderness than they had been in the past. There was, of course, no reason why he should give me, or anybody else, free seats if he didn't think it was good for business, and equally no reason why I shouldn't buy my own seats and criticize his plays if I thought it was good for the drama; but, as I explained with dignity in the next number, for *The Granta* to take its revenge in this way 'though apparently more expensive would in fact be rather cheap.' So Theatrical Notes were abandoned.

Normally the editor wrote the leading article and Motley Notes, and depended on outside contributors for such stuff as jokes are made of. I took what I think must have been the mistaken view that no contribution to which I would not proudly have put my own initials was worth inclusion. The result was, human nature being what it is and authors what they are, that I couldn't depend on anybody. When one more set of verses was wanted for the next number, and X. Y. Z.'s 'Ode to My Tailor' filled the space exactly, the fact that I was pledged to Electrodynamics for the next two hours did not prevent me wondering whether I couldn't have filled the space as exactly, and even more delightfully, myself, if I had had the time. Naturally on these occasions one takes an exaggerated view of the possibilities. Pushing Loney's *Electrodynamics* a little to one side and rattling a pencil against my teeth, I allowed various ideas to wander through my mind, the conclusion three hours later being a set of verses signed A. B. C. which endeared itself to me as X. Y. Z's had never done. No doubt it was only better in my own opinion, but, as editor, whose opinion could I consult but my own? Making a note that I should have to do eighteen hours' mathematics to-morrow to get back to schedule, I went to bed. Life was very full just then.

In the first number I began a series of dialogues which ran through the term. This series might be called the precursor (if anything as frivolous may be so dignified) of a series which appeared later in *Punch* called 'The Rabbits.' I don't want to read 'The Rabbits' now, but I can do it without feeling uncomfortable. These earlier dialogues fill me not only with unease, but with a profound surprise that they led me anywhere. Yet they did, in fact, lead me away from the Civil Service, schoolmastering, chartered accountancy, all the professions which I might have followed, into the profession of writing.

4

It was in the first week of the following term that I opened unsuspiciously a letter addressed to The Editor of *The Granta*. It was from R. C. Lehmann, its founder and ex-editor, and now for some years on the staff of *Punch*. He asked for the name of the author of a certain series of dialogues, 'of which I and many others in London have a very high opinion,' in the hope that, if it interested him, 'work of a similar nature might be put in his way.' I gave him my name.

The undergraduate of to-day will find it difficult to appreciate the thrill which I received from this letter. It must be remembered that in those days there was no 'popular press' to keep the Universities 'in the news.' Undergraduates were not asked to tell a million suburban readers what was wrong with Oxford, or why they had decided to give up religion. They only came into the London eye on Boat Race night, when it was the magistrate who told them what was wrong and what they should give up. London was not interested to know 'what the young man of to-day is thinking.' Youth, no doubt, would be served, but custom demanded that it should be served last. When it had a beard and was more than a youth, then let beards be wagged.

I had no beard; I was twenty and very young for that; but 'people in London' were talking about me. I was thrilled. There was only one person to whom I could communicate, and with whom share, that thrill. I wrote at once to Ken.

How easy I have found it to go through the world making on equal terms friends, acquaintances, enemies, and to have the persistent feeling that the only side of the equation which matters is my own. I meet Smith, I like Smith; that is all there is about Smith. I meet Jones, I detest Jones; that goes for Jones. What do they, in return, feel about me? That is their own concern. But for some reason which I cannot explain I assume that their feelings are not so definite as mine, nor so well considered. Is this because they feel less deeply than I, or because I am less worth consideration than they? I have never answered that question. The answer lies in the usual tangle of superiority complexes, inferiority complexes, conceits, modesties, mock-modesties and vanities of which modern man is composed.

Through the rivalries of our childhood and boyhood I had tried to be 'nice about it' to Ken. It did not occur to me that he was trying, with complete success, to be nice about it to me. He was nice without effort, simply because he was not so interested in our rivalry as I, because (I could almost persuade myself) he didn't even know that we were rivals, and that I had beaten him again. How could it be a humiliation to him who showed no signs of being humiliated? All these little 'victories' and 'defeats' meant no more to Ken than the winning or losing a game of beggar-my-neighbour.

I was wrong. He wrote now to congratulate me. No friend could have been more honestly delighted, no lover have paid more reckless compliments. And then for the first time he brought our rivalry into the light, showing what it had meant to him from those earliest days until now:

Whatever I did, you did a little better or a little sooner . . . And so it went on. Even after all this, I could still tell myself that I had one thing left. I should always be the writer of the family. And now you have taken that too. Well, damn you, I suppose I must forgive you. My head is bloody but unbowed. I have got a new frock coat and you can go to the devil. Yours stiffly, Ken.

> *Jenny kissed me when we met,*
> *Jumping from the chair she sat in;*
> *Time, you thief, who love to get*
> *Sweets into your list, put that in!*

UNDERGRADUATE

Say I'm weary, say I'm sad,
  Say that health and wealth have missed me,
Say I'm growing old, but add
  Jenny kissed me.

Throughout his life I never lost Ken, nor he me. Time, you thief, who love to get sweets into your list, put that in.

5

The immediate result of Rudie Lehmann's letter was the suggestion that I should write a series of sketches for *Punch.* Obviously this could not be attempted until term was over, but it was attempted then with discouraging results. Nobody had said to me, looking at a copy of *Punch,* 'You ought to edit that one day,' and if anybody had, I should undoubtedly have answered 'I will.' But there seemed to be many ways of editing a paper. This series of half-a-dozen articles went backwards and forwards between me and the Assistant Editor, Owen Seaman, for some weeks, until at last they were all to his liking. They reached the editor, Burnand, at the beginning of October. Nothing more was heard of them until May, when I made apologetic enquiries of Rudie. He wrote to Burnand, who replied that he had been very busy with his autobiography lately, and hadn't had time to give them the anxious consideration which they deserved, but that he would be going down to Ramsgate for the week-end and hoped to be able to read them in the train. Rudie waited another month or two (Burnand having met a friend in the train), and then got them away from him, and sent them to a paper called *John Bull* which had just been started as a 'rival to *Punch.*' This editorship seemed to be in more lively hands, for the series was accepted at once; but the financial arrange-

ments were equally volatile, and the paper went bank-
rupt at once. Whether before or after the first of my
articles appeared I never discovered.

But at the moment the whole of this was hidden from
me. I was beginning a second term's editorship of *The
Granta,* and I was about a hundred hours down on my
mathematical time-table. So, reluctantly but, as it proved,
wisely, I installed a co-editor, Vere Hodge, and made
him do all the work which I didn't like. Editorials flowed
from his pen as they had never flowed from mine. There
was no space, of whatever length or breadth, which he
could not turn to print. Between us we covered the
paper. I wrote whatever I wanted to write, or could
reasonably find time to write, and left him to fill up.
Probably he thought that he was writing what he wanted
to write, and leaving the blank spaces to me. It didn't
matter. We worked happily together and the space was
filled. There was a faint aroma of culture about us now,
Hodge being a Classical scholar.

6

Ken and I went to the Lakes together in August, staying at a farm-house at Seathwaite. We had decided to do
a little rock-climbing. We knew nothing about it, but
had brought a rope, nailed boots, and the standard book
by Owen Glynne Jones. The climbs in this book were
graded under such headings as Easy, Medium, Moderately Stiff, and Extremely Stiff. We decided to start with
a moderately stiff one, and chose the Napes Needle on
Great Gable, whose charm is that on a post-card it looks
Extremely Stiff. Detached by the hands of a good photographer from its context, it becomes a towering pinnacle
rising a thousand feet above the abyss. Roped together,

since it seemed to be the etiquette, Ken and I would scale this mighty pinnacle, and send post-cards to the family.

We were a little shy about the rope when we started out, carrying it lightly over the arm at first as if we had just found it and were looking for its owner . . . and then more grimly over the other arm, as one who makes for a well down which some wanderer has fallen. The important thing was not to be mistaken for what we were; two novices who had been assured that a rope made climbing less dangerous, when, in fact, they were convinced that it would make climbing very much more so. There was also the question of difficulty. To get ourselves to the top of the Needle would be moderately stiff; but it was (surely) extremely stiff to expect us to drag a rope up there too. I felt all this more keenly than Ken, because it had already been decided, anyhow by myself, that I was to 'lead.' Not only had I won the Gymnastics Competition Under 14 in 1892, but compared with Ken's my life was now of no value. Ken had just got engaged to be married. If I led, we might both be killed (as seemed likely with this rope) or I might be killed alone, but it was impossible that I should ever be breaking the news to his lady of an accident which I had callously survived. I was glad of this, of course; but I should have liked it better if it had been I who was engaged and Ken who was being glad.

We scrambled up the lower slopes of Great Gable and reached the foot of the Needle. Seen close it was a large splinter of rock about sixty feet high, shaped like an acute-angled pyramid with a small piece of the top cut off; leaving a flat summit which could just take Ken and me and (we supposed) the rope. We had practised tying ourselves on, and we now tied ourselves on. I have told how Ken kissed me once, but on this occasion we didn't even shake hands. I just started up, dragging the rope behind me.

The Napes Needle has this advantage over, from what I hear, the Matterhorn: that the difficult part is not really dangerous and the dangerous part is not really difficult. The dangerous part, as one would expect, comes at the top. One begins by forcing oneself diagonally up a flat slab of rock, the left leg, from knee to ankle, wedged in a crack, and the rest of oneself free as a trolley-bus to follow the left leg upwards. Only the re-assurance of the book, as shouted up to me by Ken, that this though difficult was not dangerous, kept me at it. No doubt my leg *was* jambed—no doubt about it, as I found when I tried to move it; no doubt I couldn't roll down the mountain without it; but the rest of my body felt horribly defenceless, and every nerve in it was saying 'This is silly, and one should stick to Essex.' With a sudden jerk which made all that the book said ridiculous, I loosened my leg and got it in a little higher up. The very slave of circumstance and impulse, like Sardanapalus, 'borne away with every breath' a little farther from Ken (which meant twice as far to fall) I puffed on . . . until a moment came when I could go no farther. Knee still in crack, heart still in mouth, body still *in vacuo,* I sidled backward to Ken.

'It's no good. Sorry.'

'Were you really stuck?'

'Absolutely. There's more in this than we thought.'

'Shall I try?'

At some other time I might have said: 'My dear man, if I can't, you can't.' At some other time I might have said: 'For Maud's sake, no!' At this time I said 'Yes, do.' I wanted to lie down.

In a little while he was back with me, and we were studying the Easy group.

'All the same,' said Ken, looking up at the Needle again.

'All the same,' said I.

'Think of Bruce.'

'I think of nothing else.'

'Say "I can do it." '

'I can do it.'

We got up.

'Suppose I came up behind you and pushed a bit?'

'What's the rope doing?'

'Hanging about.'

'Is that right?'

'Well, I don't see what else it *can* do.'

'Nor do I. I don't like the look of the dangerous bit at the top, do you?'

'It may look better when we get there.'

'Yes. Well, let's get there. Dash it, we can't just carry the rope home again. Come on.'

It was a little easier this time. I felt more like a tram and less like a 'bus; I got to the sticking-place and waited for Ken's hand to reach my foot. With its support I straightened my knee and got a handhold higher up. We went on doing this until Ken had reached the sticky place, by which time I was in sight of home. Soon we were sitting side by side on a broad shelf, puffing happily. The 'difficult' part was over.

There remained a vertical slab of rock in the shape of the lower four-fifths of an isosceles triangle. It was about fifteen feet high, and there was a ledge like a narrow mantelpiece halfway up. Owen Glynn Jones (who may have been a nuisance in the home) made a practice of pulling himself on to mantelpieces by the fingers, so as to keep in training, and no doubt it is in the repertory

AUTOBIOGRAPHY

of every real climber. We were merely a couple of tourists. When in doubt we collaborated. Ken reached up to the ledge and grasped it firmly, and I climbed up him. When I was standing on the ledge, my fingers were a couple of feet below the top.

In making these climbs it is impossible to lose the way. Every vital handhold is registered in the books, every foothold scored by the nails of previous climbers. To get to the top I wanted one more foothold and one handhold, and I knew where they were. I shuffled to the left and looked round the corner.

On the precipitous left-hand face of the pyramid, a little out of reach, there was an excrescence of rock the size and shape of half a cricket-ball. That was the handhold. Just within reach of raised foot and bent knee a piece of the rock sloped out for a moment at an angle of 45°, before resuming the perpendicular. That was the foothold. I should imagine that the whole charm of the Napes Needle to an enthusiast rests on that forbidding foothold. To a non-enthusiast, as I was at that moment, the whole charm of a foothold is that it holds the foot solidly, at right angles to whatever one is climbing up. This didn't. Could one's nails (and Jones) be trusted? When all one's weight was on that slippery-looking, nail-scratched slope, while one grabbed for the cricket-ball, did one simply disappear down the left-hand face, leaving Ken with a lot of rope and no brother, or did one's head appear triumphantly over the top? That was the question, and there was only one way of finding the answer. After all, there must be something in this rope business, or people wouldn't carry them about. If I fell, I could only fall thirty feet. It was absurd to suppose that I should then break in half; there was no record of anyone having broken in half; no, I should simply dangle for a little, assure Ken's anxious head that all that blood he saw everywhere was only where I had hit myself on the way down, and then climb gaily up the rope to safety. All this was just the give-and-take of the climber's life. All those scratches were just signs of where other people had slipped, disappeared, and come laughing back. Without the rope one would be a dead man, but with it the whole climb was child's play . . . Or just plain folly?

Oh, well . . .

It was delightful to sit on the top of the Needle and dangle our legs, and think 'We've done it.' About once every ten years it comes back to me that, in addition to all the things I can't do and haven't done, I *have* climbed the Napes Needle. So have thousands of other people. But they, probably, knew something about it.

A few days later we climbed Kern Knotts Chimney. My ideal reader of this book would be somebody just sufficiently acquainted with the subject to think that by Kern Knotts Chimney I mean Kern Knotts Crack. If I had climbed the Crack, this would have been a different sort of book. The Chimney is only moderately stiff. Blocking the top of the actual chimney, which is the second stage of the climb, is a large rocking-stone. Somehow this has to be surmounted. Our faith in Jones was now such as to—I was going to say 'to move mountains' but that would be an unfortunate metaphor. It was this bit of the mountain which was *not* going to move, according to Jones, and we trusted him. But it wobbled alarmingly. There is a technique of chimney-climbing which we didn't seem to have mastered. We had a fireside discussion as to whether it would be bad form to throw the rope over this boulder and haul ourselves up by it.

'Good heavens, you can do what you like with the rope,' said Ken. 'That's what it's for.'

'Then if you had a lasso and lassoed the top of the

Monument and climbed up, you could say you had climbed the Monument?'

'That's absurd. You might as well say——'

'What?'

'Almost anything,' said Ken, thinking hard.

'Such as?'

'Well, you'll admit that you can stand on the other man's shoulders? *That's* quite fair?'

'Of course. But a rope——'

'Then if you had a friend 475 feet high and you climbed up his braces and stood on his shoulders——'

'Oh, *shut* up. Give us the rope.'

We reached the top. It may be things like this which get you blackballed for the Alpine Club. I wouldn't know.

7

My last year at Cambridge was sacrificed to the Mathematical Tripos. The sacrifice was in vain. I had hoped that I might just get a Second, but it was not to be. As I wrote later, summing up my life:

> *The work we did was rarely reckoned*
> *Worthy a Tutor's kindly word,*
> *For when I said we got a Second,*
> *I really meant we got a third . . .*

It sounds well to say that one has got an Honours Degree; it looks well to write B.A. (Maths. Honours) after one's name; to a maiden aunt one can explain how well her nephew has done. But one cannot explain a Third Class to one's father. Father was so bitterly disappointed that for a week he did not talk to me. When I mentioned this the other day to a young friend who was waiting anxiously for the result of his Tripos, he said enviously: 'Good lord, I wish I could be sure that *my* father wouldn't talk to me for a week.' But in our family we dreaded Father's unhappy silences much more than we dreaded his anger.

When he was ready to talk to me again, we discussed the future. Was there any chance now of my passing into the Civil Service? I didn't see why not? Well, I had better begin thinking about it. So I went to London and called upon Wrens'—who with one or two 'n's,' I cannot now remember, did then, and perhaps still do, specialize in coaching for Civil Service examinations. I told them what I knew, which didn't sound much, and was advised to supplement my now rather blown-upon knowledge of mathematics with a knowledge of History. I bought a very light book on Constitutional History and took it with me every morning to the bandstand on the Westgate front. Lying in a deck-chair, I studied Constitutional History to the dreamy rhythm of the Blue Danube Waltz. Below, the sea broke gently on a highly respectable beach. It was very peaceful. . . .

I had been happy at Cambridge, and I had edited *The Granta*. The only cloud over my happiness had been the Tripos. If I never did examinations again, then I could go on being happy. I turned over another page of history and closed my eyes. Somehow I didn't see myself getting into the Civil Service.

FREELANCE

1903–1906

Chapter Ten

1

WE SAT one August evening on a garden seat at the end of the croquet-lawn, Father and I, facing the less Elizabethan wing of the house. Father had his notebook out, and was checking figures: adding this up, subtracting that, and telling me the result. Twiddling the head of a croquet-mallet between my feet, my eyes on the ground, I said 'Oh, yes,' and 'Yes,' and 'I see' in a reserved, rather obstinate voice. We were settling my future.

Father was convinced now that I was not good enough for the Civil Service. If there was a doubt in his mind, it was whether I was good enough to be a schoolmaster, to carry on this great preparatory school which he had built up. Still, he would give me the chance. A year in Germany studying the latest educational systems, a year or two at a public-school, then to Streete Court, first as assistant-master, then as junior partner, finally in full control: he had it all worked out in his notebook: the salary I should get at first, my share of income as partner, the allowance to be paid to him when he retired, the compensation to be made to my brothers for inheriting the whole patrimony, the value of the inheritance in fifteen years' time when I should be my own master, all obligations discharged. Blue-black ink, red ink, little ticks in pencils, as he checked each item: a labour of love and pride and hope that morning in his study, while I fooled about on the fashionable beach with the prettiest of the many pretty visitors to Westgate.

'Well, dear, what do you think of it?'

'It's all right. It's very generous.' I said it reluctantly. The prettiest of the pretty visitors lived in London. I was going to Germany. It seemed wrong.

'Well, you must think it over. I don't want to hurry you.'

In front of us was the long north wing, with the big schoolroom which Father had added to it when first Streete Court had climbed beyond that obstinate twenty-mark where it had stayed so long (and, it seemed, so hopelessly) . . . into the thirties and then the forties . . . and then the fifties: until now it could hold its own with all the fashionable schools of Thanet, this dream of the little Kilburn schoolmaster, B.A. (Lond.), with his old-fashioned clothes and his old-fashioned beard. He leant back, his notebook on his knees, looking over the quiet lawns to all the ugly schools through which he had struggled on his way to this loved place, and again he was on his knees to God, as he had been every night of his life, in gratitude for the fulfilment to which he had been led.

'Father?'

'Yes, dear?'

'I think I—I think I—I'd like to try to be a writer.'

'It's for you to decide.'

'Yes . . . I think I have decided.'

Father closed the notebook and put it back in his pocket. How much of heartache was hidden in it and put away for ever?

'How do you mean to set about it?'

'I thought I'd just go up to London—and write.'

'Write what?'

'Well—anything. Everything.'

'Just think a moment, darling, of all the people who

want to write, and who think they *can* write, and how very few of them——'

'Naturally I'm thinking of the very few of them.'

'We can't all be Dickenses, you know.'

'Dickens isn't the only man who has made a living by writing.'

'Even Mr Wells had to do other work for a long time before he could support himself by writing.' Father had called him 'Mr Wells' to me when I was eight; he would go on calling him Mr Wells.

'Wells hadn't got any money. I've got £300 or so. Haven't I? I mean you said—I mean I know it's your money, and it's awfully good of you, but you did say—I mean the others had a thousand pounds.'

'I think it's £320. Of course that would help.'

'But, Father dear, three-twenty, just think, I could live for three years on that if I had to, and do you mean to say that in three *years* I couldn't—why I nearly had a whole series in *Punch* when I was still at Cambridge, I mean everybody thought I was going to, and it isn't as if—I mean I did edit *The Granta,* and people do read *The Granta* in London. Besides, there's——' I stopped suddenly.

'What, dear?'

'Nothing. Anyhow I *know* I can do it. Three years!' In three years I could be editor of *Punch,* of *The Times,* of—should I? Yes, for Ken's sake—of *The Cornhill,* of anything you like, my dear Father. Look at me. There is nothing I can't do.

'Then you want to go to London and take rooms there. Would you live with Barry?'

'Good Heavens, no. Sorry. Ken will be in London this year, but I wouldn't even live with *him.* I *must* be alone.'

'You do understand, don't you, that you have no more money to come after this three hundred? And it will be too late then to be a schoolmaster. You'll just have to be a bank-clerk.'

It had always been held over us, I don't know why, this threat of servitude in a bank. Other sons might be told that they would have to enlist, or emigrate, if they failed in their chosen profession; even to sweep a crossing; but from childhood we had been taught that it was in banks that human driftwood ultimately grounded. What qualifications were necessary for a bank-clerk other than that of being a disappointment to his father we never discovered.

'Of course,' I agreed. 'But I can do it. I know.'

Father went in to tell Mother. I went in to write a letter. What I had been about to say was 'Besides, there's Harmsworth.' But I thought that I would write to him first, just to make sure.

2

Alfred Harmsworth had been a boy at Henley House. He was one of those boys who seem full of intelligence out of school hours and devoid of intelligence in them. A master's natural deduction is that the boy is idle: 'Could do better' he writes in his report. Father didn't condemn Harmsworth as idle, he condemned himself for not being able to discover where this obviously clever boy's interests lay. Harmsworth came to him one day and asked if a school paper could be started, because other schools had them, and he knew a little printer round the corner who would do it very cheaply. Father said that a school paper was a good idea, but it took up too much of a headmaster's time. Perhaps one day when he was less busy.

'That's all right, sir,' said Harmsworth eagerly. 'I'll do it all. You shan't be bothered, I promise.'

Now I think that nine headmasters out of ten would have pointed out that, even as it was, this boy was continually failing to pass the necessary examinations, and that there was an obvious use which could be made of his spare time. Father was the tenth headmaster. Here, at last, was something which the boy was keen on doing. Then let him do it. So the first number of the *Henley House School Magazine* was published: 'Edited by Alfred C. Harmsworth.' On that day, one may say, the Northcliffe Press was born.

Harmsworth, as the world knows, was a very brotherly man. Almost as soon as he was earning a living for himself he was earning a living for a multitude of brothers. At about the time when he was giving us pennies at Penshurst Place, he was particularly concerned with the education of a younger brother, Albert. While we were buying ourselves sweets in Penshurst, Harmsworth was telling Father of the struggle he was having to educate and bring up his family. Every penny that *Answers* brought in, and as yet nobody knew whether it was to be a success or failure, must go back into the paper; and yet here was young Albert——

'I'll take him for you,' said Father. 'When *Answers* is a success, you can pay me my fees, but we'll say nothing about them for the present.'

'And suppose it isn't a success?' said Harmsworth, not supposing any such thing.

'In that case we'll go on saying nothing about them.'

So Albert came to Henley House, and a delightful boy he was. Quite a good bowler too: off-break. And when, after a few anxious months, *Answers* was fairly on its feet, Harmsworth, with many expressions of gratitude, discharged his debt.

The first country house which Harmsworth bought when he was approaching millionairedom was at St.

Peter's in Thanet. A few miles way, struggling to keep his school above water, was Father, at Streete Court. Father, in adversity and prosperity alike, was grateful to God for His mercies, but he was too simple and modest to expect much from his fellow-men. Yet even he was a little hurt (when he thought of it) that the Great Man next door never drove over to see his old schoolmaster; never gave so much as an English Essay Prize to his old school. However, that was the way of the world.

But there came a day when, for the first time, he did appeal to Harmsworth for help. He was anxious about the lease of Streete Court. The freehold was not his, and any buildings which he put up, such as the gymnasium and, later, a sanatorium, became the property of the land-lord and the subject, at the end of each seven years' lease, of additional rent. It was essential that he should buy the freehold as soon as possible. The price was about £7,000.

Father had nothing. There was only one person who could help him. So Harmsworth was asked if he would buy Streete Court, and become Father's landlord until the day when Father had saved enough to buy it back from him. In this way, he would have, at any rate, security of tenure. Harmsworth replied that he had so much of his money tied up, and so many claims upon it, that he was unfortunately unable . . . and so on.

Father said nothing. It was the first occasion in his life on which he had asked for help, and he felt sad and silent and ashamed. Mother said a good deal. Harmsworth became 'that man.' Even as a boy he had always been—all the things he wouldn't have been if he had answered the letter differently. If I had said aloud 'Besides, there's Harmsworth,' Father would have shaken his head and said with a little smile 'Oh no, dear,' and Mother would have laughed scornfully and said 'That man!'

But I didn't feel quite the same about it. I did understand that one might be a millionaire, and yet not want to invest £7,000 in a particular way at a particular moment; I thought that, however good a schoolmaster Father had been to Harmsworth, it was, after all, his job to be a good schoolmaster. One isn't grateful (at least, I never see why one should be) to a doctor for curing one's influenza or to a baker for selling good bread. I thought that Father and Mother over-estimated the affection and gratitude which old pupils should feel for them. And though it was true that Father had been exceptionally kind to Harmsworth in the matter of his brother, was it not precisely to Father's son that Harmsworth would wish to repay this kindness? How delightful for both of us if he did. For to a young man who knew nobody 'knowing Harmsworth' was the best of all introductions to Fleet Street.

So I wrote to him.

It was a difficult letter to write, and I don't suppose I did it very well. I couldn't just say 'I'm coming to London, and I want a job.' Besides I was not sure that I did want a job. I wanted to be a free-lance, with (it sounds unpleasant, but it must have been in my mind) a pull over other free-lances as regards the Harmsworth papers. Most of all, I wanted some word of encouragement which I could show to Father and Mother as assurance of my capacity to earn a living; as proof also, perhaps, that I had been right and they wrong about Harmsworth. What, in fact, I said to him was that, after editing *The Granta*, I was coming to London to write, and that I hoped the fact that he had patted my head as a child wouldn't influence his editors against my articles which I might send to them. Silly, but the best I could do.

The answer came a fortnight later. It said that in Sir Alfred's absence abroad my letter had been forwarded to

Mr Philip Gibbs, the Literary Editor of *The Daily Mail*, 'to whom the articles you mention should be sent.'

I did not show this letter to Father; I did not send any articles to Mr Philip Gibbs. I felt as Father had once felt, ashamed of my own letter. Whether Harmsworth ever received it, and returned it with instructions to the office, or whether he knew nothing of it, I never heard. I told myself that I had really only written to 'that man' for my parents' sake, and that I was glad that the great name I was going to make for myself would be made without his or anybody's help. I pictured him on his knees a few years hence begging me to edit *all* his papers for him. Proudly I should refuse. . . .

3

With Mother's help I furnished two rooms in Temple Chambers at the bottom of Bouverie Street. This, I thought, would be convenient when I became editor of *Punch*. Breakfast was provided at a price; I lunched at an ABC and dined at The Cock in Fleet Street. When I was not eating I was writing: no day without its thousand words, sent off to this paper or that. I was, proud thought, a free-lance. To-day such apprenticeship seems less usual. Wordsworth, in what one might be forgiven for not recognizing as deathless poetry, writes of his 'instinctive humbleness maintained even by the very name and thought of printed books and authorship.' Humbleness is now better under control, 'the dread awe of mighty names' has been 'softened down,' and the young graduate begins his career at once as gossip-writer or critic. Perhaps it is as well; for how else could he live whose traditional playground, the evening press, has been torn from him? In my day there were eight fields open to his practice. Now there are but three, and even in these

three he may not intrude on the reservations of the qualified. For to-day genius is rewarded rather than encouraged. The 'mighty name' is acquired as a going concern.
What makes it go is of no moment to the editor.

I knew nobody in Fleet Street, but Rudie Lehmann
had given me introductions to T. A. Cook of *The Daily
Telegraph* and J. B. Atkins of *The Manchester Guardian*.
Cook had one piece of advice for me: 'Never accept less
than two guineas a thousand'; and to any free-lance of
to-day I will add: 'Never accept advice like this.' The
important thing at first is to be printed. In those days a
guinea a thousand was the usual rate, and I was thankful
to get it. So far I hadn't got it. Atkins asked me to lunch.
He was friendly and charming, and sorry that he couldn't
do much for me. He did what he could. He sent me a
press invitation to the first appearance in England of
Consul, the Man Monkey, and another to a meeting of
the Royal Asiatic Society. I did them both in one afternoon. Consul's performance struck me as the more
human, but there wasn't much in it. I may have muddled
the two 'stories' up. However it was, both Atkins and
I realized that I was not meant for a reporter.

Meanwhile my first free-lance contribution had been
accepted. Sherlock Holmes had just 'returned' in *The
Strand Magazine* after his duel with Moriarty. I wrote a
burlesque of this, which I sent to *Punch*. *Punch* refused
it, and I sent it to *Vanity Fair*. I can remember the last
two lines of the dialogue between Holmes and Watson.

'And Moriarty?' I said. 'What of him?'

*'There was no such man,' said Holmes. 'It was merely
the name of a soup.'*

To my delight the 'stamped addressed envelope enclosed' did not come back at once, and I was hopeful as
usual that, when it did, it might contain my first proof.
Ken was now in London, a qualified solicitor just enter-

ing his first office. We were dining together at a non-descript club which he had joined. Waiting for him in the smoking-room I picked up *Vanity Fair*, wondering on which page of it, one day, my parody might appear. To my utter disappointment I found that somebody had forestalled me; somebody else had written a Holmes parody. No doubt people were doing it all over England at that time. Jealously I read the opening paragraph. Dash the man, he had even got my first joke, about the Persian slipper! I read on . . . and then suddenly with beating heart glanced at the end:

' "There was no such man," said Holmes. "It was merely the name of a soup." A. A. M.'

First pale with the shock of it, then red with embarrassment, I glanced nervously round the room. My secret was out. Was everybody looking at me? Even now when I see my name in the paper, I feel that the world is intruding unduly on my privacy. I ought to be anonymous: we all ought to be anonymous. When I give my name in a shop, I give it with an ill-grace. This first appearance of my initials in a London paper which all London could read filled me with a ridiculous shame. Only for a moment of course. Then I read the article through lingeringly: line by matchless line, loving every beautiful word of it.

I read it through twice more before Ken came; once as the old gentleman in the next chair, once as his wife for whom he would go out and buy a copy, as soon as he had read it. It seemed just as good to them as it had to the author. Then Ken came in. He was, of course, as excited and happy as I. Since I was now a millionaire, we resolved to celebrate the event. After the best dinner the Club could provide, and a bottle of something to 'wash it down' (as other writers were saying), we went to the St James' Theatre and saw George Alexander in *Saturday to Monday.* In the Royal Box sat King Edward and Queen Alexandra; in the next box sat George and Mary, Prince and Princess of Wales. I tried to think that they too had just read *Vanity Fair*, and had felt that the occasion should be celebrated. Anyhow, there they were; it was a great evening. At the end of the month I received my first cheque, which was to pay for all this. Fifteen shillings.

4

These were the great days of Tariff Reform. Joseph Chamberlain was stumping the country; Arthur Pearson, his chief henchman, was putting fresh heart into the readers of *The Daily Express* and *The St James' Gazette* by telling them that Tariff Reform meant Work for All —or, if they preferred it, as they probably did, Games for All, Pianos for All, Bicycles for All and Cheaper Wool. In the music-halls Mrs Brown Potter was reciting the Tariff Reform National Anthem, which went, as far as I can remember it, like this:

I pledge my word the Empire wants Protection,
  I pledge my word that by (pom-pom) Protection we shall
      gain;
I pledge my word 'twill cure all disaffection
  (or win the next Election—or something):
  These are the words of Joseph Chamberlain.

What (if anything) this lacked in imperial vision or economic argument was forgotten in the beauty of the reciter and a communal feeling—'Good old Joe!' It is doubtful whether it made any converts.

Up to now I had not taken much interest in politics. Until the age of ten I had been a Gladstonian Liberal. Then on one never-to-be-forgotten evening Papa came into the sitting-room and announced to his family that for the first time in his life he had voted against Mr Gladstone. He sat down, breathing heavily, and Mama and Ken and I became Liberal Unionists. So we remained until I came to London.

Now it happened that in *The St James' Gazette* one evening there was an article on 'the miserable existence of the usher in a preparatory school.' This was almost the only subject on which I had any special knowledge. I wrote a reply to it which was printed, and earned my first real guinea. This settled my college for me. I would graduate in letters at St James' as had Barrie in Pall Mall, as 'Saki' was now graduating at Westminster. Always every week, sometimes every day, I sent up an article to *The St James'*. No need to wait for a proof; I dashed out and bought a copy next day, to see where my contribution was. Looking for it in vain, and feeling that if one is looking for a thing one may as well look thoroughly, I read every word of *The St James'* every evening, leading article and all. And in this way, inevitably, I became a Free Trader and a Liberal.

Father had kept on friendly terms with H. G. Wells and they often wrote to each other. Wells had asked me to Sandgate that summer; had read some of my *Granta* articles; and had said, charmingly but incorrectly, that they were just the sort of thing with which he himself had begun, save that my touch was lighter than his. I was prepared to believe most things, but not this. It was much more of a thrill to be shown the manuscript of the book he was then writing, a novel called *Kipps*. He was now coming up to London for a few days, and asked me to dine with him at the National Liberal Club. I went eagerly.

He was, as always, friendly and helpful. He advised me never to accept a job on a paper, but to remain a free-

lance. Since there was now no chance of anybody offering
me the servitude of a regular job, I promised to retain
my liberty. He said that I must join a club, so that by
reading every sort of London and provincial paper I
could keep in touch with the needs and ways of editors.
'In fact,' he said, 'you'd better join this. I suppose you're
a Liberal. Your father's son.'

I assured him that I was a Liberal, but not for the
reason suggested. Father, I implied, had ratted on us. I
also told him that there was nobody in London whom I
could ask to put me up for this or any club.

'Good,' he said. 'Then I'll propose you and we'll get
Archer to second you.'

'William Archer?' I asked in awe.

'Yes. You'll have to meet him, of course. I'll arrange it.'

A day or two later, at some horribly early hour on a
cold November morning, I breakfasted with Wells and
William Archer. Archer had more gravity than any man
I have met. In his grave, handsome presence it was useless to remind myself that Stevenson had once been delighted by the humour of his letters. One felt that
humour in his presence would have as little chance of
establishing itself as would some practical joke on a
Bishop during the final blessing. Nor was it more hopeful
to be intelligent. Archer, one felt, knew it all, and had
rejected it. They talked: wisely, profoundly, unceasingly:
together they seemed as old and as wise as God. From
time to time one of them would look to me for support
against the other, and whichever looked first would get
my support: 'Er—yes,' or 'Oh, rather,' or 'Well, I suppose in a way it is.' It wasn't helpful. Contemplating
myself from outside I got the impression of somebody
who could do nothing but eat. With every mouthful I
felt younger and more stupid; it didn't seem possible
that there could be any club for which Archer would not

blackball me. However, when he had finished his breakfast, he filled in a form to say that he had known me intimately for several years, in the course of which I had proved to be a most entertaining companion. I was elected.

For many years afterwards Archer and I would meet at the club. Neither of us had thought of this, and we didn't know what to do about it. He was as shy of me as I was of him. We said 'Hallo!' or 'Good evening' gaily, as if each of us had much to tell the other. In the silence which followed the gaiety slowly died away. After a period of intense thought a smile would light up our faces, and we would say simultaneously: 'Have you seen Wells lately?' Wells was safely in Sandgate, away from all this, and we hadn't seen him for some time. We said so—simultaneously. Then he would say, 'Well—er——' and give a little nod, and I would nod back and say, 'Well,' and we would hurry away from each other. I find that if I start wrong with anybody I never get right again. Some years later we were fellow-guests at E. V. Lucas' house in the country, and I hoped that this would bring us together; for a man may be tongue-tied in a drawing-room, but sing his heart out under the open sky. Something, however—possibly the fact that Archer wore a bowler hat all the time—kept us spiritually in London. We returned there in the body on Monday, fortified by the knowledge that our repertory now included an enquiry as to when we had last seen Lucas.

5

Back at Westgate, Father and Mother were getting anxious. I suppose it would be fair to say that the average Victorian father expected little from his son as an individual and everything from him as his father's son. As a tribute to Father the editorship of *The Times* would be a reasonable offer to make to me; as a reward for a young man who had slacked his way through public-school and University the offer was unlikely. So, however certainly with one half of his mind he was aware that my progress must be slow and difficult, with the other he was prepared for miracles. Surprisingly, there had been no miracles. Three months had gone by, and I had earned five pounds. What could he do about it? Only one thing. He wrote to 'that man.'

The first news which I got of this was the enclosure in one of Father's letters of Harmsworth's reply. It is always a temptation to glance at the enclosure in a letter before reading the letter. Unsuspecting I read: 'Dear J. V. Very well, I will see your boy for you. Tell him to ring up my secretary and make an appointment.' I was sick with indignation. How dare Father do anything so stupid? It was already settled that Harmsworth was to come, hat in hand, to me, not I to him. I didn't want him, I was getting on perfectly well by myself; I had earned over five pounds, and my last contribution to *The St James' Gazette* was so good that it was bound to be accepted. Over six pounds, then. Why should Father humiliate himself and me like this? At least he should have consulted me first. Then I would have told him of my own letter, and he would have seen how impossible it was.

Well, it was too late now. I had to go. I was shown into the Great Man's room, I sat down nervously, he spoke to me. He said that he was going to send me along to two of his editors. 'I have been careful,' he said, 'not to let them know that your father is one of my oldest and greatest friends' (and I told myself that Mother would like this), 'because I want you to make your own way. So now it's up to you.' A page boy was summoned, and I was led away.

First to Mr Arthur Mee, who, it seemed, had succeeded

Mr Philip Gibbs as editor of 'the articles you mention.'
He told me that, if I cared to send in contributions to
The Daily Mail I could address them to him personally.
I was in no mood to realize that this was a valuable concession; I felt that it just left me where I was before. We
passed on to the next editor. I have forgotten his name,
but still have a memory of shirt-sleeves and a half-smoked
cigar. He was that sort of editor, and he was responsible
for some twenty 'comics,' boys' papers and what not.
Humorous writers, he assured me with his feet up, were
in demand, but I must realize that his public did not
want anything subtle or refined. 'Funny stories about
policemen, y'know what I mean, umbrellas, knockabout,
that sort of thing.' I assured him that I knew what he
meant. I left the building. I walked across the road to
Temple Chambers. Telling myself that I mustn't let
Father think that his help was in vain, I sat grimly down
and began to write a funny story about a policeman; not
subtle, not refined. Knockabout. I wrote four hundred
words. I think I can say truthfully that those are the only
words I have ever written which I did not write for my
own pleasure. At the four hundredth word, I stopped,
read them through, and with a sigh of happiness tore
them into pieces. I was back on my own again; making,
as Harmsworth said, my own way.

6

Punch remained my goal, and I was no nearer to it.
Every week I sent something in, and every week it came
back again. It was difficult to know what to do with the
rejected contributions. If *The St James'* didn't like
'Spring in the Black Forest' (1,200 words), there was a
chance that *The Westminster* might love it; and if *The
Westminster* hated it, then it might be just the thing for

The Globe. One could go on hoping, and hope was what, of all things, I wanted. But it was difficult to feel any hope about a six-hundred word sketch which *Punch* had rejected. There seemed to be no place for it but the waste-paper basket, a place, no doubt, entirely suitable. Luckily a new weekly paper called *The Bystander* was prepared to accept verse. Its editor was not quite such a formalist as Owen Seaman; a Cockney rhyme did not sear his soul; and even though he paid no more than a guinea for a set of verses, yet the thought of a guinea consolation prize was encouragement enough. I continued to send in verses to *Punch*.

There was a legend in those days that the contributor of any joke to *Punch*, illustrated or not, received £5 for it. In April, I made my first contribution to the paper, a four-line paragraph. I might get £5, and if so I was a made man; but was it possible on the strength of one paragraph, to say that I 'wrote for *Punch*'? Hardly. However, I had little time in which to wonder. In the following week the miracle happened, and a set of verses forced itself past Seaman into the paper. I was a real *Punch* contributor at last. To consolidate my position still more thoroughly, I had a small prose contribution, a narrow column, in the next number. All was well. I had proved that I could earn a living by writing. I would be Editor of *Punch* one day. I was the happiest man in London.

Punch, like most papers, pays its contributors every month. At the beginning of May it sent me a cheque for my three April contributions. The cheque was for sixteen shillings and sixpence. It didn't seem to make sense. I wrote to Rudie Lehmann asking him what it meant. He replied: 'My dear boy, it's a damned disgrace. I am writing to Phil about it.' This was Phil Agnew, one of the proprietors of *Punch*. Phil replied, in effect, that the honour of writing for *Punch* was considered to be sufficient reward at first, but that when the honour began to wear off, then I should begin to get paid more.

Well, I had had the honour, and I couldn't afford to sustain it. There was no object now in sending contributions to *Punch*. I renounced the editorship.

Fortunately a renewed attack on *The St James'* met at last with success. I took an imaginary girl to the Zoo, to the Tower, to Earl's Court, whence we proceeded together into print. In July I went round to the *St James'* office to demand regular work. I saw myself as its literary or dramatic critic. The editor suggested that I should come into the office during August and write some of its 'Notes of the Day.' I pointed out that these were mostly political, and that I was a Liberal. 'That doesn't matter,' he said. 'We'll tell you what to write.' I replied coldly that nobody could tell me what to write. He said, 'Good afternoon.' A little later he left *The St James'* to edit a Liberal paper. Don't ask me what his politics were. How should I know?

Country Life wanted an assistant editor. So did *The Hibbert Journal*. I applied simultaneously to both. To *Country Life* I quoted my games record, my editorship of *The Granta*, and my early collections of birds' eggs and butterflies. To *The Hibbert Journal* I quoted my profound interest in philosophy and theosophy, my early collections of birds' eggs and butterflies, my games record and my editorship of *The Granta*. Neither application was successful.

Then in August I wrote what I though was a very funny dialogue about Hackenschmidt and Madrali, those famous wrestlers. I had, in fact, seen them wrestle; had paid four pounds ten for a seat; had arrived sixteen seconds late, and thus missed the first bout of fifteen seconds, but saw the whole of the second bout of a minute and a half. An expensive evening, to which some paper ought to contribute. The editor of *The St James' Gazette* refused to; so did the editor of *The Westminster*; so did every other editor in London. I dropped the dialogue sadly in the wastepaper basket. Life for a moment seemed very difficult. Suddenly I remembered that there was a paper called *Punch* which paid a few shillings for articles. Since nobody else wanted my dialogue, and since even half-a-crown, and I could hardly get less than half-a-crown, was, as they say, half-a-crown, I pulled it out of the waste-paper basket, dusted it and sent it to *Punch*. *Punch* printed it. *Punch* sent me a cheque for £2 5s.

All was well again. I had proved that I could earn a living by writing. I would be editor of *Punch* one day. I was the happiest man in London.

September saw the end of my first year as a writer. I had earned twenty pounds, and spent the whole of my patrimony.

Chapter Eleven

1

FATHER 'always used to say' (and the phrase was almost literally true of Father) that Nature meant him for a millionaire. He had a gift for extravagance. I inherited it from him. But the extravagance was combined with a Scottish common-sense and a Presbyterian horror of getting 'wrong' about money. We set our standards within our income and then enjoyed ourselves carelessly. Having thought once and for all as to what we could spend, we never thought twice about spending it. To-day I could be happy without a car, I could be happy without a country cottage, but I shouldn't be happy if I couldn't be reckless about golf-balls, taxis, the best seats at cricket grounds and theatres, shirts and pullovers, tips, subscriptions, books and wine-lists. What it comes to, I suppose, is that I prefer a dribble of smaller extravagances to one big extravagance. And when my income demanded that I should go without all the things which I have mentioned above, then I was quite happy being reckless about 'buses and butter.

So, having £300 in the bank, I spent it in my own way. A good deal on tobacco; hardly any on drink. Hansoms to Lord's, for only by hansom should one approach Lord's (ah! how much Lord's has lost since hansoms went out); but the top of 'buses (and how much London has lost since the tops of 'buses went in), 'buses everywhere else. Subscription dances. Football and cricket on Saturdays for Old Westminsters. Dinners and plays with Ken while I was still rich. I spent nothing, but the money went.

Ken had dragged out a miserable two months in an office off the Strand, discovering that the flaw in the process of becoming a solicitor was the fact that inevitably you became a solicitor. He hated it. One day he heard that there was a Department in the Civil Service for which qualified solicitors only were eligible. With one profound movement he shook off, perhaps for the only time in his life, his acquiescence; resigned; worked hard for two months, and passed into the Estate Duty Office. He was safe. He had achieved a future. Every day at one o'clock I walked down Fleet Street towards the Strand, and he walked up from Somerset House towards Fleet Street, and we met and had lunch together. I wrote of him once:

> There are who daily in the safe retreat
> Of some Department gather round and bleat
> Scandal and Art until it's time to eat;
> Return at three, and having written 'Dear
> Sir, your communication of last year
> Duly received and noted'—disappear.

His only criticism of this was that they began their letters 'Sir,' not 'Dear Sir.' But this was before the War. In the War, and afterwards, he worked himself to his death.

Now I should be able no longer to walk down Fleet Street to meet him. I had only £20 in the Bank, and I must find cheaper lodgings. I advertised for 'two unfurnished rooms with use of bath, central,' received news of furnished bed-sitting-rooms in Ponders End and maisonettes in Park Lane, refused all interest in anything from St John's Wood, and came at the end of September to Chelsea. Wellington Square, Chelsea, is now becoming fashionable; when I tell my friends that I used to live there they think that I have come down in the world. It was not so fashionable in 1904. I lived in a police-sergeant's house; I paid ten shillings a week for the two rooms at the top of the house; and the bathroom, to which I traveled every morning, had been, until lately, a sort of conservatory linking up the backyard with the ground-floor passage. There was an incandescent mantle and a smell of gas in the sitting-room, there was some sort of music-hall singer in the floor below, there was a variety of police-sergeant's children on the stairs. I paid seven-pence for breakfast, and had my other meals out. The sergeant's wife was a big, friendly soul, motherly (as she might be with the practice she had) and embarrassingly kind. Her husband had been the champion revolver-shot of the Empire, or something like it, and the two targets, right and left-hand, which hung framed in the hall, ex-plained why. I was very happy at Wellington Square, and life was exciting.

Punch was a little more remunerative now. I had an occasional essay in *The Daily News,* for which I received two guineas instead of the usual guinea. Once I got three guineas for a story in *The Westminster Gazette,* my top price so far and therefore to be celebrated with Ken in some way, and reduced, in effect, to two guineas. And then on January 17th, 1905, I went to the Bank to draw out my weekly two pounds. Two pounds just about saw me through: fourteen shillings for rooms and breakfast, another fourteen for lunches and dinners, and two shil-lings for coal—leaving ten shillings a week for teas, 'buses, stamps, stationery, doctors, dentists, games, clothes, holi-days and club-subscriptions. It was the club-subscriptions which put me out. I had lunched with Ken, my bank being in Fleet Street, and he came in with me to get the money. I was telling him proudly that I had a balance of nearly six pounds. The cashier took my cheque, went away and came back with the manager. The manager broke it to me kindly that I was overdrawn. I protested. He reminded me that I had signed a Bankers Order for the National Liberal Club subscription of six guineas, which had just been paid. I said, 'Oh!' There didn't seem to be anything else to say. We waited. He asked if I should be paying any more money in immediately. Normally I could have said with absolute conviction 'No,' for there was no hope of getting anything from a paper until the end of the month. Then I remembered that to-morrow was my birthday. Father had sent me a fiver last year. Would he do it again? Probably. I announced with dignity that I should be paying in the tremendous sum of £5 to-morrow; and my cheque was cashed.

The fiver arrived next morning, and to my dismay another one followed it a few days later. Rudie Lehmann, who was in a way responsible for my coming to London as a writer, took a delightfully friendly interest in my struggles and had to be given the latest bulletins. I wrote what no doubt I thought was a humorous account of the bank incident, and he replied with a cheque for £5 'to be repaid when your balance is on its legs again.' It was extraordinarily kind, but I didn't want the money, and I hated the idea of borrowing from anybody. So I waited a week or two, by which time a balance might be considered capable of getting on its legs, and then repaid it.

From now on I had nothing but what I earned each month. I wanted £100 a year: eight guineas a month: say three from *Punch*, two from *The News*, one from *The St James'*—that ought to be possible. It left another two guineas to come from all the other publications in London, except *The Hibbert Journal* in which I had now lost interest. Well, that also ought to be possible. What about *The Evening News* to which I had never sent anything? I sent something to *The Evening News*. C. E. Burton, the Literary Editor and most prolific verse-writer in London, asked me to come and see him.

'I liked your article, it's going in to-morrow.'

'Good.'

'It was funny without really trying.'

'That's what it tried to be,' I confessed.

'How would you like to write us an article like that every week?'

'I should love it.'

'Splendid.'

I waited. Nothing happened.

'Er—what would the—I mean, what do you——'

'Oh, a guinea.' He said it cheerfully. I said nothing. Doing his best for it he added, 'Every week.'

'It isn't very much.'

'But how re-assuring to have one *every* week. Think how glad Amelia would be.'

Amelia was the girl I took into *The St James' Gazette* with me from time to time. Also for a guinea. I blushed; not with embarrassment at the thought of Amelia, who didn't exist just then, but with pride to think that she had become real to somebody else.

'Couldn't you possibly make it thirty shillings, so that we could feel that I wasn't like the ordinary contributor?'

'I see your point. So let's say twenty-five. You could feel like that quite easily on twenty-five.'

'Yes, rather. Thanks very much.'

It didn't need three years at the Mathematical Tripos to tell me that I now had £65 a year. I had already decided that I was going to get £35 or more from *Punch*. So what? Obviously a dash to Somerset House to catch Ken before he left, and a cheap dinner together. My £100 a year was assured. We must celebrate.

2

Father was sixty in March. At sixty he would retire. He was doing this for Mother's sake: 'You know what your mother is. As long as there is any work which she can do, she has to do it. Look at the way she still does the carving! It's too much for her at her age. She has had a very hard life. Now I want her to have a rest.' And Mother said: 'It's all a lot of nonsense, dear. You know what your father is. I've never had a day's illness in my life. But your father isn't really strong. He has had a very hard life, he's earned a rest, and I shan't say any more about it.'

Father looked forward to their years of leisure more than Mother did. Except in the arts there was almost nothing, or so it seemed to him, which he could not have done, no position of responsibility which he would have been afraid to fill. Sometimes he would tell us of his plans in the event of finding himself Prime Minister, Lord Roberts, or the President of Marylebone Cricket Club: flights of imagination which borrowed reality from the fact that the conversations between Father and the necessary executive were always in *oratio recta*. 'I should send for the Chief of Staff and I should say, "Now look here" . . . ' One heard the click of heels in response and the prompt 'Very good, sir.' Though unlikely to be offered any of these posts, he was now at least available for them. He was only sixty: there were many ways in which he might discover himself. At any rate he could hear good music at last.

No doubt schoolmasters hear, or overhear, a great deal of bad music, but it is a mistake to suppose that the world of good music is closed to them. For some reason Father assumed that Covent Garden and Queen's Hall were not available until one had retired from active work and had gone to live in the country. I don't think that he had ever been, or ever did go, to a good concert: I am sure that he never saw an opera: yet somehow it was fixed in his mind that all his life he had been starved of music against his will. I have a recurring dream in which I am trying to put on my pads in order to go in to bat, and cannot, cannot, cannot get the buckles to fasten. As in a dream Father saw himself continually making for the Albert Hall and continually being thwarted. Now, at last, he would be able to get there.

All through that Spring Term members of the family were looking for its new home. Somewhere off the beaten track, so that it would be cheap and the countryside unspoilt; somewhere not too far from London, so that any of us could come down for week-ends. A combination of these virtues was not easily found. It was left to Ken and me to make the great discovery: in a village with the unsophisticated name of Steeple Bumpstead—Essex, if you liked Essex; on the borders of Suffolk, if you didn't. Father, who had lived and taught in Essex as a young man, did not wish to be reminded of it. So, at the beginning of April he said good-bye to Streete Court, leaving behind him a name which is still remembered, and the address for any who cared to write to him: 'Broadgates, Steeple Bumpstead, nr. Haverhill, SUFFOLK.'

Ken and I went down for Easter. On the Monday Steeple Bumpstead Cricket Club opened its season in the field between our garden wall and the churchyard. The cows were driven off the pitch, anything which they had left behind was removed, and a wicket was marked out. If Bumpstead lost the toss, the bearded and burly owner of the cows would open the bowling with a fast underhand which included everything from a long-hop to a yorker in one ricocheting delivery. To-day being Bank Holiday, and the morning empty, the village had drifted early on to the field with bats and balls, perambulators and dogs, and while the younger members practised un-officially in corners, their seniors stood about between the creases and discussed life. In the course of their discus-sion a sudden dispute arose between the local policeman, in uniform, and a casual soldier, also in uniform, as to their respective merits in the cricket-field. Mere assertion not seeming enough, however emphatic, it was suggested by partisans that they should settle the argument in a single-wicket match. The soldier thought it unnecessary.

' 'Im?' he said scornfully. 'Why 'e'd never get *me* out.'

'Nor 'e wouldn't get me out neither,' said the police-man.

'*Me?* Not get '*im* out? I'd do the 'at-trick on him if 'e only 'ad one stump.'

'So would I. That's what I'd do.'

'I'd knock 'im into the churchyard,' said the soldier. 'So I would. Right into the churchyard. Every bloody ball.'

'So would I too,' said the policeman. 'Into the church-yard *and* out of it. And don't you come swearing at me, when there's ladies and young children present. That's obscene language, that is. And I don't mind telling *you*, young man, that I'd knock every bloody ball—every ball o' yours, right into the church and over the church and all, so I would. *You!*'

Still talking they were led away by their supporters, and presently the policeman was standing, bat in hand, at one end of the pitch, and the soldier, ball in hand, at the other. 'Play,' said the umpire.

Twenty minutes later the policeman was still at the wicket. His score was 'o.' At least three balls had come within his reach, but he had missed his opportunities. Tired of batting he declared his innings closed. Half an hour later the soldier was still at the wicket. His score was 'o.' He had not had so many opportunities as the policeman, and he had missed them. His innings was declared closed by the hysterical spectators. The policeman went in again. Ken and I, equally hysterical, left the garden-wall for the luncheon interval.

On the way back to London next morning I was thinking of this match. 'You might make a joke about that,' said the Gnat at every opportunity, and I was equally on the look-out for articles. Having written this one, I felt that it was worth more than 25/–, more even than the two guineas *The News* might give me. Why not try, as I never had, *The Daily Mail*, which was reputed to pay enormous sums? So I tried it. The article was printed, and I was invited to call upon the editor.

'We all liked your article very much,' said Marlowe.

I tried to look modest.

'The Chief tells me that your father is one of his oldest friends.'

I tried not to look cynical.

'How would you like to come in here and edit Page Four?'

I should have thought that he was being funny, if I had not heard that this was the Harmsworth way. Page Four—the leader page—with the special articles! Arthur Mee had followed out after Philip Gibbs: a vacancy: try somebody young. Quick come, quick go.

'I should like to very much, but I'm afraid I couldn't until the end of June.'

'How's that?'

Well, at the end of April I was going up to the Orkneys for two months, to coach a distant connection of the Limpsfield uncle's, a boy of fifteen whose health was keeping him out of school for a term. It had seemed a delightful opportunity, giving me all that I wanted just then: a remunerative holiday, new experiences, copy, and an acquaintance, welcome to one who had never

been north of Keswick, with my ancestral country. How
gladly would I have sacrificed it all now.

'It's all fixed, is it?'

'Well, yes. I said I would.'

'End of June, what? I daresay we can keep the place
warm for you. Can you write up there?'

'Oh, rather. I mean to.'

"Well, send us some more articles, and we'll keep it
open until you come back.'

I floated out of his room. I floated down Fleet Street.
I had got a job! On one article! Incredible! If only I
could take it on at once—if only the Limpsfield uncle had
never married—if only I hadn't been such a fool—— But
never mind. At the end of June I should be an editor.
Silly young men would write silly young letters to Harmsworth, and their silly private letters would be 'handed on
to Mr A. A. Milne, to whom the articles you mention
should be sent.' Perhaps I would see them, if their fathers
were importunate enough; tell them kindly, with my feet
up, that they could send their contributions to me personally and not to the Editor. And every week I should
print a brilliant article by myself, just to show them how
it should be done.

None of this happened. I sent an article in as soon as
I got to Orkney. My place-warmer wrote that he didn't
think it suitable for *The Mail* (how wise he was), and
that he had handed it on to *The Evening News,* for
whom, he understood, I was writing. This seemed to me
such impertinence that I sent in no more articles. Nor
did I hear again from Marlowe. My association with *The
Daily Mail* was ended.

3

I have said that once every ten years I remember with
pride that I am one of the many, or not so many, who

have climbed the Napes Needle. Once every twenty years I remember, not exactly with pride, but with a slight lifting of the chin, that I am one of the few, or very few, who have spent a night alone on a desert island.

There the island was, perhaps a few hundred acres of it, half-a-mile from the mainland, its only inhabitants seafowl. We landed one afternoon and walked about it; found an eider-duck's nest, surprised a few rabbits, and rowed home to tea. At dinner that evening I said that I should like to stay there one night. Nobody knew why; I didn't know why myself, but I supposed that there 'might be an article in it.' Sometimes we fished at night. It was easy for the others to drop me on the island after the fishing and to send somebody over for me next morning. I landed with a rook-rifle, a rug and a flask of brandy.

There was no shelter anywhere. I wrapped myself in my rug and snuggled down into the heather. As long as I lay still the world was still, but every movement of mine filled the sky with the deep-breathed sound of wings, as if a sudden storm had blown up and died away again. The night was too dark for sight, but the nearness of all that life was faintly menacing. I turned from one cramped position to another as quietly as I could. . . .

The dawn came early and with it a gentle rain. I drank the brandy. The brandy had been part of the joke; like the rifle, a concession to romance. Now I was glad of it. Rifle under the arm, I walked down to the shore. I followed the coastline until I had caught up my footsteps—how many people, I thought, have done that? I did it again. It didn't seem so original this time. I sat on a rock and looked out to sea, my rifle on my knees. Nothing happened. . . .

I decided to shoot a rabbit. Since I was using a rifle I supposed that I should be allowed to shoot it sitting.

Well, it was my island and I could make my own laws:
I would stalk a rabbit until I got it into a sitting posture,
and then we should see. This took time, but time was
what I wanted to take just then. It was appreciably nearer
breakfast when we got into the required positions: the
rabbit sitting up outside its hole, polishing its whiskers,
I on my stomach, a suitable distance off, my finger at the
trigger. I fired. The rabbit looked up at the noise, noticed
me, and trotted into its hole to tell the others. I hadn't
killed it, but I could tell myself proudly that I had distracted it.

I fetched my rug and went down to the landward side
of the island. The grey lifeless air melted into the grey
lifeless waters, I could see no land, but soon I should hear
the creak of oars, and from the mist would come the
rescue for which I waited now as eagerly as any authentic
castaway. Soon—in about two hours—it came. I lit a pipe,
and went down to the beach to meet it.

Naturally I made an article out of all this. It was too
long for *The Evening News*, and apparently too bad for
every other paper. But the experience was not wholly
wasted. At dances that autumn I would tell my partner
that I had once spent a night alone on a desert island
. . . and get her surprised attention for a moment.

4

In April, as I should have said before, I had had my
first book published. Rudie, who continued to feel
responsible for me, introduced me to Barry Pain. Barry
Pain, who thought in little shilling books, said: 'Why
don't you make a little shilling book out of those
St James' articles?' I said that there weren't more than
half-a-dozen anyway. 'Then write some more. You could
call it *Lovers in London*. It would look well on the book-

stalls.' It wouldn't, I thought, look as well as *Eliza*, that best of all shilling books, but it would be a good thing to have done. So I did it; Barry Pain's agent sold it for me; and it was published by Alston Rivers: paper cover 1/–, cloth cover 1/6.

Owing to the misplaced optimism of somebody I got £15 in advance of royalties, which was more money than I had seen for a long time. I also got one or two reviews. *The Sheffield Daily Independent* said (and I have been interested in the paper ever since): 'The only readable part of this book is the title,' which was more damping than it knew. A few years later E. V. Lucas read it, and suggested that I should buy back the publisher's rights, add some more chapters, and re-publish it at six shillings. So I borrowed Mother's copy, read it, and hastily bought back all rights in it for £5. I didn't want to re-publish it in any form, but I was terrified lest the publishers might. Sometimes now I see it advertised in booksellers' catalogues. It is marked, thank God, '*very rare.*'

I had had a dozen contributions in *Punch* in the first half-yearly volume, and in the autumn I was asked (this time officially) to write a series. I wrote it. It wasn't very good, and it wasn't very bad. By the end of the year I had made about £120, and had lived on it. It seemed that the present could take care of itself; but what of the future? Where should I be in five years' time? Normally I should not have wondered; but I was sitting in Battersea Park, in a pair of tight boots, on a mild February day which seemed to make them tighter, and I preferred to think of anything rather than of the walk back to Wellington Square. What could I look forward to—after getting these boots off? At twenty-four one must be certain of fame at thirty. How could I achieve fame at thirty? Only, it seemed, by writing a novel: a real novel: a six-shilling novel which would be the talk of every dinner-table.

Sitting in my slippers before the fire I resolved to begin my novel on Monday. I would retire into the country to write it, as many a young writer had retired before. I would give myself up exclusively to my novel. It would be called (this is all I remember of it) *Philip's Wife*. Why, I do not know. To prove to myself that this was no empty resolution I wrote to *Punch*, warning it that it must not expect any contributions for the next few months, as I was retiring into the country to write a novel, a novel to which I was giving myself up exclusively. My letter went, of course, to Owen Seaman, my contacts with Burnand being limited to the one we had so nearly made in the train. A note came back from Rudie: 'Owen showed me your letter. Don't come to any decision about leaving London until you hear from him.'

Two days later, on another mild February day in another pair of boots, I made my way to the *Punch* office. I had been there once before, to have a few words with Seaman in the Assistant Editor's room. Probably I had suggested a visit, feeling that this would establish me more firmly in his mind as a contributor. This time the suggestion came from him, and the meeting-place was the Editor's room. Burnand had finally retired to Ramsgate.

The new editor made as little of the occasion as he could. In his new position he wanted somebody to relieve him of the worst of the donkey work: somebody who came in for, say, a couple of afternoons a week and sorted out the contributions: naturally I should be on trial at first: naturally I couldn't expect to be put on the *Punch* table immediately: obviously this and obviously that: but what it came to, however he glided over it, was—How would I like to be Assistant Editor of *Punch?*

It didn't seem possible.

'The Proprietors thought, seeing that they wouldn't require your full time, that £250 a year would—er—meet the case.'

That didn't seem possible either.

'As regards your own contributions, they would be paid for at double rates, and naturally we should expect you to contribute every week.'

I tried to look grateful, eager, but not surprised, while doing simple arithmetic in the head. It wasn't coming out. I put the arithmetic by for the 'bus, and looked grateful, eager, but not surprised.

'Normally, of course, you would send them straight down to the printer, but I think perhaps that just at first you had better let me have a look at them before they go.'

Nothing that was going to happen 'just at first' mattered now, I was so certain that I should get everything I wanted in the end. Hadn't I always said that I would be Editor of *Punch* one day? Or hadn't I? I couldn't remember. Anyhow I was going to be.

'Of course,' I said eagerly to everything.

'You'd better start on Tuesday. I don't come on Monday.'

'Right,' I said, wondering how I could possibly live until Tuesday.

I left the office. It appeared on the 'bus that I should be getting £500 a year. I had been living happily on £120 or less. How delightfully extravagant one could be with £500 a year. Could it be true? Could I have misheard the figures? Should I go back and ask for it all again? Perhaps in writing this time. No, it was true. I wanted to think of all that it would mean, of all that I would write to Father, of all that I would tell Ken, but I could not think for happiness.

Just as it had seemed wonderful to be editing *The Granta* after so short a struggle, so it seemed wonderful now to be, at twenty-four, Assistant Editor of *Punch*. In fact I had no need to be so surprised at myself. My real achievement in either case was to be not wholly the wrong person, in the right spot at the right moment. When Seaman was Assistant Editor, the Editor was travelling about the country writing his reminiscences. The new Editor proposed to live in his office chair and devote himself to his paper. The new Assistant Editor would have none of the responsibilities which Seaman had had, his position would be one of more subjection and less dignity. Clearly, then, he must be a young man; clearly he must be a young man who was already a journalist, but not a journalist bound to another paper; he must be himself acceptable as a contributor; and, not least important, he must possess, for the Editor's peace of mind, a degree of presentability such as was only conferred, it was thought, upon the whiter students of the larger colleges at Cambridge. I met all the conditions. Two years earlier I should not have been acceptable, two years later I might not have been available. Burnand resigned at the exact moment, and I had, I must suppose, the field to myself.

ASSISTANT EDITOR

1906–1914

Chapter Twelve

1

Although I was (undoubtedly) Assistant Editor of *Punch*, I had not been given a seat at the *Punch* table. The *Punch* Dinner, at which the cartoons for the next number were planned, was held every Wednesday evening at seven on the floor below the editorial offices. Wednesday was a busy day, and I was generally in my room when the diners began to congregate. Most of them would put their heads in to say 'Good evening'; some of them would stay for a little talk; just so (one felt) would kindly uncles who had come to dine look in on the nursery to say good night to the children, before joining the other guests in the drawing-room. I was too young to dine downstairs. There was no precedent for putting a child of twenty-four on the historic Table. There was also no precedent for removing anybody from the historic Table, once he had carved his initials on it. Any Proprietor of any paper might quail at the thought of giving me a seat at the Table at twenty-four and finding me still there at seventy-four.

This, however, was not the reason given for my exclusion. The business of the dinner was the discussion of the cartoons. My political competence was doubted; my political competence (said the Proprietors) must be proved before I could come downstairs. When the Shade of Nelson was saying to John Bull: 'The ships are different, but the spirit of the men remains the same,' what would Milne be doing? Sucking his thumb in the corner and saying 'Who was Nelson?'—or making the idiotic suggestion that the legend should be: 'The walls of England are no longer wooden, but the Heads of the Admiralty remain the same.' Encouraged by Seaman I thought out cartoons by myself in the nursery, which he took down to dinner to show the grown-ups how serious I could be. Sometimes they were used just as I had suggested them; sometimes they were adapted; but I remained upstairs.

A year or two later, I emphasized my value to the Table in a more striking way. The first copy of *Punch* was printed on the Sunday morning, and sent to the Editor. The machines continued to go round, and other copies to tumble out of the press, but it was not too late for any small correction to be made, if such were necessary; a harmless error in the first five thousand copies could be eliminated from the remaining hundred thousand. It was our final precaution against the misprints which we derided in others. This first copy came to whichever of us was in London or nearer to London for the week-end. Imagine, then, my horror to discover one Sunday that not a simple comma but a whole cartoon had got out of place. The 'senior cartoon' (Partridge's) was in the front of the paper, the 'junior cartoon' (Raven-Hill's) in the middle. I hurried round to the office and became authoritative. The copies which had been printed must be scrapped, the pages must be set again, with the cartoons changed. The printer insisted that this was the order in which the pages came down to him on Friday night. That might be so, I had corrected each page separately and had never seen them together, but if it were so, then the Editor had made a mistake. Did I accept full responsibility now? Absolutely. So the machines stopped work at my word, and I, in the silence, felt extremely important, and wondered how much I had cost the Proprietors.

A good deal, I hoped. For it appeared that at the Wednesday dinner Partridge's cartoon, having been drawn in advance before he went on holiday, and being in consequence untopical, had been deliberately made the junior cartoon. I had deliberately, and at some expense to the Proprietors, made it the senior cartoon. This, I felt, was the best argument for my admission to the Table which I had as yet produced. The argument was not effective, but in recognition of the fact that I was spending about three times as many hours at the office as had been bargained for, my salary was raised by fifty pounds.

Friday was my busy day. I sat down after breakfast to make my own personal contribution to *Punch*: a gay (I hoped) article of twelve hundred words, with a smile in every paragraph, and a laugh in every inch. (I was paid by the inch.) I might have sat down for this purpose on Sunday, Monday, Tuesday, Wednesday or Thursday morning; I regretted now that I hadn't; but it was too late. By four o'clock on Friday my article must be sent down to the printer, and the knowledge that it must be finished by four o'clock on this very day made both the writing of it possible and the writing of it earlier impossible. Ideas may drift into other writers' minds, but they do not drift my way. I have to go and fetch them. I know no work manual or mental to equal the appalling heartbreaking anguish of fetching an idea from nowhere. The expression of it in writing is comparatively easy. A sort of agraphia may come over me sometimes: a terrifying inability to compress thought into a sentence: but normally I can follow up an idea with an enjoyment, at times lazy, at times eager, which may awake no echo in the reader's heart, but is doubtless audible to him. First, however, the idea. On Friday morning at 9.30 I sat down to search for it.

At 11.30, my brain in ruins, I was still searching. At 11.30 I was telling myself that even if I did find it, I had to find fifty-one more before the year was over; and that if I stayed on *Punch* until I was seventy, as everybody seemed to do, then I should have to find about 2,500 ideas before I died. Yet now, in my prime at twenty-four, I couldn't even find one. Why hadn't I become a schoolmaster?

At twelve I was saying: 'Well, it's not very good, but I may as well begin, and see what happens.' I began.

At 12.30 I was saying: 'It's not so bad.'

At 1.30 some variation of the idea came to me, and I began again. It was now definitely going to be good.

At 3.30 it was finished. I dashed to the *Punch* office, sent it down to the printers, and went out again in search of something to eat.

Soon after four I was back in the office, criticizing a play to which I had been the night before, and writing a book-review. By five o'clock I was 'doing the paragraphs.' The paragraphs were cuttings from other papers, with appropriate comments. (As an example: 'Peacock and Peahen for sale: unrelated: 1906 chicks,' with the comment: 'Then it's quite time they *were* related.') After I had really got the thing going, cuttings poured into the office from all over the world, and I enjoyed myself enormously with them. Some, of necessity, were unprintable. I liked the one, and carried it about with me for a long time, which said of George V on his yacht: 'The King has a delightfully keen sense of humour, and it is a joy to hear his hearty laugh when a sailor runs across the deck and catches his toe in a ring-bolt.' We were much too loyal to print this sort of thing, but loyalty can be carried too far. An enthusiastic clergyman wrote to his local paper of a never-to-be-forgotten experience which he had just had. 'Our Great Leader' (Mr Balfour, no less) had travelled to Edinburgh the night before, and his train had stopped at the local station for a few minutes. 'Probably I was the only person in the neighbourhood in possession of the information. I hurried round on my bicycle, and for five minutes had the inestimable privilege of gazing upon the face of the revered statesman.' Unfortunately Seaman's loyalty extended to Our Great Leader, and the picture of Balfour wondering, under that fixed gaze, who the lunatic was remained my private joke.

The paragraphs were finished by six o'clock, and I had the day's contributions to go through. These consisted of articles or verses, jokes for illustration, and press cuttings. Few of them were of any value. The possible paragraphs I kept for the following Friday, and the best of the other contributions were passed on to the Editor with appropriate comments. Sometimes a joke would be 'going the rounds,' and a hundred people would send it up, most of them alleging that it had happened to themselves last Tuesday. When Winston Churchill talked about a 'terminological inexactitude,' every other envelope contained some supposedly humorous substitution of this phrase for the more ordinary word 'lie.' When Tommy Bowles won a famous City of London election, the number of people who probed to its depths a joke based upon 'a game of bowl(e)s' was only less than the number who thought it made the matter clearer if they described it as a game of 'bowls (Bowles).' One old gentleman wrote: 'Dear Sir, On my seventy-seventh birthday last week a young friend of mine who is a great footballer'—(and 'footballer' was crossed out, and 'cricketer,' in pencil, substituted)—'said to me, "Seventy-seven not out!" I think this is clever wit.' It was difficult in this welter of clever wit to keep one's head; difficult not to feel, on one day that anything which didn't try to be funny was funny, and on the next that nothing would ever be funny again.

At seven o'clock my own proof would come up. It was, and I never know why this should be so, an entirely different article in print, and, as such, needed critical appreciation. I gave it this, I finished off the contributions, and went out to dinner at eight.

At ten o'clock Owen and I were back in his room. The paper had been set and the pages were beginning to come up. They came up three or four at a time. Every now and then I managed to get hold of one, and then waited . . . and waited . . . for the next one. All Owen's past life (or something) came before his eyes as he corrected a page of *Punch*, but through it all he read doggedly, very slow, very sure, until I wanted to scream: 'For Heaven's sake, what's it all about? Time isn't a thing you do this to.' I suppose it was because my day had been so frantic until now that I could not bear these wasted hours. Leisured idleness is a lovely thing, but idleness without leisure is an invention of the devil. They think highly of it in the army.

By one o'clock we were through. It had been interesting to cut ten lines out of somebody else's article, and annoying to have to cut two out of my own. I had verified a quotation, explained the point of one of the paragraphs——

'Not more than twenty people will see it. Can't you make it clearer?'

'Easily. But it will spoil it for the twenty.'

'We can't edit a paper for twenty readers.'

'Wouldn't it be heavenly if we could? . . . Is that better?'

'H'm. It isn't too clear now.'

'One must keep it funny somehow.'

'Oh, well, all right. You may find a better one to-morrow.'

'Can I have some more pages?'

'Can't you find anything to do? You'd better pick out some books.'

'Right.'

—had had a long talk with Owen, gone into my room and picked out half a dozen books for review, read them all, lit my tenth pipe, and been in time for the next page. By one o'clock we were through. I went back to bed.

On Saturday morning the corrected pages came back for final correction. We were due at the office at eleven. I got there at ten, had all the pages to myself, corrected them, and waited impatiently for Owen to come. I was playing cricket at twelve, or I was catching an 11.40 into Sussex for the week-end, or I was going to Lord's, or Twickenham, or—— Anyway——

'I've done all the pages.'

'H'm. Do you want to get off?'

'Unless there's anything else I can do?'

'When's your train?'

'11.40.'

'Plenty of time. You'd better enter up the books.'

'I have.'

'What about that paragraph? You were going to find a better one. Anything in the post?'

'Three. They're on your desk.'

'Right. Well—good luck,' and with it that sudden charming smile which turned him in a moment from a cold schoolmaster into the delightfully warm-hearted human being which in fact he was.

He was a strange, unlucky man. All the Good Fairies came to his christening, but the Uninvited Fairy had the last word, so that the talents found themselves in the wrong napkin and the virtues flourished where graces should have been. Humour was drowned in Scholarship, Tact went down before Truth, and the Fighting Qualities gave him not only the will to win but the determination to explain why he hadn't won. There is a story of him as a golfer, making an excuse for every bad shot until he got to the last green, when he threw down his putter and said: 'That settles it. I'll never play in knickerbockers again.' It could have been so delightfully said— but it wasn't. He had, truly, a heart of gold, and if it had been 'concealed beneath a rugged exterior,' as so often it is in novels, it would have been more patent to the world than the veneer which was so nearly gold allowed it to be.

If anybody, reading this, says: 'And now, to make the portrait complete, I should like to know what he thought about *you*,' he would be justified. I must have maddened him. I did ask him once whether he was happier with my successor, a man of his own age, than he had been with me, and he said that there was nothing much in it; which meant, of course, that he preferred the other. 'You had a much lighter hand with the paragraphs, and you didn't let so many bad contributions get past you, but he is tidier and more businesslike, and he doesn't want to dash away on Saturday mornings.' He might have added, 'And you were an unpatriotic Radical, and he is a patriotic Conservative.' For my politics also maddened him.

Owen was one of the many non-party politicians of those days who took the strictly impartial view that all Radicals were traitors and all gentlemen Conservatives. He did honestly believe that *Punch* under his editorship was a non-party paper. At the Table Rudie Lehmann and E. V. Lucas did their best for Liberalism, but Rudie had been there so long that he had almost given up hope, and E. V. had always a sardonic tolerance for his opponents and a quick recognition that 'the sense of the Table' was against him. Lehmann, of course, had German origins; Lucas, poor fellow, had never been to a Public School or University; their politics could be understood. But Milne was in a different case. Sheer, wilful wrong-headedness. A young man from one of the Eight Public Schools and the Only University, who certainly dashed off on Saturdays, but dashed off to play cricket at country houses—it was ridiculous.

It may seem odd, but politics were like that in the great days of Lloyd George's Penal Budgets, when income tax soared up to—was it 1/10 in the pound?—and a super tax, if you can believe it, was actually put on employment-giving incomes of over £5,000 a year. In all my contacts on dance-floors, cricket-fields and at country houses in those days it never failed to be assumed that I shared my companion's estimate of the Government's perfidy.

Owen discovered all too soon that I didn't. I had given up submitting my contributions to him before sending them to the printer, but until I was on the Table he had a right of veto over them. Over the contributions of members of the Table he had none. When the slogan of the day was *'We want eight* (battleships) *and we won't wait,'* and Navy Leaguers were crying for Three and Four-Power Standards, without which we were at the mercy of our enemies, I suggested to Rudie Lehmann that he should re-write the Ballad of the Revenge on the assumption that Sir Richard Grenville had refused to put to sea until he had a 53-power standard:

And the sea went down, and the stars came out in the wake
of the setting sun,
And ever the gallant fight went on 'twixt the Fifty-three and
the One.

When the pages came up on Friday, Owen was more slow, more thoughtful over them than he had ever been. At last he said, in his most cold voice: 'Have you seen

Rudie's verses?' Naturally I said that, though I hadn't seen them, I knew what they were about as I had given him the idea. 'Then,' said the cold voice. 'You have done *Punch* and your country a great disservice.' Possibly; but in those days I resented the assumption that Englishmen could only be accepted as lovers of England if they discussed Germany in terms either of adulation or of terror. Unfortunately, the war, which made the world safe for democracy, and England fit for heroes to live in, did not succeed in changing permanently the stigmata of patriotism. Once again the true-blue Englishman feels this profound admiration for Germany: an admiration too profound for anything but the very deepest bomb-proof cellar.

I am too old now to resent it, but I do find it funny.

2

Being now a man of means (or so it seemed to me) I moved from Wellington Square to a flat which had the high-sounding address 'St James' Park Chambers, Queen Anne's Gate,' but which was more easily identifiable by cabmen as '31 Broadway, Westminster.' It had its inconveniences. In order to get to the long living-room in front, it was necessary to pass through either of the two rooms at the back; which gave visitors an immediate acquaintance with one's bedroom or one's bathroom, as preferred. In these days this might be supposed to strike the right note of intimacy at the start, but in those days one kept something in reserve. I decided, therefore, to sleep in the bathroom, or, as I chose to put it, to have the luxury of a completely fitted bath in my bedroom. The other room thus became the ante-room or library. Through this visitors were shown, little knowing that for their sakes I was sleeping with the geyser. Luckily I had got used to the smell of gas in Chelsea.

Ken was married and living on two hundred pounds a year in Ealing. Always once and often two or three times a week I went down to dinner with them. While Maud stayed at home and boiled the potatoes, Ken and I would go out and buy all the things at the grocer's which we would have bought so gladly at Westminster: sardines, tongues, tinned fruit, soft drinks and, more adultly, cherry brandy. Then while Maud washed up, we men sat in front of the fire, replete, and smoked and chattered. So it was often, but not always. There were days when Maud was not well enough for domesticity, and then it was for the men to take over her responsibilities. Many a time we have gone to the butcher's and moved on equal terms with him from one undressed and much-slapped piece of beef to another, and haggled for four pounds of rolled ribs, and taken our booty back, and cooked it, Mrs. Beeton watching from the top of the oven, roast with two veg., and served it up triumphantly, no better beef on any table in England. Did I 'lead,' as I did on the Napes Needle, or is it just my infuriating habit to assume that I did? I can't remember; perhaps Ken was the better cook of the two. But I remember that I made an article out of some such dinner a few days before I got on to *Punch*, which I sent (I suppose by request, though it seems strange) to the Manchester *Sunday Chronicle*. Unfortunately in Manchester, or in this part of Manchester, it is customary to demand an account from the contributor, detailing the number of words or lines for which payment is requested. I read my article at the National Liberal (how right Wells was to say that I should find it useful) and then went out to buy a copy for the making of the account. A second contribution was sent up, and was published (as I suppose, since it was never returned to me) on a Sunday when I was out of London. Thus I never saw it in print, was unable to make out an account, and in fact, did not get paid for it. With an income of £500 a year I was not bothering then about a trifle like that; but if *The Sunday Chronicle* cares now to send the money, with thirty-two years' interest, to the Children's Country Holiday Fund, it has my permission.

The weekly article in *Punch* left me with a certain amount of time but very little inspiration for other work. Owen used to suggest that I should spend the time in writing serious articles for the reviews; so did Father. As schoolmasters they felt that I was not taking full advantage of my education. Owen made it perfectly clear in his verses that he was a classical scholar, but there was nothing in any of my cricket sketches to indicate that I could even work out a bowling analysis. Consider the literary members of the Table. Lehmann was in Parliament, Lucas had written a life of Lamb, Graves was assistant-editor of *The Spectator*. Could I not also show that beneath the mask of levity there dwelt a serious purpose, or a knowledge of quaternions, or something?

The answer was that the levity was no mask put on for the occasion. The world was not then the damnable world which it is to-day; it was a world in which imaginative youth could be happy without feeling ashamed of its happiness. I was very young, very light-hearted, confident of myself, confident of the future. I loved my work; I loved not working; I loved the long week-ends with the delightful people of other people's delightful houses. I loved being in love, and being out of love and free again to fall in love. I loved feeling rich again, and having no responsibilities but only the privileges of a benevolent uncle. I loved hearing suddenly that some Great Man, full of serious purpose, had loved my last article. And if anybody says that all this is a misuse of the much misused word 'love,' well, it is, but I like misusing it, for it conveys my simple happiness. Those (as I said when I collected under one title four books of *Punch* contributions; and as Wordsworth had said earlier; and as Osbert Sitwell was to say later), Those Were The Days.

In short I was gay, and the gaiety could not be kept in. If to please my elders I had exposed the inner life of the quaternion in *The Quarterly Review*, it would have been a gay exposure, shocking to the academic mind. It is assumed too readily, I feel, that a writer who makes his readers laugh would really prefer to make them cry, and that he is only making them laugh because, as a 'professional humorist,' he is paid to do so. When, many years later, critics took to calling me 'whimsical,' they assumed, easily and naturally, that 'whimsy' was something which I had heard from Barrie was profitable, and which I stuck on my writing here and there, as one sticks stamps on a postal order to give it a higher value. I doubt if this mode of writing is practised so freely as is supposed. It is too difficult. A writer's job is to express himself in prose or verse, and this is what most of us are doing. We are not laboriously expressing somebody else's personality in order to please a publisher or annoy a critic.

3

In 1910 I was allowed downstairs. Graves presented me with a knife with which to leave my mark on the Table, and I achieved a modest and monogrammatic A. A. M. which is already, I dare say, a hieroglyphic to him who sits in my place. Who was this, he wonders and nobody now can tell him. Yes, Bernard Partridge is still there, the only survivor of my time, he sat just opposite, he may

remember. Milne, wasn't it? And in a little while somebody will be saying: 'What were his initials?'

In those days the initials were better known. Indeed,
I could claim that they were the most popular which ever
appeared in *Punch*, inasmuch as they were divided, when
I retired, among two other contributors, Anthony Arm-
strong and Archibald Marshall, for whose work I have
received a good deal of credit. An article by 'A. A.' on a
Dutch cheese he had once met brought me an unexpected
gift from Holland which I accepted thankfully, knowing
how impossible it was to forward anything so ill-shaped
for forwarding as a Dutch cheese. It was always a regret
to me that Marshall didn't write more about champagne
or golf balls. For *Punch* readers are delightfully respon-
sive. At a crisis in the war I wrote some pathetic verses
called 'The Last Pot,' and never lacked for marmalade
again. When I had exhausted the benevolence or the
larders of English women, the nearer colonies and the
more distant Dominions took up the torch, so that the
Empire became for me a place in which marmalade is
always setting. Whether through kindnesses like these, or
from letters, or just from an awareness hard to justify or
explain, the regular *Punch* writer did feel peculiarly at
home with his readers, sure of their instant response. Just
as a theatre company can play better to a warm house
than a cold house, so does the 'professional humorist' ex-
pand in the warmth of the reception which he knows is
awaiting him. As a writer I expanded happily.

As a member of the Table I provided my own warmth.
The dinner was a long one and a good one; we drank
champagne who liked it; we smoked cigars or pipes; we
talked and could have gone on talking. But from the
other end of the Table Owen said, 'Well, gentlemen,'
and we turned reluctantly to the business of the evening.

The cartoons. The very political cartoons. And in those days politics made me extremely warm.

With its large circulation in the Shires, the Vicarages and the Messes of England *Punch* was almost compelled to be True Blue. To-day the distinction between Blue and Red is not so marked; ultra-red is indistinguishable from ultra-blue, and everything complementary is some shade of purple. But those were the days when Lord Willoughby de Broke swore that blood would flow beneath Westminster Bridge (I think I am right about that, but it may have been Waterloo Bridge) before the Parliament Bill became law; and an Ulsterman called O'Neill threw a book at Winston Churchill (this being one of Mr Churchill's Liberal periods) across the sacred floor of the House of Commons; and Lord Winterton bobbed up continually, calling out, 'Manners, there, manners'; and Duchesses bound themselves by a terrible oath never to lick stamps for a little Welsh attorney; and 'well-known Harley Street physicians' solemnly exhibited in the more Conservative press the seeds of poisoning which lurked in the gum of Insurance stamps if Duchesses licked them, but not apparently in the gum of postage stamps such as are continually licked by common people. It all seems ridiculous now; it seemed to me ridiculous and indecent then; and being young and impatient and sure of myself (or, as I said, young), I found it difficult not to get over-heated at those interminable discussions which followed the over-heating *Punch* Dinner.

4

When Owen went off to the Riviera or Scotland, E. V. Lucas came into the office as acting-editor. He had as many concerns outside *Punch* as Owen had few, and consequently was as quick as Owen was slow. After the paper was put to bed on Friday night, Owen had nowhere to go but home, and a lonely home at that. E. V. had a hundred mysterious activities waiting for him. Only once as we walked down the Strand together did he vary his usual, 'Well, I'm going this way. Good-night,' in preface to one of those disappearances to which I was now used, and which had all the air, even if they took him no further than the Garrick Club, of a prelude to adventure. On this occasion he suggested that I should come with him, and for the first time in my life I passed through the stage door of a theatre. What theatre I cannot remember, save that it was a theatre of varieties. We found ourselves in the dressing-room of one of the great comics of the day, I have forgotten which. He and E. V., it seemed, were dear old pals. I was introduced. My presence there was so surprising to myself that I supposed he had wished to meet me, but my name meant as little to him as would that of Keats or any other dear old pal. We got on splendidly together. I didn't say anything because I had nothing to say; I didn't drink anything because I had nothing to drink, except whisky, which I have never liked. But his flow of professional high spirits swept me up equally with Lucas, the dresser, and a couple of other men whom he seemed to think I had brought with me; his eyes appealed with no less confidence to mine than to theirs for appreciation and support; and when I left it was with the knowledge that there was always a drink waiting for me (old boy) whenever I liked to drop in. I never saw him again.

When Lucas died, I wrote this of him in *The Times:*

He could not be called 'the writers' writer,' as—was it Spenser? E. V. would know: why can't I ask him?—as Spenser was called the poets' poet, but he was the writer most loved as a man by other writers; in part because he was free from the unlovable vanities and jealousies which other writers indulge. Nobody was so instantly appreciative of the work of his fellow-craftsmen, nobody was so little cumbered about his own. Listening to him among his contemporaries, the conversation all of books, a stranger on the outskirts of his company would still wonder why the wittiest and the best-informed of them all did not himself try authorship. In fact, his writing, though so necessary to him, was in no way an expression of himself. No essayist of his quality has had so little to say of the world within him, so much to say of the world around him. To pass from a knowledge of his books to a knowledge of the man was to find oneself neither on familiar ground nor on treacherous ground; it was to explore a new country, as exhilarating and as firm of outline as his own beloved Downs. To be a writer and to have him for a friend was to feel that whatever one wrote was written in a special sense for him; so that the thought 'E. V. will like that' gave one a new conceit of the last paragraph, a new confidence for the next. With the same assurance one would save for him the little gleanings of the week: ridiculous things, odd things, fine things, damnable things: heard, read, discovered: thinking, 'I must tell E. V. that,' knowing that his comment would give just that extra flavour to one's own emotion. He had the dry sparkle of his favourite wine, and brought to his companion the same sense of ease and well-being, the same satisfaction with oneself, the same stimulation to be wiser and wittier than one really was. Now E. V. is dead; now it is the morning after. The world is not so good a place as we had thought it. We are not such fine fellows.

Through the thirty years of my friendship with him, beginning from the days when he first came into the *Punch* office as Acting Editor, I was encouraged by him to think that I was a good writer. Anybody who likes may differ from him, including myself at times, but I know that I am a better writer for his appreciation than I should have been without it. Owen was as guarded in his praise as a preparatory schoolmaster, who fears always the retort: 'If my son was as clever as you said, why didn't he get a scholarship?' When I had written half-a-dozen articles, he would say, 'Isn't it about time you wrote some verse again?' which in a way (let us look on the bright side) was a compliment to my verse; and after three sets of verses he would say, 'It's about time you did another series, isn't it?' which could be taken (thank you, Owen) as a compliment to my prose. If these were compliments, they were all that I extracted from him. But E. V. knew that you can't be light and gay and off-hand and casual and charming in print unless you are continually re-assured that you are being some of these things. If I had any value to *Punch* it was because sometimes I was some of these things, and E. V.'s praise helped me to give the air of doing it all easily—which is the only air to give writing of that sort.

At this time he was contributing, over the initials V. V. V., a weekly commentary to *The Sphere* called 'A Few Days Ago.' When he wandered off to Florence, he asked me, with the editor's acquiescence, to take his place. So, for the six weeks of his absence, I commented on the world (religion and politics barred) over the initials 'O. O. O.,' and at the end of them was given the freedom of *The Sphere* for a weekly essay over my own name. I wrote these essays for two years at three guineas a time, and then retired, feeling at a temporary loss for subjects, politics and religion being barred. After a year's rest I asked if I might come back, being then engaged to be married and more aware of the importance of money. Clement Shorter expressed his delight in the nicest way; but after six months the Proprietors of *Punch* offered to pay me what *The Sphere* was paying me if I stopped writing for it. This doesn't sound like a tribute, but I suppose in a way it was. Shorter again was nice about it, and let me go. After the war, when I had left *Punch* and had to earn a living somehow, I suggested to Shorter that I should make another return to *The Sphere,* but this time for six guineas. Once again he agreed, with the politeness of one whose only object was to serve me. I have always thought of him as the best editor for whom I have worked. We never met; he never wrote to me, save when I retired from or returned to the paper; but in some way he always gave the impression of having the completest confidence in his contributors.

5

It was in 1910 that I published what I think of now as my first book: *The Day's Play,* a collection of *Punch* articles. E. V. suggested that, since I had parodied the title, I should send a copy to the author of *The Day's Work.* When I said that I didn't know Kipling, and couldn't imagine the author of the famous and recently-published line 'The flannelled fool at the wicket, the muddied oaf in the goal' being interested in a book full of cricket and lesser games, E. V. assured me that Kipling was 'not like that,' and that he would write me a charming and appreciative letter back. I should have loved a charming and appreciative letter from Kipling, but had to wait twenty years for it; for in those days I couldn't regard it as possible that young writers should introduce themselves in this way to older writers whom they didn't know. The school tie wouldn't hear of it; it was 'bad form.' However, each Wednesday when we met at the dinner, E. V. would say, 'Have you sent your book to Kipling yet?' until at last I had to promise him that this next week I really would. So I sat down to write the accompanying letter: 'Sir,' I began ... It was, it had to be, one of those let-

ters in which the case for the importance of the addressee
and the unimportance of the addressor is slightly over-
stated. Kipling himself once answered Tennyson's praise
with the words: 'When a private is praised by his General
he does not presume to thank him, but fights the better
afterwards,' although the parallel of a corporal not thank-
ing his colonel but fighting the better afterwards would
have done justice to the situation. My letter beginning
'Sir' and enclosing my own modest volume expressed not
only an unrestrained admiration for the great man's own
work, but the assurance that it was from him alone that I
had drawn my first enthusiasm for literature, and that it
was to the peak whereon he sat that I was lifting my eyes,
content if I could master only so much as the few first
gentle slopes. (Or whatever. I don't keep copies.) When
I had written this, I read it through, and decided that it
was so utterly false that I simply could not let it go. I
admired much of Kipling, but not like that. The only
writer whom I did admire at all like that in those days
was Barrie. So, not wishing to waste the letter, I sent it
and the book to Barrie. He wrote a 'charming and appreciative' letter back. He elected me the 'last member' of
his cricket team, the Allahakbarries. He asked me to
lunch. That was how I got to know him. Even after
twenty-five years I wished that I had not forced myself
on him, but had been introduced in the ordinary way.

6

In 1913 Owen Seaman's god-daughter, Dorothy de
Sélincourt (Daphne to friends), was persuaded to marry
me. Owen had taken me to her coming-out dance, and
we had gone about together in a way common enough
now, but less usual in those days. When I wanted a present for a sister-in-law or a new suit for myself, I would

summon her to help me; when she wanted a man to take her to a dance she would ring me up. She laughed at my jokes, she had my contributions to *Punch* by heart before she met me, she had (it is now clear) the most perfect sense of humour in the world; and I, in my turn, had a pianola to which she was devoted, and from which I could not keep her away. We might have gone on like this for ever. One day we found ourselves in a boot-shop.

'Any sort of boots or just boots?' she said.

'Ski-ing boots,' I said proudly. 'This is a great day in your life.'

'I bought mine yesterday.'

'What for?'

'Ski-ing.'

'Where? Hampstead Heath?'

'Switzerland.'

'But that's where *I'm* going!'

'Well, there's plenty of room for both of us. I'm going to a place called Diablerêts.'

'Dash it, so am I.'

'What a very small——'

'Don't say it. Are you at the Grand?'

'Yes. What fun. I've got a pair of orange trousers.'

'I shall be wearing a red carnation in my button-hole. We're bound to recognize each other. What are you like with a lot of other people about?'

'Heavenly.'

'So am I. I do hope we shall like each other.'

We did. The 'other people about' made everything different. I proposed to her at eleven o'clock one morning in a snow-storm. I had to, because she was going back to London that afternoon, where also there were other people, and it was clear to me now that it was my mission to save her from them.

This is the autobiography of a writer, not of a married

man. My next book was dedicated 'to my collaborator who buys the ink and paper, laughs, and in fact does all the really difficult part of the business,' and it is as a collaborator that Daphne plays her part in this book.

We were married in June, and took a flat in Embankment Gardens, Chelsea. I was now getting eight guineas a week for my contributions to *Punch,* which was then the top price for writers on the staff. When I stopped writing for *The Sphere,* the Proprietors compensated me by raising my salary to £500, so that with double pay for Almanacs and Summer Numbers, and a trickle of royalties from the books, I was making about £1,000 a year. We were very comfortable and very happy. I had met the Williamsons (C. N. and A. M.) a year or two before at a luncheon-party, and romantic Alice Williamson had made me promise that, when I fell in love or got married or did any of those things, I would introduce the lady to her. So, after our return from a rather cold and bleak honeymoon on Dartmoor, we asked them to dinner. They returned our hospitality (if you can call it that, the cook-general being temperamental) by offering us their villa at Cap Martin for a second honeymoon. The offer, as we discovered when we got there, included not only the villa but the staff, the food, the cellar and even the cigars, together with letters of introduction to everybody and the company of that delightfully wheezy bull-dog Tiberius. It was a noble piece of hospitality, but Alice Williamson was an American, to whom such gestures are natural.

7

My friend Alderson Horne, at whose house in Sussex I had spent so many delightful week-ends, was putting on his first play. Disguised as Anmer Hall he has since become the high light of what critics call the uncommer-

244

cial theatre, by which is meant the theatre which hasn't got to make both ends meet. In those days most plays were preceded by 'curtain-raisers': one-act plays which entertained the cheaper seats while the stalls were finishing their dinners: acted, mostly, by the understudies. Alderson, either from friendship or because he thought I had an unrevealed talent for such things, asked me to write the curtain-raiser.

For some years now I had been trying to catch a glimpse of the middle-aged man who writes this book. What should I be in 1930, in 1940? Still writing for *Punch*? Editor of *Punch*, perhaps. Nothing (I felt) which I wrote for *Punch* in 1930 would be better than what I was writing now. I had by this time mastered the technique (the tricks, if you like to call them that) of the 'humorous' sketch; I couldn't expect to become 'funnier'; and the gaiety and light-heartedness would gradually become less gay, less carefree. Having made a reputation, however small, by 1910, it was silly and unexciting to spend the rest of one's life trying to keep the spots off it. It was true that to be editor of *Punch* was a career in itself, but should I be allowed to do what I liked with *Punch*? No. And would it be a good thing for *Punch* if I were? No. Its secret was that it was a National Institution. Did I want to edit, could I edit, a national institution? I thought not. In any case the editorship would not be vacant for another twenty years . . . another thousand humorous articles . . . the best of them no farther on than the best of those which I had already written.

Then how escape?

Obviously, and only, by writing in my spare time novels or plays on which ultimately I could depend for a living. When should I begin? There was only one day— to-morrow—and to-morrow—as is its habit, never came. Then I married, and, it seemed, became more tied to my surroundings. Could I give up the certain income; could I renounce my collaborator's great ambition for me, the editorship of *Punch?* I didn't see how I could. Nor (it being Friday morning, and Jane having had a temperament the night before) did I see how I could endure to go on for ever like this. Something would have to happen some day.

So, when Alderson asked me to write a curtain-raiser, I told myself that it was happening now. I was going to be a dramatist.

I wrote a one-act play called *Make-Believe,* a title which I used later for a full-length children's play. My collaborator sent it off to Alderson and bought a new dress for the first night. After a few exciting days the play came back again. The reason given (and there is always a kindly reason given) was that the characterization was too subtle for understudies to put over the footlights; it needed a star cast. Quite possibly Alderson didn't like it.

So what? Should I try another manager, or should I try another play? Could I write plays or couldn't I? I didn't know. But probably Barrie would know. I sent *Make-Believe* to him. Barrie said that without any doubt I could write plays, and sent it on to Granville Barker. Barker wrote to me enthusiastically, accepted the play for production and added, 'But the important thing is that you should immediately write me a full-length play.' The thing had happened. I was escaping. I was going to be a dramatist.

But, as it turned out, I was to escape in other circumstances. War was declared.

AMATEUR SOLDIER

1914–1918

Chapter Thirteen

1

I should like to put asterisks here, and then write: 'It was in 1919 that I found myself once again a civilian.' For it makes me almost physically sick to think of that nightmare of mental and moral degradation, the war. When my boy was six years old he took me into the Insect House at the Zoo, and at the sight of some of the monstrous inmates I had to leave his hand and hurry back into the fresh air. I could imagine a spider or a millipede so horrible that in its presence I should die of disgust. It seems impossible to me now that any sensitive man could live through another war. If not required to die in other ways, he would waste away of soul-sickness.

I was a pacifist before 1914, but this (I thought with other fools) was a war to end war. It did not make the prospect of being a soldier any more attractive. There was an extraordinary idea among the elderly that 'being a soldier' meant just no more than 'risking your life for your country,' and that the man who was unwilling to do this was a coward, and that the man who was willing to do this was a hero. To people like myself the Great Sacrifice was not the sacrifice of our lives but of our liberties. Ever since I had left Cambridge I had been my own master. I fixed my own hours, I was under no discipline; no bell rang for me, no bugle sounded. Now I was thirty-two, married, with a happy home of my own and engaged happily in work which I loved. To be a schoolboy again, to say 'Yes, sir' and 'No, sir' and 'Please,

sir' and 'May I, sir?' was no hardship to schoolboys, no
hardship to a million men in monotonous employment,
but it was hell itself to one who had been as spoilt by
good-fortune as I. However, again I was fortunate.
There are Colonels and Colonels; I met only the one
sort of Colonel. If a special order had gone round the
British Army: 'For your information and necessary action: Milne is joining us. See that he is given the easiest
and best possible time, consistent with ultimate victory,'
I could not have had more reason to be grateful to my
commanding officers.

As the result of an introduction from Graves I was
commissioned to the 4th Battalion of the Royal Warwickshire Regiment, then stationed at Golden Hill in
the Isle of Wight. In the orderly room I said 'Sir' to the
Adjutant, whose uncle I called 'Charles' on the *Punch*
Table. It gave me no compensating thrill that elderly
sergeants who knew all about soldiering said 'Sir' to me.
It was a reserve battalion, into which the Colonel had
persuaded many of his personal friends, some of whom
were married. After six experimental weeks in which I
learnt to be just a little, but not much, like a soldier,
Daphne joined the married strength, and from then on,
whenever it was possible, she shared the war with me.
Through a variety of accidents I became Signalling Officer. After a nine weeks' course at the Southern Command Signalling School I really knew something about
it, with the result that I was kept at home as an instructor
until July 1916. As a specialist officer I was, I thanked
Heaven, independent again. Nobody in the battalion
could tell me anything about signalling (except my sergeant, and he only when we heliographed from one range
of hills in the Island to another, and he thought he was
back in India); I was excused—or excused myself, it was
never clear which—orderly officer's duty; never saw my

company commander from one week to another; and
having the whole battalion behind me on route marches
could almost imagine that I was taking a brisk country
walk in civilian knickerbockers.

Mrs Williams, the Colonel's wife, mother of five children and the regiment, only to be described as a 'perfect
dear,' became great friends with Daphne. They put their
heads together and organized an entertainment for the
troops, one of the features of which was to be (whether
the troops liked it or not) a little play in which Daphne
and the Colonel's children would act. The play would
be written by the Signalling Officer. My collaborator was
detailed to break the news to me. I said that I was much
too tired in the evenings to write anything. She said that
she would do the writing; all I had to do was to lie in an
armchair and tell her what to write. Easy work. So we
wrote a 'little play': about a Prince and Princess and a
Wicked Countess (Daphne) and a magic ring. Some of
the dialogue seemed to us rather funny, and my collaborator said, as she has so often said, 'You mustn't waste
this.' But there seemed to be nothing to do with it, since
it was no more than one scene in a children's play.
'Write a book round the people in it,' said my collaborator. 'I've never written a book,' I protested, 'not
straight off.' 'Well, now's the time to begin,' she said.

So after I had come back from my signalling course,
and rejoined the battalion which had now moved to Sandown, and we had taken the prettiest cottage in the town
with lilacs and cherry-trees in the garden, I dictated the
book: a long fairy-story called *Once on a Time*. There
are, I think, some good things in it, but few people have
read it, and nobody knows whether it is meant for children or for grown-ups. I don't know myself. But it was
the greatest fun to do. We began every evening at half-
past five, I in my chair before the fire, my collaborator,

pen in hand, brown head bent over table, writing, waiting, laughing: it made the war seem very far away, it took us back to our own happy life in London. On Sundays—for I seem to have excused myself Church Parade too—we went for long walks over the cliffs with lunch in our pockets, and the characters in the book came with us, listening to us as we settled their fate for the next chapter.

It was a great moment when the last word was put down on paper. I had thought that I could never write more than two thousand consecutive words, and I had written sixty thousand. I had written a book. It was finished. Spring was here, and now, save for this trivial business of soldiering, I was free, I could take a holiday, I could rest.

But I couldn't. In a week my collaborator was saying, 'What shall we do now?' We had to do something. I couldn't just be, of all stupid things, a soldier. What should we write?

Not a book. We had written a book. What about a play? *The* play, the full-length play which I had been going to write before the war.

So I wrote a Comedy in Three Acts, called *Wurzel-Flummery*.

In one of those *Sphere* articles I had referred to the unimaginative way in which millionaires leave their money. 'How much more amusing,' I wrote, 'to leave £20,000 to each of fifty acquaintances on condition that they all take the same ridiculous name. Fifty Spiffkinses in the same club, just because you said so.' This idea came back into my mind suddenly and was made the theme of the play. The ridiculous name was Wurzel-Flummery. We imagined Dennis Eadie, who had played the irresponsble clergyman so delightfully in *The Honeymoon*, playing the solicitor. Barrie, who had promised to give me any introduction I wanted, read the play, praised and criticized it, and sent it to Eadie. Eadie asked me to lunch with him at the Carlton Grill to 'talk it over.'

How happily I went to the Colonel to ask for a day's leave, how readily he granted it, how excitedly next morning we went to the station together, my collaborator and I, how fondly, how hopefully we waved good-bye to each other, how eagerly she waited on the platform for me as my train came back. The news was as good as could be expected. Eadie seemed really keen on the play, and wanted to do it, but there was just something not quite right with it. 'If I knew what it was, I would tell you, but I don't. I just feel that there's something. Why don't you ask Barrie? Or read it through again yourself. It's so nearly right.' I said that Barrie had already made one or two criticisms. 'Well, there you are; he would know. And when you've got it right, send it back to me. I want to do it.'

Who could say fairer than that over one's first play? We had a happy dinner together, chattering excitedly, building the wildest castles in Shaftesbury Avenue. At half-past ten we went to bed, still chattering. At eleven there was a heavy knocking on the front door. Our servant slept out. I went down, knowing what it was. An orderly saluted and said that the Colonel would like to see me in the Mess. I was for France in forty-eight hours.

Somewhere in the waste land round the Somme I opened a letter from Daphne, written from Burnham-on-Crouch where she was staying with her mother. Enclosed in her letter was a note from Gerald du Maurier to Barrie. For better or worse *Wurzel-Flummery* had had to stay as it was, and since Eadie didn't like it as it was, some other manager must be approached. It had always seemed possible, now in this dead country it seemed certain, that this was all I should have to leave to my collaborator. So Barrie had sent the play to du Maurier, and here was du Maurier's answer.

'Dear Jimmy,' he wrote, 'I like it enormously; I know his work in *Punch,* of course. If I were in this for fun, I would do it like a shot, but there's no money in it.'

For some reason, his name perhaps, his technical perfection as an actor, the fact that he was George du Maurier's son, I had always thought of Gerald as an artist, who did things 'for fun.' How else could one write, paint, compose, act, engage in any of the arts? When one knew him, one knew that the stage meant nothing to him but a means of getting money; he never pretended otherwise; but somehow it was a shock to make the discovery at this particular moment, in this particular place.

2

I was attached to the 11th Battalion of the regiment, then commanded by Lieut.-Colonel C. S. Collison. If I quote again from *The Times,* it is not because I do not dislike quoting myself, but because I dislike still more paraphrasing anything which I have already written.

All who served under Colonel Collison in the 11th Battalion of The Royal Warwickshire Regiment will have heard with deep regret of his death, and those of them who had the honour of his friendship will feel that some small tribute should now be paid to his memory, even if it be by the least of his subalterns. But it was a privileged subaltern who, by the accident of being a signalling officer, was attached to the H.Q. mess, and thus admitted to the intimacy of his company. To a young, anti-military, 'literary man,' hating the Army, and prepared to resent all Regulars, he was a revelation. Handsome, debonair, the ideal monocled colonel of fiction, with all a soldier's love of soldiering and traditional faith in the value of military service, he added to this conventional equipment a fastidiousness, a feeling for beauty, and a humorous, detached irony which made him the most invigorating company imaginable. He called you by a nickname, but he was your colonel; his humour asked for humour in return, but his military façade kept you from taking liberties; he was intimate and aloof, human and astringent; in his manner always on parade, in his mind always alert for companionship.

How such a man became a colonel, or a colonel remained such a man, was a mystery. However many lives in his loved battalion the 'tin hat' had saved, he never could accustom himself to its lack of aesthetic appeal. He was all for smartness; but a subaltern who had thought to please him by having his hair cut particularly short during the Battle of the Somme was advised 'not to go about looking like a convict when peace might burst upon you at any moment.' When he lamented the men's habit of answering, as it seemed, every question with the words 'I couldn't say, Sir,' he was not regretting their ignorance, but being harrowed by the unchanging texture of its expression. He was a good soldier, and if he wanted to do something obviously necessary, which a good soldier could not do without higher authority, he did it; and then, like a good soldier, applied for leave to do it. When he was commanding his battalion at Chatham in the first rumour-fed days of the War, and was ordered to repel invasion by establishing a series of sentry-posts 'facing,' as he put it, 'the hostile town of Maidstone,' it was not his to reason why. He established them. 'But, of course, I withdrew them directly the General had gone'—and of course he would.

Thinking of him again, of those far-off days from which these memories have drifted back to me, I turned to some of the letters which I had then written, wondering how much of my feelings for him I had put on paper. I seem to have fallen for him, as they say, at once. On my first day up the line: 'I had about an hour's talk with the C.O. last night; he is a delightful person.' Ten days later, after we had come out of action: 'The C.O. is heavenly; I love him; frightfully funny in a particular way of his own. He was in grand form to-night; in fact, we all were; at least, he made us think we were.' And so on, panegyrically, until his health sent him back to England, and to the wife of whom he had said to me once: 'I write to her every day, because I have dinner every day. If there's time to have dinner there's time to write to your wife.' My last reference to him is this: 'The C.O., as you know, left for England on Monday, and to-day (Sunday) I had a box of 50 Coronas from him: with apologies that he couldn't afford 100 owing to the extortions of the mess president (myself). Pretty quick work, and isn't he a dear?'

A dear! Shall that be his epitaph? It seems the most unlikely one for a good soldier, the most unsuitable one for this particular ironic soldier; but at least it tells of the real affection which he inspired in one grateful subaltern. Moreover, it would amuse him. So let it stand.

I had been sent, with the military efficiency of those days, to a battalion which had already a signalling officer, a new man just appointed, called Harrison. I had spent eighteen months learning to be a signaller, and of bombs and rifles and the ordinary routine of the platoon officer I had forgotten what little I had known. The brigade was just going into action. It proposed to capture the Switch Line at Bazentin-le-Petit, or what once was that village. When this business was over, the Colonel would recommend my transference to some battalion which wanted those eighteen months' training; meanwhile I could go into action with the signalling officer and add some practical knowledge to all the theory which I had assimilated. As soon as we had got into the reserve trenches I went into the signallers' dug-out to introduce myself; I liked signallers and felt at home with them. I meant to have asked a thousand technical questions, but found myself engaged in a long discussion with Lance-Corporal Grainger about books. He was a Welsh miner, as well educated as most of them are, quiet, friendly, charming. We found that we shared a passion for Jane Austen.

The attack was timed for midnight. On the day before, Harrison and three men, with me hanging on 'for training,' ran out a line to the front trench by a devious route, for we had been told that the existing line would never stand against the opening counter-barrage. On the way we fell into a burst of whizz-bangs, and Harrison was knocked out. We got him back to the first-aid post, I reported to the Colonel, and became signalling officer. At four o'clock next morning we went out again, this time by the ordinary communication trench, such as it was, and laid a line, elaborately laddered according to the text books, and guaranteed to withstand any bombardment.

H.Q. was in a deep German dug-out, facing, of course, the wrong way. In an adjoining dug-out was the H.Q. of the East Lancashires with whom the attack was being made. In the space between these two underground rooms were my signallers. At eleven o'clock that night the Colonel, the Major, the Adjutant and I sat round a table by candle-light smoking and talking, waiting for our barrage to begin. But the Germans, who knew all about it, began first. And the line went.

The sergeant-major of the East Lancashires went up the steps with some idea, I suppose, of getting information, and was blown out of existence before he reached the top. My signallers announced this, and added that the line to Brigade was also down. We sat there completely isolated. The depth of the dug-out deadened the noise of the guns, so that a shell-burst was no longer the noise of a giant plumber throwing down his tools, but only a persistent thud, which set the candles dancing and then, as if by an afterthought, blotted them out.

From time to time I lit them again, wondering what I should be doing, wondering what signalling officers did on these occasions. Nervously I said to the Colonel, feeling that the isolation was all my fault, 'Should I try to get a line out?' and to my intense relief he said, 'Don't be a bloody fool.'

It was about two o'clock in the morning that a runner got through. The attack, as was to be expected, was a complete failure. In his Company, So-and-so and So-and-so were killed—I remembered them, two boys under the apple trees in the little village where I had joined them in billets; we had dined in the garden to the gramophone, and there were peaches which one of them had fetched from Amiens, and the war was just a happy picnic to them, the guns rolling so far, far away in the distance that one would never catch up with them—no, sir, he couldn't say about the captain—no, sir, *he* was all right, but he couldn't rightly say about any of the others, it had been coming over something cruel.

'All right,' said the Colonel.

'Am I to go back, sir?'

'No.' He caught the Major's eye. The Major got up and strapped on his revolver. It was all too clearly the moment for me to strap on mine. Perhaps somebody else would do *Wurzel-Flummery*—afterwards.

'Use your common-sense,' said the Colonel. 'If it's impossible, come back. I simply cannot lose three signalling officers in a month.'

I promised, but felt quite unable to distinguish between common-sense and cowardice. The whole thing was so damned silly.

I told my sergeant that we were now going to run out a line, and asked him to pick two men for me. I knew nothing of the section then, save that there was a lance-corporal who loved Jane Austen, unhelpful knowledge in the circumstances. He said at once: 'I'll come for one, sir,' which I thought was sporting of him, although it was obviously wrong for both of us to go. He picked on another man, a company signaller who had joined head-quarters for the occasion, and we attached ourselves to the Major. We dashed. The Major went first—he was going to 're-organize the troops'; I went second, God knew why; the sergeant and the signaller came behind me, running out a line neatly and skilfully. No ladder-ing now, no text-book stuff, it was just dropped any-where. From time to time the Major flung himself down for a breather, and down we flopped and panted, wonder-ing if he would get up again. To our relief each time he was alive, and so were we. We passed one of the signal-stations, no longer a station but a pancake of earth on top of a spread-eagled body; I had left him there that evening, saying, 'Well, you'll be comfortable here.' More rushes, more breathers, more bodies, we were in the front line. The Major hurried off to collect what men he could, while I joined up the telephone. Hopeless, of course, but we could have done no more. I pressed the buzzer, and incredibly heard Daffy's slow, lazy voice: not my Daffy in England, but Corporal Daffy, ex-gardener from Buxton, with the gardener's heavy drooping mous-tache and heavy stoop, unalterably a civilian. There was only that one other voice in the world which I would have sooner heard.

I asked to speak to the Colonel. I told him what I knew. I ordered—what were telephones for?—a little counter-bombardment. Then with a sigh of utter con-tent and thankfulness and the joy of living, I turned away from the telephone. And there behind me was Lance-Corporal Grainger.

'What on earth are *you* doing here?' I said.

He grinned sheepishly.

'You weren't detailed, were you?'

'No, sir.'

'Well, then——'

'I thought I'd just like to come along, sir.'

'But *why?*'

He looked still more embarrassed.

'Well, sir, I thought I'd just like to be sure *you* were all right.'

Which is the greatest tribute to Jane Austen that I have ever heard.

3

We put in a week at Loos after the Somme, and were then due for a long rest. In billets at Philosophe on the way out I heard for the first time the name of the Divisional General: Gleichen. Was he still Count Gleichen or had he already become Lord Edward Gleichen? I cannot remember. After the war we found that he and Lady Edward were neighbours of ours on Ashdown Forest, and we became so friendly with them that Lord Edward and I exchanged books, he giving me *London's Open Air Statuary* and I giving him *Winnie-the-Pooh*. It is doubtful if the history of the British Army can record any similar exchange. I had heard Owen Seaman talk about him, and now, hearing his name again, wondered if we should ever talk about Owen Seaman. My more military companion was horrified at the idea of a General talking to a Second Lieutenant; it would practically mean that we had lost the war; so I let it go for the moment. At La Comté, our rest-village, the telephone rang in the H.Q. mess one night, the Adjutant leapt to his feet, announced in an awed voice, 'The General, sir, from Division,' and handed the receiver to the Colonel. 'Yes, sir,' said the Colonel several times. 'Thank you, sir.

Good-bye, sir.' He came back to the dinner-table and surveyed me through his eye-glass.

'You're lunching at Division with the General, Punch,' he said.

'When, sir?'

'To-morrow. You're taking me with you. Do you mind?'

'Actually, no, sir.'

'It's a little hard,' he sighed, 'to have had to wait for this until one of my subalterns puts in a good word for me.'

'Bad for discipline,' said the Major, trying to look as if he meant it. When, a little later, he went on leave for ten days, he spent one of them travelling backwards and forwards across Essex, just to see Daphne for a moment and tell her how well I was. That was the sort of field-officer I served under in the War.

I explained that my editor knew Gleichen. It was accepted as an explanation rather than an excuse. 'They're sending a car for you at twelve,' said the Colonel, lighting a cigar. 'For God's sake don't leave me behind.'

We went back into the line at Bully-Grenay, hoping to spend the winter there, but the 'blood-bath of the Somme' was not quite full, and at Beaumont Hamel there was to be yet one more display of G.H.Q.'s bulldog tenacity. The battalion's objective was called—and it was the only attractive thing about it—Beauregard Dovecote. If ever any place looked a death trap on a military map this did. But it rained and rained and rained. At the last moment the attack was postponed. The troops should have been disappointed about this, but weren't; they marched westwards, singing loudly. It went on raining; one never ceased to be wet through. We fetched up eventually at Doullens; the sun came out; the H.Q. staff was photographed, and all was gas and gaiters. For a week or two we rested, trained and wrote home saying that we were in the pink. At some sort of field-day I was introduced (if that is the correct military word) to the new Divisional General. He told me that Signal Officers must be extremely careful not to risk their valuable lives; I agreed with him cordially. Gleichen had been given employment at home, his name being too German for the patriotic press. I wished mine had been Müller.

I had my men out on a little hill one morning, and was walking as usual, from station to station to see how the messages were coming through. It was a warm November day, so warm that each station seemed a mile, rather than a few hundred yards, from the next, and I wondered how I could drag my legs there. At lunch in the H.Q. mess I went to sleep; spent the afternoon and evening sleeping in front of the stove; and when I went to bed was given the usual couple of aspirins by the M.O. Next morning my temperature was 103. The M.O. went off to arrange for an ambulance to take me to the clearing station. By the time I was introduced to it again, the thermometer was soaring up to 105. Next day the battalion got the order to move; the attack was to begin. My sergeant came to say good-bye to me. I handed over my maps, commended the section to his care, wished him luck, and went to sleep again. He was lucky. He only lost a leg.

Ten days later I was at Southampton. Some kind woman offered to write a telegram for me. It was to Daphne, saying that she would find me in hospital at Oxford. I woke up one afternoon and saw her at the end of the bed, crying.

4

We were back at Sandown. January 18th was my birth-day. In addition to letters from the family there was one from J. M. Barrie. Surprising. How did he know that—he didn't know. He wrote to say that Boucicault was putting on two one-act plays of his in a Triple Bill, and that if I could turn *Wurzel-Flummery* into a two-act play, it might be used to complete the programme. One could hardly imagine a more exciting birthday present.

The three plays came on at the New Theatre in April, *Wurzel-Flummery* in the middle. Dot Boucicault played the solicitor, Nigel Playfair the pompous M.P. I got thirty pounds a week for the eight weeks of its run. We went up for the first night with forty-eight hours' leave, were introduced to Irene Vanbrugh, and asked by Dot to write a play for her. Next morning I was asked by Alfred Butt to write the forthcoming revue for the Palace Theatre. Dazzled by the financial prospects I started off gaily, but it soon became clear that, even if we had noth-ing else in common, Butt and I were beginning to share the same misgivings about our partnership. I couldn't possibly write the revue he wanted, he couldn't possibly want the revue I was writing; so, to the relief of both of us, we said no more about it.

Meanwhile the War Office was getting on with the war. Our battalion was a unit of the Portsmouth Garrison, and had, like other battalions in the garrison, its own signal section. It was now decided to establish a sig-nalling school at Fort Southwick at which all signallers of the garrison could be trained together. The school was divided into four companies, of one of which I was to be in charge. Reluctantly Daphne left Sandown and the regiment, and took a cottage at Portchester. I should have a two-mile walk up to the Fort every morning at

7.30, and a two-mile walk down every evening which would get me home at 5.30. Then, after tea, we could begin Irene's play.

Unfortunately the play which I had in my mind offered no possible part to her. I tried to forget about it and think of something else. It was no good; the only way to forget it was to write it. So I wrote (or, more accurately, dictated to my collaborator) a play called *The Lucky One*. The Theatre Guild did it in New York some years later, but it has never been put on for a run in London. I used to think it was my best play; well, I suppose it was once; but now I see that I just wasted a good idea. I wish I hadn't thought of it so soon.

Again I tried to write 'Irene's play,' but again I thought of something else first. The result was a one-act play called *The Boy Comes Home*. We enjoyed writing it, but there seemed to be nothing much to do with it. If only I could write the play which Boucicault wanted. But Daphne was becoming concerned about my health; I got tired so easily. Well, it was a tiring life, getting up at 6.30, walking two miles up hill, running a company for eight hours (which included teaching ploughboys the theory of induced currents), walking two more miles and then doing my ordinary work of writing for another five hours. And I knew the cure for it. I wanted to go to sleep for a whole year.

However, she begged me to see the M.O. at the Fort. I saw him, and he sent me down to the Military Hospital at Cosham, I was kept there for a night, thumped all over in the morning, and passed on to the Convalescent Hospital at Osborne for three weeks.

And there I really did rest. Life at Osborne seemed to me then, and has seemed so at times since, the ideal life. One would not expect Osborne House to be beautiful; it was not; but the surroundings are perfect. There was a nine-hole golf course running down to the Solent, there were croquet lawns, there was an excellent library of light novels. Our duty was to see the M.O. in charge of our section on every other morning. The food was incomparably better than anything we had had lately. We ate, slept, read, played games gently, and wished it could go on for ever. I know of nothing which gives one so complete a feeling of luxurious rest as settling down to a novel in a deck-chair immediately after breakfast, with the knowledge that one is safe from the reproaches of conscience. And if this were the day when Daphne was coming over to tea, then life had at the moment no more to offer.

I managed to get another three weeks' sick leave after I left Osborne, and then we returned to Portchester. But the war had been going on in our absence. The battalion was now under orders for Dover, which took it out of the Portsmouth Garrison and removed its signallers from Fort Southwick. There was a chance that I might ultimately get a job in the War Office; in any case Daphne would not come to Dover with me, where there were nightly air-raids. If we were to write Irene's play together, we must write it in the next week. On Thursday at 5.30 I settled into a deck-chair in our little garden, saying, 'I shall now think of something.' By dinner-time I was ready. At 8.30 I began to dictate *Belinda*, and by Tuesday evening it was finished. My collaborator took charge of it while I went off to Dover. A week later I got a telegram from Boucicault: 'I like the play, my wife likes the part, I would like to do it.'

5

Belinda came on in April 1918. It synchronized with the most desperate moments of the war, it lived through

the worst air-raid, and it died gamely nine weeks later.
In the circumstances it was difficult to regard its ill-
fortune as a matter of much importance. I was now in
the War Office, wore the green tabs of Intelligence and
wrote (horrible word) 'propaganda.' I had been marked
for Home Service by a succession of medical boards, with
the recommendation of 'sedentary work.' If there is any
work more sedentary than writing I do not know it;
moreover, by a happy accident, it was the only work for
which I was mentally fit. I had a room to myself and
wrote pretty much what I liked. If it were not 'patriotic'
enough, or neglected to point the moral with sufficient
hardihood, then the Major supplied the operative words
in green pencil.

Arthur Bourchier saw *Belinda* and wrote to ask if I
had written anything which might suit him. I said 'No,'
but he insisted on reading *The Lucky One* and *The Boy
Comes Home*. He sent back the first, and passed on the
second to Owen Nares. Nares came to dinner, play in
hand, our first actor guest. He wanted to do it at the
Victoria Palace as a music-hall turn, but his time was
strictly limited to twenty-three minutes, and this would
play for twenty-seven. He suggested cuts: four minutes:
four pages: I didn't want to cut, and I knew that the
Victoria Palace would be too big for it. As it happened,
Nigel Playfair had just arranged to put it on at a charity
matinée. Somehow I felt that if it were played once in a
reasonably sized theatre, I should be content. So, having
been told by my agent that I couldn't expect more than
five guineas a week for it, I wrote to him now to say that
I insisted on fifteen, feeling that if Nares turned it down,
so much the better. I showed the letter to my collaborator, who said indignantly: 'Fifteen! You ought to have
twenty'; so I added, not really meaning it, 'P.S. On
second thoughts twenty.' My agent took it seriously,

asked twenty and got it. After Nares had played it at the Victoria Palace, it was incorporated in a revue at the Palace. In the spring Godfrey Tearle toured the provincial music-halls with it. After which all the boys in the amateur world came home with it . . . and continue so to come.

AUTHOR

Chapter Fourteen

1

THE war would be over any day now—what was I going to do? Duty (I thought) called me back to *Punch;* inclination to this new life in the theatre. I was certainly not established in the theatre; £311 from *Belinda* was the most I had made out of a play. Could I be sure of a living as a dramatist? Wasn't I in a way pledged to *Punch,* which for the first three years of the war had paid me half my assistant-editor's salary? The answer to the first question was 'No,' to the second 'Yes.' I would go back to *Punch* for three years; then I should feel free. And by that time I hoped to have proved that I could live on the theatre.

But on Armistice Day I forgot all this. The war was over and I was going back to my old job. Once more I should sit in that dusty little office sorting out good jokes from bad; once more have fun with the paragraphs, be (oh so happily) bored at the Wednesday dinners; once more (on Thursdays) take Daphne with me as unofficial secretary to clear up the week's arrears of work. She loved it; I loved it; and I had promised her to be Editor one day. I was going back.

Demobilization, we were told, would be quicker if we could produce a letter from our employers to say how eagerly they longed for us to return to them. I hurried round to the *Punch* office for my letter. I burst in on Owen Seaman. He looked up, surprised. 'Hallo?' he said. 'I've come back,' I announced dramatically.

271

AUTOBIOGRAPHY

It sometimes happens that a man, being engaged to marry one girl, falls in love with another. Shall he, can he, break his plighted word to Isobel? No, the Montmorencies never break their plighted words. He has an anguished parting from Norah, the lovely girl he met on the boat; she too will make the great sacrifice; whatever the cost to themselves, Isobel's life must not be wrecked. Manfully he returns to Isobel, is shown into the drawing-room . . . and is told falteringly by the dear girl that in his absence she has found happiness with another. Will he be so brave, so noble as to release her?

And what does he say? He says with the utmost indignation, 'Damn it, she's jilted me!'

So, when I said, 'I've come back,' and Owen, instead of falling on my neck, said coldly, 'Oh!' and when it appeared the Proprietors had neither expected nor wanted me back, being not only very well satisfied with my elderly substitute, but also a little annoyed that I had written plays, not *Punch* articles, in my spare time; when, in short, it became clear that I was free to do whatever I liked, which is what I have always wanted to do, I said bitterly and ungratefully to myself, 'Kicked out!' But I did know that within a few hours I should be delighted.

We were very considerate with each other. Owen's one wish was to serve my interests, mine to serve *Punch*. Of course (he said) my place was open to me, there was no question of that, but it seemed a pity that I should waste my time on the mechanical work of sub-editing when I could write such brilliant plays. Of course (I said) I should like to devote myself exclusively to playwriting, but after *Punch's* generosity to me I could not possibly put the paper to any inconvenience. Was he sure—very politely he made it clear that he was. My only doubt, I said—and then stupidly murmured something about

Daphne's ambition for the future. This took him off his guard, and it was not until the third attempt that he found words which made it seem rather a compliment that, whatever happened, I should never be Editor. That settled it. I arranged to send in my resignation to the Proprietors.

'That doesn't mean from the Table, of course,' he said. 'You'll still be on the staff and write every week.'

But that was what I wouldn't do. What I wanted was just the opposite: the mechanical work and the salary, coupled with a free mind for the theatre.

'I'll think about it,' I said, 'and let the Proprietors know.' But I had no doubts. I wrote and resigned from the Table. They were very nice about it. They told me to drop in to dinner when I liked, and drop in to the pages of *Punch* when I liked. For six months or so I dropped in occasionally. Then I dropped out.

It happened that we were dining that night with W. L. George and his wife. Daphne was dressing when I got back and in no mood for conversation. It was not until we were in the taxi that I told her that I was not going back to *Punch*. She burst into tears. She was still crying quietly to herself when I paid off the taxi. We walked round the dark and silent square, beneath a rain-laden sky which threatened to fall at any moment, while she tried to get control of herself. I promised her that we shouldn't starve, I promised to make a success of the theatre. It was a little like telling a woman whose loved cottage has been burnt down that you will build a more expensive one on the ruins. It doesn't really comfort her at the time.

There was one other guest at the Georges', and we didn't need an introduction to tell us that it was beautiful Lillah McCarthy. When the five of us sat round the dinner-table the talk was general. Naturally I had Miss

McCarthy on one side of me. We left a few minutes after her, and caught her up again at High Street Station. We travelled to Sloane Square together.

Three days later I had a letter from her. She said that she was just starting in management, and that Barrie had suggested that she should ask me for a play. Would I have tea with her on Tuesday to discuss it?

We were very much excited about this. It seemed possible that we shouldn't starve after all.

'Why didn't she ask you the other night?' wondered my collaborator.

'Not in front of the Georges.'

'Well, when we were alone afterwards.'

'Not with the train making all that row.'

Daphne agreed that you couldn't shout at a man across an Underground carriage, 'Will you write me a play?'

'Besides,' I said, 'she probably hadn't seen Barrie then.'

'Yes, that's possible.'

'Also it's more than possible that she never heard my name.'

'Oh, I think she knew who you were. It must have come out somehow.'

'If you want a bet, I'll bet she didn't.'

'All right, I bet she did.'

'I'll ask her on Tuesday, and let you know.'

'Rather fun if she didn't. *Think* of her surprise when she sees you!'

This was Friday morning. We had all been given six weeks' leave from the War Office, after which we had to rejoin our regiments for demobilization. I retired to my room to think of a play for Lillah McCarthy. It was wonderful to be thinking in the morning again. By Tuesday afternoon I had written the first act of a comedy which was to be called *Mr Pim Passes By*. I could now definitely promise Miss McCarthy a play. I went round to tea with her, full of hope.

She was charming. I told her about the play, and she asked me to send it to her manager, A. E. Drinkwater, as soon as it was finished. We talked, we had tea. . . .

I said good-bye.

She said how delightful it had been to meet me.

I said: 'Well, of course, we did meet last Tuesday.'

She said: 'Oh—did we?'

Since then I have never expected my name or my face to mean anything to anybody. It saves a lot of anxiety.

2

Demobilization was not difficult. I rejoined the regiment at Crowborough, where, as a sedentary soldier, I not only lived comfortably at the Beacon Hotel, but found a comfortable stool in the demobilization office from which I could call attention to the hard case of Lieut. A. A. Milne. In little more than a week I was in respectable clothes again.

Mr Pim Passes By was finished and under consideration by Drinkwater. A children's play, *Make Believe,* had opened Nigel Playfair's management of the Lyric, Hammersmith. In the summer, I had written a play called *The Great Broxopp* which was now being sent round. The future of the English theatre seemed assured, but our own present needs demanded some sort of regular weekly income. I had re-established relations with *The Sphere*—but was six guineas a week enough? Luckily at this moment Lord Lee bought *The Outlook,* engaged E. V. Lucas as a contributor, and asked him to suggest a dramatic critic. He suggested me; and I, when asked, suggested six guineas a week again. It seemed a nice reasonable sum.

Lee had not yet presented Chequers to the nation but lived there himself, and to Chequers my collaborator and I went for a week-end. Just what Daphne was doing there I don't know; we were supposed to be discussing the opening number of *The Outlook*, but I took a verbal 'you' as plural, and said that 'we' should be delighted to come. If now I happen to mention that I once spent a week-end at Chequers and anybody assumes that a Prime Minister was my host, no doubt it adds to the interest of the conversation.

I was dramatic critic of *The Outlook* for six weeks before I discovered that the position was impossible. One could not damn a manager's play and then send him a play of one's own; still less could one praise it and then send him a play of one's own; least of all could one tell other dramatists how to write plays when one's own imperfect plays were available for comparison. So I resigned —I was getting good at this—but still wrote occasional essays for the paper.

In the intervals I wrote a detective-story. I had read most of those which had been written, admired their ingenuity, but didn't like their English. Their characters (in as far as they existed as characters, which was anæmically) continually 'effected egresses,' instead of 'going out.' The detective 'carefully selected' a cigarette from his case (something which no human being has ever done) before telling his colleague what his impressions were when he first had 'cognizance' of the affair. I wondered if I could write a detective-story about real people in real English. I thought it would be 'fun to try,' my only reason for writing anything. The result would have passed unnoticed in these days when so many good writers are writing so many good detective-stories, but in those days there was not so much competition, and *The Red House Mystery* had a surprising success. One eager American editor came over to London and made a contract giving me £2,000 for the serial rights of my next one. I still have that contract somewhere, whether valid now or not I cannot say, for my 'next one' was a book of children's verses, and subsequent works have made as little claim on his bank roll. Sometimes I think it would be fun to try again . . . and then there seem to be so many other things to try. As it might be, autobiography.

3

Daphne was in a nursing home in May. One afternoon I found Irene with her. Dot Boucicault had announced that he wouldn't put a play on in London until theatre rents had gone down. In the autumn they were having a season at Manchester.

'Isn't it about time you wrote me another one?' said Irene.

'Dot said he wasn't going to——'

'Well, if we had the right play—one can always change one's mind.'

'Would he really like to read one?'

'Of course he would. Part for me?'

'Yes.'

'Better than Belinda?'

'I hope so. You'll see.'

Drinkwater had been unable to make up his mind about *Mr Pim Passes By*. A week ago I had made it up for him. That evening I sent the play to Boucicault. He signed an agreement which gave him the right to try it out for a week in Manchester. On January 4th, 1920, it came to London.

I have attended many first nights in the miserable *rôle* of author, but never one like that. The house was so delighted to see its loved and lovely Irene back again that in sheer happiness it extended its favour to the play. Calls went on continuously, there were continuous cries for 'Speech!'—the author was pushed on and pushed off; and still Dot and Irene were bowing. As I sat in the wings among the stage-hands wondering if it were true, a very weary voice behind me said: ' 'Ere, go on and give 'em a speech, guv'nor, and let's all get 'ome.' So that was all it was. I imagined him when he got home.

'Late to-night, Bill.'

'Yus, we 'ad a success.'

And forty million people in England equally stolid. However, that didn't prevent us from enjoying it.

4

In August of that year my collaborator produced a more personal work. We had intended to call it *Rosemary*, but decided later that *Billy* would be more suitable. However, as you can't be christened William—at least, we didn't see why anybody should—we had to think of two other names, two initials being necessary to ensure him any sort of copyright in a cognomen as often plagiarized as Milne. One of us thought of Robin, the other of Christopher; names wasted on him who called himself Billy Moon as soon as he could talk, and has been Moon to his family and friends ever since. I mention this because it explains why the publicity which came to be attached to 'Christopher Robin' never seemed to affect us personally, but to concern either a character in a book or a horse which we hoped at one time would win the Derby.

When he was three, we took a house in North Wales for August with the Nigel Playfairs. It rained continuously. In the one living-room every morning there were assembled Five Playfairs, Three Milnes, Grace Lovat-Fraser, Joan Pitt-Chatham, Frederic Austin, and a selection of people to whom Nigel had issued casual invitations in London before starting north for what he supposed to be his Welsh castle. In a week I was screaming with agoraphobia. Somehow I must escape. I pleaded urgent inspiration, took a pencil and an exercise-book and escaped to the summer-house. It contained a chair and a table. I sat down on the chair, put my exercise-book on the table, and gazed ecstatically at a wall of mist which might have been hiding Snowdon or the Serpentine for all I saw or cared. I was alone. . . .

But sooner or later I should be asked what I was writing. What was I writing?

About six months earlier, while at work on a play, I had wasted a morning in writing a poem called 'Vespers.' I gave it to Daphne, as one might give a photograph or a valentine, telling her that if she liked to get it published anywhere she could stick to the money. She sent it to Frank Crowninshield of *Vanity Fair* (N.Y.) and got fifty dollars. Later she lent it to me for the Queen's Doll's House Library, and later still collected one-forty-fourth of all the royalties of *When we Were Very Young*, together with her share of various musical and subsidiary rights. It turned out to be the most expensive present I had ever given her. A few months after this, Rose Fyleman was starting a magazine for children. She asked me, I have no idea why, to write some verses for it. I said that I didn't and couldn't, it wasn't in my line. As soon as I had posted my letter, I did what I always do after refusing to write anything: wondered how I would have written it if I hadn't refused. One might, for instance, have written:

There once was a Dormouse who lived in a bed
Of delphiniums (blue) and geraniums (red),
And all the day long he'd a wonderful view
Of geraniums (red) and delphiniums (blue).

After another wasted morning I wrote to Miss Fyleman to say that perhaps after all I might write her some verses. A poem called *The Dormouse and the Doctor* was the result. It was illustrated by Harry Rountree; proofs had come to me in Wales; and with them came letters from both illustrator and editor saying: 'Why don't you write a whole book of verses like these?'

So there I was with an exercise-book and a pencil, and a fixed determination not to leave the heavenly solitude of that summer-house until it stopped raining . . . and there in London were two people telling me what to write . . . and there on the other side of the lawn was a child with whom I had lived for three years . . . and here within me were unforgettable memories of my own childhood . . . what was I writing? A child's book of verses obviously. Not a whole book, of course; but to write a few would be fun—until I was tired of it. Besides, my pencil had an india-rubber at the back; just the thing for poetry.

I had eleven wet days in that summer-house and wrote eleven sets of verses. Then we went back to London. A little apologetically: feeling that this wasn't really work: feeling that a man of stronger character would be writing that detective-story and making £2,000 for the family: a little as if I were slipping off to Lord's in the morning, or lying in a deck-chair at Osborne reading a novel, I went on writing verses. By the end of the year I had written enough for a book.

It was only after the book was in the publisher's hands that Owen Seaman heard about it. Probably Lucas, then chairman of Methuens, had mentioned it casually. Owen asked if *Punch* could print some of it, and I told him, reluctantly enough, that he could use what he liked, for I feared that as a 'reprint from *Punch*' it might not get the attention which would be given to a new book. However, the publication of some of the verses had two good results; it confirmed my opinion that Shepard was the right illustrator for the book, and, with the first appearance of *The King's Breakfast*, gave the publishers an idea of its ultimate reception. This was enthusiastic beyond all imagining, both in England and America. In the ten years before it went into a cheap edition half a million copies were sold.

It is inevitable that a book which has had very large sales should become an object of derision to critics and columnists. We all write books, we all want money; we who write want money from our books. If we fail to get money, we are not so humble, nor so foolish, as to admit that we have failed in our object. Our object, we maintain, was artistic success. It is easy to convince ourselves that the financial failure of the book is no proof of its artistic failure; and it is a short step from there to affirm that artistic success is, in fact, incompatible with financial success. It must be so: for how else could we be the artists we are and remain in our first editions? If any other artist goes into twenty editions, then he is a traitor to the cause, and we shall hasten to say that he is not one of Us.

All this is commonplace. What has been particularly irritating about the sales of the Christopher Robin books (even though the irritation has produced no more intimidating retort than the writing of the name 'Kwistopher Wobin') is that the books were written for children. When, for instance, Dorothy Parker, as 'Constant Reader' in *The New Yorker*, delights the sophisticated by announcing that at page 5 of *The House of Pooh Corner* 'Tonstant Weader fwowed up' (*sic*, if I may), she leaves the book, oddly enough, much where it was. However greatly indebted to Mrs Parker, no Alderney, at the approach of the milkmaid, thinks 'I hope this lot will turn out to be gin,' no writer of children's books says gaily to his publisher, 'Don't bother about the children, Mrs Parker will love it.' As an artist one might genuinely prefer that one's novel should be praised by a single critic, whose opinion one valued, rather than be bought by 'the mob'; but there is no artistic reward for a book written for children other than the knowledge that they enjoy it. For once, and how one hates to think it, *vox populi, vox Dei*. The position can only be saved by asserting that it isn't the genuine voice of the people. It is the illiterate mothers who speak. Even so, it might be held that mothers have their own particular qualifications for speaking.

In fact I know that a great many children did, and do, like *When we Were Very Young*. I think that such merit as attaches to the verses for this (as distinct from the illustrations to which the book is so obviously indebted) was won by taking pains: more pains, perhaps, than is usual. Whatever else they lack, the verses are technically good. The practice of no form of writing demands such a height of technical perfection as the writing of light verse in the Calverley and *Punch* tradition. *When we Were Very Young* is not the work of a poet becoming playful, nor of a lover of children expressing his love, nor of a prose-writer knocking together a few jingles for the little ones, it is the work of a light-verse writer taking his job seriously even though he is taking it into the nursery. It seems that the nursery, more than any other room in the house, likes to be approached seriously.

Whether I have added to technique that 'wonderful insight into a child's mind' of which publishers' advertisements talk so airily, I wouldn't know. I am not inordinately fond of or interested in children; their appeal to me is a physical appeal such as the young of other animals make. I have never felt in the least sentimental about them, or no more sentimental than one becomes for a moment over a puppy or a kitten. In as far as I understand their minds the understanding is based on the observation, casual enough and mostly unconscious, which I give to people generally: on memories of my own childhood: and on the imagination which every writer must bring to memory and observation. Again to avoid paraphrasing myself I shall quote here from a Preface to Parents, which I wrote for a particular edition of the verses.

In real life very young children have an artless beauty, an innocent grace, an unstudied abandon of movement, which, taken together, make an appeal to our emotions similar in kind to that made by any other young and artless creatures: kittens, puppies, lambs: but greater in degree, for the reason that the beauty of childhood seems in some way to transcend the body. Heaven, that is, does really appear to lie about the child in its infancy, as it does not lie about even the most attractive kitten. But with this outstanding physical quality there is a natural lack of moral quality, which expresses itself, as Nature always insists on expressing herself, in an egotism entirely ruthless.

Now it seems to me that the writer who is trying to put a child upon paper must keep these two outstanding facts about children before him, and endeavour to preserve his sense of proportion. A sentimental painter might leave out the wart on Cromwell's face; but the biographer who, priding himself on his realism, calls attention to the wart every time he mentions the face, is just as falsely sentimental, since any small blemish on the face of one we know soon passes unnoticed. A pen-picture of a child which showed it as loving, grateful and full of thought for others would be false to the truth; but equally false would be a picture which insisted on the brutal egotism of the child, and ignored the physical beauty which softens it. Equally false and equally sentimental, for sentimentality is merely an appeal to emotions not warranted by the facts.

AUTOBIOGRAPHY

To avoid equally these two sentimentalities is the difficulty in front of the writer. It is easy (at least, I suppose it is easy, if one is a painter) to paint a beautiful child, but it is not easy to describe one. Any attempt to do so will become either conventional or indescriptive. But it is possible to give what one might call 'an air of charm,' particularly when writing in verse, to any account of a child's activities, and it seems to me that this 'charm,' if one can convey it, should have as much chance in the printed page as in real life of hiding from the sentimentalist the uncharming part of a child's nature: the egotism and the heartlessness.

I shall now expose my own egotism by giving one or two examples of how I have tried to do this.

The mother of a little boy of three has disappeared, and is never seen again. The child's reaction to the total loss of his mother is given in these lines:

> *James James*
> *Morrison Morrison*
> (*Commonly known as Jim*)
> *Told his*
> *Other relations*
> *Not to go blaming* him.

And that is all. It is the truth about a child: children are, indeed, as heartless as that: but only in one sense have I made a song about it.

In *Buckingham Palace* Christopher Robin is taken by his nurse to see the changing of the guard. She tells him about the soldiers and the Palace and the King, and at the end of it all he has only one question to ask: 'Do you think the King knows all about Me?' Could egotism be more gross? If you were to take an author up to your most admired friend—as it might be Lindbergh—and on the way were to whisper to him of all the wonderful things your hero had done, would you not be disgusted if his only remark were, 'Do you think Lindbergh knows all about Me?' But since a child of three can say these things, and be innocent and charming enough to make them sound innocent and charming, so then, in the poem, if a true picture is to be given, the egotism must be there for the unsentimental to find, but there must also be charm enough to give it at least a surface covering.

Finally, let me refer to the poem which has been more sentimentalized over than any other in the book: *Vespers*. Well, if mothers and aunts and hard-headed reviewers have been sentimental over it, I am glad; for the spectacle in real life of a child of three at its prayers is one over which thousands have been sentimental. It is indeed calculated to bring a lump to the throat. But, even so, one must tell the truth about the matter. Not 'God bless mummy, because I love her so', but 'God bless Mummy, I know that's right'; not 'God bless Daddy, because he buys me food and clothes,' but 'God bless Daddy, I quite forgot'; not even the egotism of 'God bless Me, because I'm the most important person in the house,' but the super-egotism of feeling so impregnable that the blessing of this mysterious god for Oneself is the very last thing for which it would seem necessary to ask. And since this is the Truth about a Child, let us get all these things into the poem, and the further truth that prayer means nothing to a child of three, whose thoughts are engaged with other, more exciting matters; but since the Truth about a Child is also that, fresh from its bath, newly powdered and curled, it is a lovely thing, God wot, why then, let us try, however inadequately, to get at least a hint of this upon paper, so that, if possible, the reader, no less than the spectator, may feel that Beauty is hovering. . . . For some day we may be describing a Scientist Shaving and calling it *Matins,* and then there will be no need to wait upon Beauty.

5

Winnie-the-Pooh was written two years later, and was followed by a second book of verses and, in 1928, *The House at Pooh Corner*. The animals in the stories came for the most part from the nursery. My collaborator had already given them individual voices, their owner by constant affection had given them the twist in their features which denoted character, and Shepard drew them, as one might say, from the living model. They were what they are for anyone to see; I described rather than invented them. Only Rabbit and Owl were my own unaided work. These books also became popular. One day when Daphne went up to the nursery, Pooh was missing from the dinner-table which he always graced. She asked where he was. 'Behind the ottoman,' replied his owner coldly. 'Face downwards. He said he didn't like *When we Were Very Young.*' Pooh's jealousy was natural. He could never quite catch up with the verses.

It is easier in England to make a reputation than to lose one. I wrote four 'Children's books,' containing altogether, I suppose, 70,000 words—the number of words in the average-length novel. Having said good-bye to all that in 70,000 words, knowing that as far as I was concerned the mode was outmoded, I gave up writing children's books. I wanted to escape from them as I had once wanted to escape from *Punch;* as I have always wanted to escape. In vain. England expects the writer, like the cobbler, to stick to his last. As Arnold Bennett pointed out: if you begin painting policemen you must go on painting policemen, for then the public knows the answer —Policemen. If you stop painting policemen in order to paint windmills, criticism remains so overpoweringly policeman-conscious that even a windmill is seen as something with arms out, obviously directing the traffic. These last ten years in which I have been writing plays, novels and invocations against war are littered with affiliation orders on behalf of all the 'juveniles' born so lovingly and with such complete absence of labour into the book-world. If I didn't put my name to them, 'that,' as the King of Hearts said, 'only makes the matter worse.' It proves that my spiritual home is still the nursery, that I am still thinking of policemen. As a discerning critic pointed out: the hero of my latest play, God help it, was 'just Christopher Robin grown up.' So that even when I stop writing about children, I still insist on writing about people who were children once. What an obsession with me children are become!

Chapter Fifteen

1

IT HAS been my good fortune as a writer that what I have wanted to write has for the most part proved to be saleable. It has been my misfortune as a business man that, when it has proved to be extremely saleable, then I have not wanted to write it any more. It has been my good fortune as a husband that I have been encouraged to be a writer, not a business man.

I like writing, by which I mean that I like putting down certain words in a certain order. Because it gives me no pleasure when I am writing a play just to put down 'Exit Smith,' and less than no pleasure to put down, as I read the other day, 'They exit together,' I gratify myself by taking as much time and trouble over stage directions which may never be seen as I should over an inscription in stone on an inescapable monument. This is due, not entirely to that pride or self love which makes a woman wear pretty knickers even if nobody is going to discover them, but to a laziness which at times approximates to torpor. I hate writing; by which I mean that I hate the business of putting down words with a pen. Unless I can get some sort of 'kick' out of them I can hardly bring myself to the drudgery of inking them in. To spend two days in writing a difficult letter to *The Times* is not work but continuous excitement; to spend five minutes regretting my inability to give the prizes away at St Etheldreda's is to live again through all the wasted hours in form and lecture-room.

AUTHOR

When I read one of those 8/6 novels whose weight well qualifies them for a permanent place in literature, I never find myself thinking 'How boring this is to read,' but always 'How boring this must have been to write.' This is no criticism of the book either as a work of art or as a work of interest. I doubt if any 8/6 novel could be as dull as parts of *Paradise Lost*, but the author of *Paradise Lost* in his most uninspired moments is leading an exciting life. So is the author of what you have thought the most unhumorous 'humorous book'; for he, plainly, was amused. From time to time I feel that the writer of the 8/6 novel which I am reading was neither amused nor interested, and I envy him the staying-power which kept his pen at work.

In the beginning of that abortive revue which I designed for the Palace Theatre I wrote what I thought of as a lyric, to be sung by the comedian of the company. It was, in fact, a set of light verses, as clever as I could make them. Sir Alfred Butt, profoundly shocked, pointed out that there was a laugh in every line. I agreed complacently, 'But you can only have a laugh in the *last* line of a verse,' he protested. I asked why. He explained, quite convincingly, why a song went backwards and forwards across the footlights more effectively this way; and I explained, quite unconvincingly, why I was unable to write three lines which were just any old words, in order to introduce one line which was worth writing. This was about the moment when we began to say good-bye to each other. Probably I thought that I was being an artist, but I know now that I was just being lazy.

It is, no doubt, this laziness which has made me try so many different forms of writing.

2

The most exciting form of writing is the writing of plays. There is, however, this to be said against it: that, when once the play is written, the author is never really happy again until it has been taken off. One writes a book; a publisher is waiting for it; a date of publication is fixed for it. The book will be printed just as one wrote it, exact to the last comma. Whether criticism blows fair or foul, the book remains in being; it is there for anyone to read.

One writes a play; no manager is waiting for it; the play may be sold this year, next year, sometime, never. Being bought, it may be produced this year, next year, sometime, never. If produced, it will not be produced, exact to the last eyebrow, as the author saw it, for the reason that its characters live in the author's imagination, and that, even if they have autotypes in real life, it is extremely unlikely that these will be actors and actresses by profession, available for this production. Finally, when some version of the play has been launched, a puff of foul criticism, a week of fog, a few days of crisis, a 'bus strike, the sudden indisposition of the leading man may be enough to sink it for ever. Even if the play runs, every visit to it brings to the author the realization that this is not the play which he had thought he was writing. Oh, well—next time perhaps. The play comes off, and he loses himself happily in a world of his own imagination, peopled by characters for whom no alien flesh and blood need be sought; he writes a novel.

I take down a novel at random from my shelves; I open it at random. I read this:

The page followed him in silence into the Abbot's house, where, stepping into the first apartment which he found open, he commanded one of his attendants to let his brother, Master Edward Glendinning, know that he desired to speak with him.

It may be Scott's fault rather than mine that at first I supposed it was the page who was brother to Master Edward. If you felt that way too, then we can write: 'Followed by the silent page he entered the Abbot's house, where . . . ' and all will now be clear. Perhaps my thesis will also be clear, which is this: that a novel continuously demands from the author paragraphs, sometimes whole pages, in whose composition no delight can be taken. There is no kick whatever to be got out of writing: 'Stepping into the first apartment which he found open, he commanded one of his attendants to let his brother, Master Edward Glendinning, know that he desired to speak with him.' Wodehouse, desiring to convey the same scene, might have written: 'Seeping into the first apartment,' and by so writing would have chosen his word and have given expression to his art. But Scott could do nothing but stud the words down his pen and look forward to Sir Halbert Glendinning's next speech. ('Thou mayest have remarked, stripling, that I have but seldom distinguished thee by much notice. . . .') Whatever the words now, they are words which must be sought for: particular words to suit the occasion, the character of the speaker, and the state of the person addressed. However ill-chosen, their choosing keeps the writer at full stretch. He gets value for his labour.

For one who insists on full value a play is the thing. So strongly do I feel this that, when I write a play, I write all the dialogue first, without a single stage direction and then reluctantly turn novelist. There is a certain amount of fun to be got from the description of the characters, from the hints at their emotions which a dramatist must give; but it is dreary work to record the position of a window or a fireplace, and the number of telephones on a desk. With the opening scene of Act II bubbling over in one's mind one cannot impede oneself with upholstery. 'Stepping into the first apartment which I find open,' I plunge into dialogue. I see the room as I write . . . and if I must, I will tell you about it afterwards.

I said just now that dialogue in a novel had to suit the occasion, the character of the speaker, and the state of the person addressed. In playwriting it offers an additional stimulus to the author: it has also to suit the audience. Stage-craft, of which we hear so much, is merely the art of making things easy for the audience. Realistic dialogue makes things difficult for an audience, for the reason that it is both boring and allusive. Here is a slice of life.

> *Husband:* Well, what do you think?
> *Wife:* I don't know. (*Thinks for a minute.*)
> *Husband:* It's for you to say.
> *Wife:* I know. (*After a long pause.*) There's Jane.
>
> *Colonel in third row of stalls strikes match to see who Jane is. She isn't in the programme. Who the devil is Jane? He never knows.*)
>
> *Husband:* You mean the Ipswich business?
> *Wife:* Yes. (*Telephone bell rings.*) That's probably Arthur.
>
> (*Clergyman in fifth row of stalls strikes match to see who Arthur is. He's not in the programme either.*)
>
> *Husband:* Monday. Much more likely to be Anne.
> *Wife:* Not now.
> *Husband:* Well, you anyway.
> *Wife:* Oh, all right. (*Exit for ten minutes while Husband reads paper.*)
> *Husband (as she comes back):* Anne?

Wife (in a voice): 'Give my love to the dear boy.'
Husband: 'No darling, *not* like chickens.'
Wife: Of course. What are you doing on Friday?
Husband: Trevors. Why? *(He sneezes.)* Damn, I haven't got a handkerchief. *(He gets up. At the door he says:)* Oh, by the way, I'd better ring Morrison. *(Exit. Wife writes a letter and then picks up paper. Husband returns.)*

Wife (from paper): Myrtle's engaged! Fancy!
Husband: Yes, I meant to have told you. I saw John at the club.

> *(Two old gentlemen strike matches.)*

Wife: Who is he?
Husband: Bar, I think. Listen, darling, we *must* decide.
Wife: It's difficult. *(After a long pause.)* Oh, well, let's——

> *(Enter Maid.)*

Maid: There's a policeman downstairs, sir, wants to see you.
Husband: Oh Lord! *(He goes out for five minutes while the audience waits breathlessly. Now the drama is moving. . . . He returns.)*
Wife: Car?
Husband: Some fool turned the lights off. Let's see, *what* were we talking about? Damn, I left my pipe downstairs.

> *(He goes out.)*
> *(And if the audience goes out too, who shall blame it?)*

That is how real life is lived. It is clear that natural behaviour, natural dialogue, must be dressed up before it can recommend itself to an audience. The only truth which is demanded from the dramatist is truth to character. Subject to this truth he is required to present in the refracting mirror of the stage such distortion of real life as will best reflect his meaning. Remembering that the playgoer, unlike the reader, can never turn back, one sees that playwriting becomes an exciting sort of game, in which one has to defeat the apathy, the preconceptions and the defective memory of one's antagonist. It may interest my reader in the upper circle if I illustrate with a play of my own some of the fun and the dangers of this game.

3

A play can be based upon Theme, Story or Character. If you base it upon a theme, then you must invent a story which will illustrate the theme; if you base it upon a character, then you must invent a story which will exhibit the character. The story is necessary in any case, and will be the main interest for many of the audience, but it will not necessarily be the main interest for the author.

The Truth About Blayds was based upon a theme. It was not a Story of Literary Life, nor a Study of a Literary Fraud. My interest in it was the interest which I took in this problem: What happens in a religious community when its god is discovered to be a false god? To work out this problem I could choose any community, any god, convenient to me. A tribal god on an island, a national hero among his countrymen, a churchwarden in a chapel —if the devastating truth were known, who would still be faithful, who unfaithful? And faithful to what? The Truth or the God? I decided to illustrate the theme with the story of a great poet; showing the reactions of his family to a death-bed confession that he had lived on the work of a long-dead contemporary, in his lifetime unknown, unpublished.

I made the family as representative of a religious community as I could. The High Priest, secretary, son-in-law

and official biographer to Blayds: his wife, taking her
beliefs at secondhand from the priest: her sister, the true
believer who had sacrificed everything for the Faith: the
detached critic, old suitor of the sister's, who accepted
intellectually rather than spiritually: the grandchildren,
dragged reluctantly to church, scoffing, unbelieving. One
knew them all, and it was interesting to watch their characters come out in the fierce light which beat upon the
dead Blayds, the self-confessed fraud to whom willingly or
unwillingly they had given their lives. It was interesting,
that is, to me; but it could only be interesting to the audience if it believed as completely as I did in the Blayds
legend. It would never do if the audience were saying to
itself all through the discussion: 'But how could anyone
have been taken in? Who could have thought for a
moment that he was a great poet?'

Blayds, then, must be seen and believed in: authen-
tically a Great Man.

Now nothing is so difficult to put on the stage as a
Great Man; and of all great men the most difficult to
project across the footlights is the literary genius. For it
is obvious that a character in a play can never be wiser or
wittier than the author of the play. The author may tell
himself that in real life no genius is uniformly wise or
witty: that the great writers whom he himself has met
have shown nothing of their peculiar quality in conversation. This may be so. Barrie told me of an occasion when
he was present at a gathering of young authors all very
busy talking about style. An older man sitting aloof in a
corner, but listening intently, was asked to contribute to
the discussion. He confessed uncomfortably that he had
never thought about the subject: he would rather listen
and learn what he could: he really would have nothing to
say of any value: they all knew much more than he did.
Fearing to be drawn more deeply into the argument,

he added that he had to go now, and slipped out. 'Who *was* that?' Barrie was asked. Barrie, who had brought him there, explained that it was Thomas Hardy. But not a Thomas Hardy who could have made the crossing of the footlights. For stage life, as I have said, can never hope to be real life, but only life which seems real in the unreal conditions of the theatre.

The genius, in fact, must carry immediate conviction of his genius to the audience. Taciturnity is not enough. But if the author be not himself a genius, how is he to create one?

The usual way, the obvious way, what seems at first the only way, is to let the audience get the measure of the hero's greatness through the eyes and by the tongue of the hero-worshippers. Only so, within the limits of the stage, can one be assured that he climbed Everest, swam Niagara, or won the battle of Waterloo. But having been as critic to all those plays in which, for the opening ten minutes, the minor characters acclaim the heroic deeds of the next character on the programme . . . and then in comes to a burst of applause dear old George Alexander, or Tree, or Arthur Bouchier . . . looking just the same, now that they are the Great Chemist, as they did last week when they were the Great Financier . . . I realized how difficult it was to establish genius by this means. It is an instinct with all of us to resent unbridled enthusiasm for the unknown. True, my genius was an old man of ninety, whose hoary locks would disguise his Green Room origins and lend him that aura of immortality which surrounds almost any writer on his ninetieth birthday; I had nothing to fear from the actor if I could give him the entrance to make, the words to say. But how could I?

Well, I began with Royce, the critic, come to present an address of congratulation to the Great Man. All is set for the usual opening; now we shall hear what a Great

Man he is. But Royce is received by Oliver, the sceptical grandson, for whom Old Blayds is merely a nuisance. They are joined by Septima, the granddaughter, and between them, to Royce's great embarrassment, the young people make the whole Blayds theology ridiculous. The audience, inclined at first to sympathize with them, begins to resent their intolerance. From feeling that a genius might well be a nuisance to his grandchildren, it wonders if the grandchildren might not well be a nuisance to him. Marion, their mother, comes in. For her, Blayds is God indeed. Now the audience sees the other side of the picture: the slavish, meaningless hero-worship. Might that not be even more of a nuisance for the genius? If the grandchildren's attitude is wrong-headed, isn't their mother's attitude even more wrong-headed? Which is the more intolerable to Blayds?

To Blayds the genius? Already without realizing it, the audience is beginning to accept the fact that he *is* a genius.

For I have even dared to give a sample of his genius. The fact that Tennyson wrote *The Charge of the Light Brigade* and Wordsworth wrote *The Idiot Boy* lent me confidence, but an audience would not be sharing my recollection of such lesser masterpieces. They would want the genuine thing. Very well, they shall think that they are getting it.

> *Septima, seventh dark daughter,*
> *I saw her once where the black pines troop to the water—*
> *A rock-set river that broke into bottomless pools. . . .*

Unconsciously Royce quotes the hackneyed words in response to the girl's name: they have a swing to them: for a moment they sound like poetry; but before the audience can give its critical attention to them, Septima says casually to Oliver, 'Noll, I'll trouble you,' and holds out her hand for the shilling which passes with the reaction of each new visitor to the introduction. 'Damn it, Royce,' says Oliver, feeling in his pockets, 'I did think *you* would be able to control yourself.' The audience chuckles, in sympathy with any daughter of Tennyson's called Maud, any son of Byron's called Harold, and any granddaughter of Blayds' called Septima.

Now comes the High Priest, the fussy little son-in-law, dictating answers to the letters of congratulation; choosing a select list of callers for the Press: 'three Society, three Artistic and Literary, and two Naval, Military and Political.' The 'health'—where shall they drink the health? In here? The letter from Queen Victoria—shall Royce be allowed to hold it in his hands? Yes, perhaps just for a moment. If this is not the household of a Great Poet, what is it?

Lastly comes Isobel, who sent her lover away twenty years ago, in order to keep alive the spark of the Great Man's genius. For twenty years she has tended him: was it worth it for the great poetry he had written?—was it worth it for the life she has lost? She wonders to Royce, who was her lover all those years ago. The audience wonders too, accepting Isobel's judgement of her father. He was indeed a great poet, and she was right; he was indeed a great poet, but she was wrong.

And so to Blayds. For half-an-hour we have been assuming that he is the last of the Great Victorians: here he comes, magnificently to the eye the last and greatest of the great Victorians. What are to be his opening words? What *can* they be which will do justice to his godhead? If Shakespeare and Aeschylus collaborated to find a speech for him, the audience would think it unworthy. What, then, will they say to a speech of mine? 'We believed in him until you made him speak to us; we should have remembered that no character can be greater than the author.' Still, he has to say something. . . .

He says it . . . and immediately the High Priest whips out a pencil and makes a note of it on his cuff. The audience breaks into laughter, telling itself how infuriating it must be for genius to have its simplest remark recorded. From now on he is free to speak at my own level, and still be a genius.

The health is drunk, the address of welcome is presented, Blayds talks a little of the friends he loved; Tennyson, Whistler, Swinburne, Meredith. Now he is alone with Isobel; the excitement of the occasion has died, and old age rushes in on him. He has something to confess—now! now!—before it is too late. 'Listen, Isobel,' and, as he begins, the curtain comes down. . . .

The curtain goes up; now my play begins. 'What happens in a religious community when its god is discovered to be a false god?' We have established him as a god; now he is to be revealed as a false god; now we shall know. We have got the necessary, but unsignificant, First Act out of the way, now we can command the audience's interest for the development of our theme. . . .

But it was not so. I discovered, when it was too late, that I was fighting a losing battle against that First Act. I had taken too much care over it. I had established the Great Man so firmly that for most of the audience Blayds, the living Blayds, was now the play. The audience had seen him, had believed in him, and wanted to go on seeing him. As consolation, the critics told me that it was the best First Act ever written, but there, for most of them, the play ended. It might be the best First Act ever written, but there, for me, the play began. For me the play was based upon Theme, for the audience upon Character; and the result seemed to be just a Story which had petered out.

4

Writers are often asked if they force themselves to write every day or if they 'wait for inspiration.' It is not suggested (as far as I know) that they say to their wives at breakfast: 'If I am not inspired by eleven o'clock, dear, I shall want the car'; nor that, being in the middle of a novel, they sit with closed eyes at their desks, waiting for assistance before they start the fifth chapter. It is in the details of conception that the layman is interested, not in the pangs of labour, nor the nourishment of the child when born. In short, is the baby ever accidental?

For myself I have now no faith in miraculous conception. I have given it every chance. I have spent many mornings at Lord's hoping that inspiration would come, many days on golf courses; I have even gone to sleep in the afternoon, in case inspiration cared to take me completely by surprise. In vain. The only way in which I can get an 'idea' is to sit at my desk and dredge for it. This is the real labour of authorship, with which no other labour in the world is comparable.

My process of conception is something as follows. After hours, days, weeks of labour (the metaphor is standing on its head, but no matter)—after weeks of anguish, during which I am nobody's friend, the germ of an idea comes into my mind. It is considered and rejected as old, foolish or inadequate. I go on thinking . . . more weeks pass . . . it seems as if I shall never write again. A pity that that idea which I had three weeks ago wasn't any good . . . or wasn't it? No. Hopeless. I go on thinking for another week. . . . What about that idea which I had four weeks ago? . . . N-no, not really good. I go on thinking. . . . Damn it, *what* about that idea which I had five weeks ago? Is it any good or isn't it? And if it isn't, why does it keep coming into my head, pushing out all the much better stories which are knocking for admittance. How can I possibly think, if I'm always thinking of this silly idea about a dead man? And then I throw my hand in. There is only one thing to do: get this impossible nonsense out of the system. It may not be a play at all; good, then I shan't have to bother about it any more. Anyhow, let's begin to write. Hooray, I'm writing again . . . and somehow the idea develops itself.

How do ideas first show their heads? In various strange ways.

Plot 1. It would be rather exciting if a man had died on one suddenly; and the police want to know all about him, and the one thing which can't be given away is the reason why he had come to the house. So Husband and Wife have to make up a story. But they can't. Their brains won't work. And the minutes are going by, and Authority is on its way, and they stand there desperately trying to think against time. Mightn't that be dramatic?

That became *Michael and Mary*.

Plot 2. It's no good. I shall never write again. A pity, because Dennis Eadie has asked for a play, and Harrison wants a play for the Haymarket, and if only I could think of an idea, then I could write a play and Harrison would put it on, and then we should all be at the Haymarket on the first night, waiting for the curtain to go up, and wondering what it was going to be about. . . . Terribly exciting, waiting for the curtain to go up and wondering— an empty stage, a big hall, and then a knocking at the door. Who is it, who is it? A butler—rather a mysterious butler, isn't he?—walks solemnly across the stage and draws the bolts. I always think that that's the most exciting way of beginning a play. Strangers, wayfarers, coming into a strange house. It *is* rather a strange house: is it an hotel? Well, of course, that's what they'd naturally ask, the people at the door. 'Is this an hotel?' And what does the mysterious butler say? Suppose he said, 'A sort of hotel, my lord'? . . .

That became *The Dover Road.*

Plot 3. God moves in a mysterious way his wonders to perform, he plants his footsteps on the sea and rides upon the storm. Grand hymn that, why did it suddenly come into my head? And why did I never see before what an absurd *non-sequitur* it is? I mean the first two lines are all right by themselves, and so are the second two, but they don't mix. In effect he begins by saying that great events from little causes spring, or whatever the line is, and then . . . It's ironic the way things do happen like that. Or the other way about. Little events from great causes. What's the Latin? *Parturiunt montes nascetur ridiculus mus.* Is that right, or shouldn't it be a pentameter? The little gods must have fun, deciding what mountains are to be in labour in order that our ridiculous little wishes shall be gratified. Here's a woman wants to hang a pair of curtains in her house, but her husband won't let her, and the little gods say, 'All right, darling, you *shall* hang your curtains,' and then they get into a corner and chuckle together, and arrange the most frightful shocks for both of them . . . and up go the curtains.

That became a play called *Green Curtains*, until it suddenly occurred to me that a better title would be *Mr Pim Passes By.*

Plot 4. This interval of labour between the end of one 'work' and the beginning of the next, when (as Wells put it picturesquely to Daphne once) I am in the basket again, is not only agony for myself but a tribulation to those who live with me. Indifference to my suffering is as much resented as anxious enquiries as to how I am 'getting on.' Nothing which anybody can say or do is right.

But once there was no interval.

I had just finished *Michael and Mary*. It was summer,

we were at our cottage in Sussex. My collaborator walked into the village with the precious play, to register it to New York where a manager was waiting for it. She was to come back by way of the fields, and I would meet her. I hate the business side of writing, even though my agent spares me most of it; as I walked I wondered unhappily if we should have the usual wrangle about film-rights. The more I thought of it, the more unwarranted did a manager's claim to a share of film-rights seem to me. I would not give way, but I shrank from the arguments and letters which my resistance would entail. . . .

We met at the stile and sat down for a little.

'I've been thinking,' I said, 'about these damned film-rights.'

'Oh, but you always keep those.'

'No, listen, this is a sudden idea. It might be funny. You see, A writes a book and sells it to B who takes half the film-rights, and C dramatizes it and takes half the dramatic rights including the film-rights, and an English manager D buys the play, including the American rights and of course half the film-rights, and sells it to an American manager E, who naturally insists on half the film-rights. And the film-rights are eventually sold for whatever it is. So what?'

'A doesn't get much of it,' said Daphne cautiously. 'Does each one get half of what's left, or how does it work?'

'Well, that's the point. Suppose A had never written anything before, and drew his own agreements up, very carelessly, then each new gangster might get, or assume he was getting, half of the full sum paid by the film company, so that if the company paid £1,000, A would have to hand over £2,000—for his own film-rights.'

'So the more he sells it for, the more he loses.'

'Exactly. It might easily happen. Well then, suppose

the man has insisted on one thing in all his agreements—
let's say he's very keen about films and wants to be sure
that it is done, or isn't done, by an English company, with
or not with, Ronald Colman or somebody—well, anyway,
he remembers suddenly that, according to all the agreements, the final word as to which company shall be allowed to make the film is his. And the play is a terrific
success, and film offers pour in, and the five of them meet
to discuss which offer shall be accepted. And A refuses to
consider any of them. Because he's just had an offer from
his dentist to buy the rights for a penny. And he produces
the letter—and four ha'pennies. . . .'

'What happens?'

'They all sign new agreements taking 10 per cent. each.
He's got them. There you are: in the old *Punch* days
that would have been next Friday's article.'

'Oh, but you mustn't waste it! Couldn't you make a
short story of it?'

'Well, yes, I suppose you could.'

'Promise you will? You will, won't you?'

'I dare say. I must do some short stories some day. They
might be fun.'

'Just *begin* this one after tea, just so as you don't forget
all about it.'

'I'll write the first paragraph, if you like.'

'Will you promise?'

'Absolutely.'

So after tea I wrote the first paragraph. At dinner I
said, 'I think I'll finish that story now I've begun; it won't
take long.'

'Is it going all right?'

'I think so. *I'm* liking it.'

At the end of the week Daphne said, 'How's the story
getting on?'

'Just on five thousand words.'

AUTHOR

'How long is a short story?'

'About five thousand.'

'Then you've practically finished it?'

'Well, actually I haven't begun yet. The plot isn't even in sight. I suppose we shall get there one day.'

'What happens if you don't?'

'Then you've written a novel, I suppose.'

'Is that how novels are written?'

'Don't ask me. I don't know how anybody writes anything. I'm just writing about two people, and having the time of my life. We shall probably know more about it by the end of the year.'

By the end of the year it was quite clearly going to be a novel called *Two People*.

How conceited of the man to refer to his books and plays as if we had read them all and knew what he was talking about! Or the other way round if you like. How modest of him to assume that only those who know all his books and plays could possibly be reading this.

Chapter Sixteen

1

Young Friend: And to what, sir, do you attribute your success?

Author: Don't call me 'sir.' I hate being called 'sir.' I'm not as old as all that.

Y.F.: Sorry. And to what—if you'd just get your back to the light . . . and I think a hat . . . thank you— And to what, young man, do you attribute your success?

A.: Meaning by 'success'?

Y.F.: Anything you like. The fact that I bought your last book—I mean got it from the library—I mean it's on my list—dammit, you know quite well what I mean.

A.: Well, as long as it's clear that I don't mean more than you do.

Y.F.: That's all right. You see, what I think you ought to give us now—last chapter and all that—is Something for the Little Ones. A few Helpful Words on Speech Day. Advice to Young Man about to make his way in World. Sum it all up. What's the secret?

A.: There's only one rule.

Y.F.: Well?

A.: *Never take advice.* Of all sad words of tongue or pen the saddest are 'Why did I listen to Tomkins?'

Y.F.: That doesn't rhyme.

A.: If his name were Benjamin it would.

Y.F.: But do you really mean it?

A.: Absolutely.

Y.F.: And that's why you're where you are?

A.: Wherever that is—yes.

Y.F.: How do you know you wouldn't have been much more successful if you had followed other people's advice?

A.: I don't. But you didn't ask me to what I attributed my failure.

Y.F.: In other words you've always done what you wanted to do, and haven't listened to other people?

A.: In other words I've listened to other people, and then tried to do what I wanted to do.

Y.F.: Which wasn't what *they* wanted you to do?

A.: Not as a rule.

Y.F.: And that's your advice to young authors—young men generally.

A.: Yes.

Y.F. (after profound thought): You do see, don't you, that if they take your advice, then they *won't* take your advice, which means that they *will* take advice, which means that—this is getting difficult.

A.: I know. It's a difficult world.

Y.F.: Oh yes, that reminds me. Oughtn't you to tell us how much more difficult Life has become since you were a boy? Something about the leisurely ease of The Good Old Days. *Laus temporis acti* and all that.

A.: Well, for one thing we didn't pronounce it like that in the good old days.

Y.F.: Splendid. Anything else you've noticed?

A.: Well——

Y.F.: Come on, this is the last chapter. Tell us What You Believe, or What's Wrong with World, or something.

2

A very clever young man was telling Reinhardt how to produce Shakespeare. None of this elaborate spectacle,

none of this gorgeous scenery. Just simple black curtains.
That was the way to do it: so much more artistic. Reinhardt nodded encouragingly. 'It is also easier,' he said. I
have a theory that what is wrong with the world (or, quite
possibly, what is right) is that to-day everything is 'also
easier.' Let me give a few examples of what I mean, and
if it be said that I am choosing examples to prove my case,
the answer is that this is exactly what I am doing.

In what I shall call 'my day' anybody who wanted to
earn a living as a singer had to learn to sing. In tune. It is
hard work learning to sing—in tune. So now you needn't.
You croon. The convention that crooning is singing enables all those people who cannot sing, but wish to earn a
living by singing, to do so without going through the
labour of learning to sing. In my day dancing was waltzing, and waltzing was not only hard work but was something which had to be learnt. To-day, with a minimum
of fatigue and an entire absence of technique, it is possible to claim that one is dancing. Drawing is difficult. A
famous drawing-master of my day used to go round the
work of his pupils, saying to each one as he compared the
work with the model, 'It is always a good thing to be
something like.' It is also a difficult thing. Modern technique, both in painting and sculpture, avoids the difficulty of being something like; just as modern hot music
avoids the difficulty of disclosing a new tune. In my day
poets said what they had to say in song. This song (poetry
it was called) demanded rhyme or, at least, rhythm from
its devotees, and in consequence was hard work. It was
obvious, therefore, that if you were going to improve
poetry you would improve it most comfortably by omitting the things which were difficult to manage—rhyme
and rhythm—and concentrating on what might come to
anybody, inspiration. In my day a novelist who wanted
to put down the thoughts in his hero's mind, as often he

might want, would spend hours of hard work reducing
them to an orderly grammatical sequence in which they
could be easily followed. The modern, so much admired,
technique allows you to throw them on to the paper just
as they came into the hero's mind (which means just as
they came into the author's mind), and if there is any hard
work to be done, it must be done by the reader. And the
latest technique of all seems to throw the work on the
proof-reader.

So much for the arts. I could stop there, but I shan't.
In my day beauty in women was for the favoured few, for
it demanded such rare gifts as a beautiful complexion,
beautiful hair, beautiful features. Nowadays it is no
longer difficult to be beautiful. Complexions, hair and
features can be bought. The modern world has accepted
the convention that obviously-painted lips and obviously-
gummed-on eyelashes are beautiful, and beauty is within
the reach of all. Even men need no longer be ugly; they
can emphasize their ugliness with a beard and become
'striking.' It is, let us admit, not always easy to grow a
beard, so we must look forward to the day when gummed-
on beards will be admissible. In my day there was something called Society, into which (unless you were born
there) it was almost impossible to enter; and if you were
outside it, as I was, you read about it in the society papers
with awe or indifference or an assumed contempt. Terrible for modern youth to think that there was any reser-
vation, however contemptible, to which it had not the
right of entry. To-day a study of the society papers shows
that there is no barrier through which the sports car of
the gigolo has not crashed, no frontier over which the
passports of the interior decorator ('special peculiarities'
and all) will not take him.

I shall now drag the moss out of my hair, and regard the
matter dispassionately. Is it a good thing or a bad thing

that the arts and graces are now so much easier to achieve? First let me admit, before it is 'pointed out' to me, that it is still difficult to be a *good* crooner (if there is such a thing) or a *good* ball-room dancer; indeed, it is obvious that a modern expert in the rumba, the lumbar, and the black bumba has need to be more expert than the old-fashioned expert in the waltz. No artistic standards could make Weatherley's drawing-room ballads of greater literary value than the best modern free-verse, nor even of greater literary value than such early examples of free-verse as Caesar's Commentaries. Pretty girls, in spite of their make-up, are still pretty, if less kissable; and who cares anyway if men are ugly and Society is dead? Yet the modern eagerness to lower standards and abolish 'form' remains a distress to the mossy. It is as if democracy had said, not: 'The arts and graces shall be open to all,' as it has every right to say, but: 'Achievement in the arts and graces shall be the perquisite of all,' which is nice for all of us, but not so good for the arts and graces. Sometimes I think it is a pity that, having gone so far, we do not go further, and say: 'Achievement in sport shall be the perquisite of all.' As a golfer I should like to be able to look contemptuously down upon the old-fashioned practice of raising the golf-ball in the air, and to abolish the old-fashioned rule which says, how foolishly, that the player who does the hole in the least number of shots shall be the winner. It is more in keeping with modern ideas (and it is also easier) to go from one point to another in a straight line rather than in a parabola, and the playing of eight shots expresses your personality, which is really all that matters, much more completely than the playing of one. But alas! in sport you can only feel superior to the champions of the past by beating them at their own game and under their own rules. In the arts you can denounce the target, change the rules, aim in a different direction, hit nothing, and receive the assurances of your friends that you are the better man.

The abolition of form. Looking for something else, I have just come across a letter dated 'April 12th, 1929,' which begins: 'Several months ago I wrote to you, but have not yet had a reply.' These unanswered letters turn up from time to time and cause an acute remorse, tempered by the happy reflection that it is now too late to do anything about it. This particular letter, however, had so nearly been answered as almost to excuse me. It was from one of those earnest Americans who are engaged upon what may or may not turn out to be a text book for schools, and who wish to make it as authoritative as possible by getting other people to do the writing for them. In this case it was to be a text book on 'the technique of the drama,' and the technique was to be provided (free) by dramatists. Would I answer the following questions? Well, apparently I did. That is, I scribbled answers in pencil against the questions, and presumably intended to have them typed and sent to him. But apparently I didn't. Reading them again I see that the fifth question and answer are strangely appropriate to my theme.

5. Don't you think that the present conventional form of play structure and the physical limitations of the stage hinder the dramatist from expressing himself as freely and as fully as he might in the cinema form?

Answer. Certainly. One is also hindered by the conventional form of the sonnet. How much more freely and fully Wordsworth might have expressed himself about Westminster Bridge if he had been writing a guide-book.

This passion for freedom untrammelled by form is attributed by Deans to the evil influences of Bolshevism and other red perils. Unfortunately I cannot share their conviction that Bolshevism is a synonym of lawlessness. On the contrary I associate it with an excess of law, a complete sacrifice of the right to self-expression, and a passion for filling up forms. In poetry the totalitarian state is best symbolized by the *villanelle*, which may be described as a reiteration on two notes: as it might be 'Hail, Hitler' and 'To hell with Russia,' or the other way round. But free verse seems to be the corollary of free speech, which is the attribute of democracy. Form: craftsmanship: all difficulties imposed from without, such as 'It's a good thing to be something like,' or the three walls of a stage; all these are barbed-wire fences which stand between democracy and the green slopes of Helicon. Away with them!

Well, what about it? In middle-age we not only forget that we are no longer young (which is not surprising, since we are always telling ourselves how young we are keeping), but we forget that our contemporaries are also middle-aged—which is astonishing since we are always telling ourselves how old the poor fellows are getting. Thus I found myself saying the other day that the extravagances of this cosmetic age proved finally that women adorned themselves for women only, not for men; in proof of which I assured my company that without exception every man I knew preferred a clean face to a painted one. And then I realized that the men whose support I was quoting were (naturally) my friends and contemporaries, and that possibly the modern young man did not agree with me. To him, it may be, blood-red finger-nails, even blood-red toe-nails, are beautiful. Yet he must admit that it is an easy way of being beautiful, and he will allow the middle-aged to think that he is easily pleased. We shall continue to think also that a society which is satisfied with crooning and hot music is easily pleased.

So in conclusion it may be asked: If the young are

easily pleased nowadays, is that not a good thing rather than a bad thing? Perhaps it is. There is little enough reason for happiness in the world to-day; let us be thankful that there are so many causes of pleasure. We have made the world a wilderness, and it is ridiculous to blame those whom we have put into it (accidentally as often as not) for being satisfied with the little we have left them to find there.

> *A Book of Free-verse underneath the Bough,*
> *A Saxophone, a Gin and It—and Thou*
> > *Beside me crooning in the Wilderness—*
> *Oh, Wilderness were Paradise enow!*
> *Praise be to Allah.*

3

As for 'What I Believe,' I put this into print once at the request of a Bishop: the only Bishop who ever came into our house. (When he left, we found five threepenny-bits on the sofa. We gave them to the Salvation Army, and tried to take our minds off the matter, but of course we couldn't help wondering.) This confession of faith formed one of a series of pamphlets, and may so remain. I wrote another pamphlet once called *Peace With Honour*. This also need not be paraphrased here. I find it very hard to convince those who are concerned with political and social activities that, unless one is professionally a Public Speaker, one does not want to say the same thing over and over again in different ways. If one has written it once, one has said it as well as one can—for ever. This must be true of most writers; I may be unique in not wanting to say anything aloud at any time. At one of my few public appearances I made a speech which, with the many others made on that occasion, was broadcast to the world. Or so I was told by my neighbour when I sat down: 'Fancy,' he said, 'they heard you in Honolulu!' Daphne was sitting a table or two away, and when we met afterwards I told her proudly that they had heard me in Honolulu. 'Good,' she said, 'I'm glad they heard you somewhere.'

Well, to those who have been reading this book I have now been audible for quite a long time. It would be as well to sit down. But before I do so, there is something which I should like to say.

Every writer who has put his name to the back of one book or the front of one programme has surrendered some part of his privacy to others. He is not on that account the servant of the public, as the actor so clearly considers himself to be, but at least he and the public are now on visiting terms. In private life we are all very much at the mercy of visitors, and we have to decide for ourselves in what size of lettering the WELCOME on our door-mats shall be displayed. So, too, the writer must decide to what extent he shall leave himself at the mercy of the public. To answer personally every letter he receives: to sign autographs and copy out verses whenever he is asked: to provide unpaid contributions for anybody's magazine: to make a speech, take a chair, give away prizes at anybody's bidding: to read and advise upon all the plays sent to him, to help place all the manuscripts submitted to him, to write quotable advertisements for all the books given to him: to accede, in short, to all the strange requests made (I suppose) of every writer, this is to be, not merely the servant but the very slave of the public. On the other hand one has been lucky, one has owed much to the encouragement and kindness of established writers, and one should make some sort of repayment. It may well be that my balance is still a debit one; that the WELCOME on my door-mat has not been so conspicuous as it should have been; that I have ignored too many requests, refused too many invitations. With all these unanswered letters behind me, I cannot help feeling that I have behaved with seeming discourtesy to too many people. If some of them happen to be reading this, I ask their pardon. And to them and to all other readers, I shall say *Au Revoir,* hoping that we may meet again.